UNDERSTANDING BUSINESS: ORGANISATIONS

This book – *Understanding Business: Organisations* – is one of a series of four readers which constitute the main teaching texts of the Open University course *Understanding Business Behaviour* (B200). The other titles are: *Understanding Business: Environments*, edited by Michael Lucas; *Understanding Business: Markets*, edited by Vivek Suneja; and *Understanding Business: Processes*, edited by David Barnes.

This course is one of three core courses which are compulsory elements in the Open University's BA in Business Studies. In addition to the compulsory courses, students who are working toward this degree also study courses which include topics such as Economics, Organisational Change, Design and Innovation and Quantitative Methods.

The approach of *Understanding Business Behaviour* (B200) as an introductory course in Business Studies is innovative. The traditional approach employed by courses in this area is to offer introductions to the key social science disciplines: sociology, economics, law, etc. This course uses another approach: it focuses not on disciplines but on key elements of the business world: environments, markets, processes and organisations. This still allows for the discussion of relevant social science theory and research but organises this material not by the logic of academic structures and disciplines but by the logic of business applications and relevance.

As with all Open University courses, students are not only supplied with teaching texts; they also receive comprehensive guidance on how to study and work through these texts. In the case of B200, this guidance is contained in four Study Guides which are supplied to students separately. These guides explain the choice of readings, identify key points and guide the students' work and understanding. A core feature of the guides is an explicit focus on the identification, development, deployment and testing of a series of business graduate skills. These include study skills, cognitive skills of analysis and assessment, IT, and numeracy.

Each student is allocated a local tutor and is encouraged to participate in a strategically integrated set of tutorials which are held throughout the course.

Details of this and other Open University courses can be obtained from the Course Reservations Centre, PO Box 724, The Open University, Milton Keynes, MK7 6ZS, United Kingdom; tel: +44 (0) 1908 653231; e-mail: ces-gen@open.ac.uk

Alternatively, you may visit the Open University website at http://www.open.ac.uk where you can learn about the wide range of courses and packs offered at all levels by The Open University.

For information about the purchase of Open University course components, contact Open University Worldwide Ltd, The Berrill Building, Walton Hall, Milton Keynes, MK7 6AA, United Kingdom: tel.+44 (0) 1908 858785; fax: +44 (0) 1908 858787; e-mail: ouwenq@open.ac.uk; website: http://www.ouw.co.uk.

SERIES INTRODUCTION

It is hardly necessary to justify the study of business, or to over-emphasise the importance of a knowledge and understanding of business organisations and their functions, or of the environments of business. The world of business is the world in which we live and work, every aspect of which may well be on the verge of fundamental change as a result of the Internet and converging communications technologies. It affects us as consumers, workers, voters, citizens, whether of nations, unions of nations or of the world. We have to understand it. We have to understand how organisations work and their core processes. This involves an understanding of their impact on employees and consumers; how markets work (and don't work); the role and nature of business environments and how these impact on business organisations (or vice versa).

This book is one in a series of four readers which bring together classic and seminal materials, many of them summaries and reviews, which are designed to achieve the teaching objectives of the Open University course *Understanding Business Behaviour* (B200) – a core course in the Open University's BA in Business Studies. The volumes are organised in an innovative way around four key areas of the world of business: environments, markets, processes and organisations.

The volumes have been designed to supply a selection of key introductory materials in each of these areas of business applications and, with the use of appropriate study guidance, to allow the identification, development, deployment and practice of a range of skills required from Business Studies courses in general. Therefore, while they constitute the core teaching resources of this Open University course, they would also make admirable selections for any course concerned with these areas. They are not intended to be cutting edge or fashionable. They are designed as a resource for anyone seeking an understanding of the nature and development of the world of business.

Each of these volumes has been edited by an individual member of the course team. But in a very real sense they are collective products of the course team as a whole. That is why all the members of the course team deserve recognition and acknowledgement for their contribution to the course and to these collections. The course team consisted of:

David Barnes, Hannah Brunt, Rob Clifton, Mike Conboy, Martin Dowling, Gill Gowans, Carol Howells, Jacky Holloway, Bob Kelly, Mike Lucas, Alison Macmillan, Chris Marshall, Jane Matthews, Konrad Mau, Terry Morris, John O'Dwyer, John Olney, Anthea Rogers, Judy Rumbelow, Graeme Salaman, Dawn Storer, Jane Sturges, Vivek Suneja, Tricia Tierney, Richard Whipp.

Two other members of the team deserve special mention for their enormous contribution to the course as a whole and to the work of managing the course team and the processes involved in assembling and organising these collections: Chris Bollom and Georgina Marsh. To them, many thanks.

UNDERSTANDING BUSINESS: ORGANISATIONS

Edited by
GRAEME SALAMAN
at The Open University

Taylor & Francis Group

NEW YORK AND LONDON

In association with

The Open University

First published by Lawrence Erlbaum Associates, Inc., Publishers

First published 2001
by Routledge
605 Third Avenue, New York, NY 10017
4 Park Square, Milton Park, Abingdon, Oxon OX14 4RN

*Routledge is an imprint of the Taylor & Francis Group,
an informa business*

British Library Cataloguing in Publication Data
A catalogue record for this book is available from the British Library

Library of Congress Cataloging in Publication Data
Understanding business organisations / edited by Graeme Salaman.
   p. cm.
   Includes bibliographical references and index.
   1. Industrial organization (Economic theory) 2. Organizational change. 3. Industrial
sociology. 4. Work. I. Salaman, Graeme.
   HD2326 U53 2000
   302.3′5—dc21   00–042478

ISBN 13: 978-0-415-23856-4 (pbk)
ISBN 13: 978-0-415-23855-7 (hbk)

CONTENTS

FIGURES AND TABLES

FIGURES

TABLES

ACKNOWLEDGEMENTS

The author and publishers would like to thank the following for granting permission to reproduce material in this work:

Blackwell Publishers Ltd, for excerpt from Christopher Mabey, Graeme Salaman and John Storey, *Human Resource Management: A Strategic Introduction*, 2nd edition, first published by Blackwell Publishers Ltd, 1988. Copyright © Christopher Mabey, Graeme Salaman and John Storey, 1998.

International Thomson Business Press, for excerpt from David Needle, *Business in Context*, 2nd edition, published by Chapman and Hall 1994, 1995, 1996. Copyright © 1989, 1994 David Needle.

Longman Group Ltd, for excerpt from Graeme Salaman, *Work Organisations: Resistance and Control*, first published by Longman 1979. Copyright © Graeme Salaman, 1979.

Macmillan Press Ltd, for excerpts from Paul Thompson and David McHugh, *Work Organisations, A Critical Introduction*, 2nd edition. Copyright © Paul Thompson and David McHugh 1990, 1995; Paul Thomson and Chris Warhurst, *Workplaces of the future*, first published by Macmillan Press, 1998. Copyright © Paul Thompson and Chris Warhurst.

W.W. Norton & Company Inc., for excerpt from Richard Sennett, *The Corrosion of Character: The Personal Consequences of Work in the New Capitalism*. Copyright © 1998 by Richard Sennett. Used by permission of W.W. Norton & Company Inc.

Oxford University Press Inc., for excerpt from C. Wright Mills, *White Collar: The American Middle Class*. Copyright © 1951 by C. Wright Mills. Reprinted by permission of Oxford University Press Inc.

M.E. Sharpe Inc., for excerpt from Graeme Salaman, *Work Organization and Class Sructure*, originally published in England by William Collins Sons & Co Ltd under the title *Class and the Corporation*. Copyright © Graeme Salaman, 1981.

Random House Inc., for excerpt from Paul Kennedy, *Preparing for the 21st Century*. Copyright © 1993 by Paul Kennedy. Reprinted by permission of Random House Inc.

John Wiley & Sons Inc., for excerpt from R. Ashkenas *et al.*, *Boundaryless Organization: Breaking the Chains of Organizational Structure*. Published by Jossey Bass, 1995.

Every effort has been made to contact copyright holders for their permission to reprint material in this book. The publishers would be grateful to hear from any copyright holder who is not here acknowledged and will undertake to rectify any errors or omissions in future editions of this book.

INTRODUCTION

This is a book to be used to inform and support teaching. It is a sort of teaching text, but an unusual one. It consists not of the usual interpretation, guidance, review and assessments that properly characterise teaching texts, but of a collection of materials that can be used to support and illustrate such analysis. This volume is a small portable library, a replacement for a reading list. And this is exactly the role it plays in an Open University course, where it constitutes the teaching materials for an introductory module on organisations and where it is accompanied by a Study Guide which directs, supports, guides, encourages and tests students' work and learning on these materials.

The subject addressed by this collection is organisational analysis. The level is introductory. This has had significant implications for the choice of materials to be included. They have been chosen because they carry and sustain a developing and emerging narrative. This narrative, which comprises three sections, is described below. The narrative element is important because it means that the chapters of this volume have been selected not only for their individual contributions but for their collective contribution, and for the way they relate to each other and to the broader argument. So the links between these selections are important: in some cases this relationship is one of support and development. In other cases it is one of dialectic and difference.

Increasingly, academic programmes are being required to address not only issues of content and knowledge, but of skills. The course for which this volume supplies the teaching materials is explicitly committed to developing skills, and the selection in this volume reflects this commitment. Teachers who wish to develop skills will find that the choice, order, progression and interrelationships between these materials supplies a fruitful basis for the identification and development (and if necessary testing) of such key cognitive skills as identifying arguments from texts, summarising arguments, assessing arguments and contrasting and comparing different positions. This volume is introductory. It establishes the fundamentals of thinking about and theorising about organisations. It is not indifferent to fashion (and some later selections engage directly with current fashions in organisational restructuring) but its first priority is to establish some continuing and underlying issues in organisations and in our understanding of organisations. Many of these have historic roots in the history of organisations and their continuing and fundamental features and tensions, and in organisation theory. This is the reason why some of the selections here are drawn from work over the last twenty or so years or even more: they are classics or they are about classics and as such they identify and deal with the fundamental, long term issues of organisation and organisation theory. But there is an important implication of this: some of these chapters, particularly the older ones adopt the convention, widely current when they were written but now unacceptable, of referring to workers as male. To the modern reader this seems strange, and it is strange. It undoubtedly reflected a degree of sociological myopia whereby female workers were overlooked and under-studied and male workers – often workers in traditional male-oriented industries – were seen as paradigmatic. It is not a sufficient excuse, although it is probably the case, that writers who referred to workers as male were using this as a convention rather than because they failed to recognise that many workers were women.

This collection is about modern organisations, how they are structured and how they work and how and why they are changing. It is also about the main ways in which researchers and writers on organisations have tried to understand them.

This is an important distinction: between organisations as phenomena – as things that exist in the world like BT or Coca-Cola – and the theories or explanatory frameworks people (including managers and consultants) use to try to describe and understand them. We use these models and theories to try – with greater or lesser success – to understand what organisations are like and how they work. They are the lens through which we view organisations. But unlike an ordinary lens, these don't simply allow us to see organisations, they also define what we see – what we notice, what we ignore, the shape and nature of the object of analysis. If we are to increase our understanding of organisations we need to recognise and be able to assess and discuss the explanatory tools we use for this purpose. Organisations do not 'speak for themselves'. They can only be explained in terms of some theory – some way of knowing and talking about them. Wittgenstein, the philosopher, said, famously, that 'the limits of my world are the limits of my language'. In other words everything in the world – including organisations – is defined by the ways in which we see and understand and label it. But organisations are not only *explicable* in terms of theory (or *theories* for there is more than one) they also, unlike atoms and bacteria, *produce* theories about themselves, and these theories – these views of organisations and what they are like and why managers do what they have to do – often carry or claim considerable authority. This is one important way in which the subject matter of this book differs from other phenomena we try to explain: the phenomena seek to account for and to legitimate themselves.

This makes the task of the book interesting. One implication is that theorising about organisations – offering explanations of how they work and why they are structured in the way they are – becomes potentially a political activity since it fits or clashes with the authoritative statements of powerful members of the organisation.

The first section of this reader is entitled *Organisations and why they matter*. It consists of four chapters. Its first concern is to establish what the modern business organisation is like and why these organisations matter. It is thus concerned to establish the foundations for the module as a whole by showing the nature (and importance) of the phenomenon we are dealing with – and some of its main variations.

Second, this section addresses some of the historical and cultural contexts of modern business organisations. It is intended to 'problematise' them – i.e. to show that they are something that needs to be explained; that although we may take them, and all their elements and their consequences, as 'normal', they are not. They are in fact a product of – and to some extent a determinant of – a particular historical and cultural period. And they depend on a number of assumptions and values which we may see as normal but which many people elsewhere in the world would not, and which our forefathers certainly would not. Assumptions for example about the priorities in life, about what work means to us, about the conditions under which this work takes place – and *for whom* it takes place.

This first section pays special attention to the implications of the modern business organisation for individuals, both in their private lives and as employees. The meaning of work for employees of the modern work organisation – a theme explored by two of the chapters in this section – is a powerful way of exploring the cultural implications and underpinnings of the modern organisation, since it closely affects their identity, their well-being, their relationships, their way of life. It therefore illustrates the impact modern organisations have on those who work in them.

Section 2 is called *Understanding organisations*. It has five chapters. First we give an historical overview of the modern organisation, starting in the early nineteenth century and finishing in the present. This section makes a number of basic points: that many of the key features of the modern organisation were established very early in its development; that it represented a basic and for many a brutal break with previous forms of work organisation; that it created a new sense of work itself with new values associated with it; that the history of the modern organisation can to some extent be seen as a movement around a small number of key themes or tensions – the need for control of workers but the limitations of control; the benefits of bureaucracy and the problems associated with it, and so on.

A second theme of this section is the various ways people have tried to make sense of, and to understand what these organisations are like and how they work. The development of the modern organisation was closely associated with the development of a number of different and competing views or theories of these organisations. It is hardly too much to say that the development of organisations was one of a number of major causes and inspirations behind the development not only of theories of organisation but of theories of modern society. As chapter 6, 'Classic theories of bureaucracy' shows, the three major theories developed to explain the rise, structure and action of the early large-scale organisation – bureaucracy – were also capable of application to the societies within which they developed. And this was no coincidence. These early theorists were alive to the point that the existence of modern organisations heralded a major change in the host society. The modern organisation defined the nature of modern society.

The close association between the modern organisation and theories of organisation also reminds us of another point made by a number of the chapters in this section: that theories of the modern organisation not only differ, and they actively compete. They contest with each other.

Section 3 is called *Changing organisations*. It consists of five chapters, and is concerned with organisational change. It describes some of the major ways in which modern organisations are changing. But it does more than this: it also encourages you to consider and assess these changes. One of the striking features of organisations – particularly recently – is the way they are changing and changing apparently radically and with increasing rapidity. Take the process of consolidation for example – one company buying or merging with another. The process of consolidation in many industries – banking, oil, insurance, car manufacture, airlines, for example – is dramatic. Each merger or acquisition means a dramatic process of internal change as two organisations in the same business (more or less) but different in structure, culture and internal processes are brought together to make one new one. But much change is driven not by external developments but internal ones: as managers seek to gain competitive advantage in one way or another (reduced costs, improved quality) by some programme of internal change. Section 3 is about these programmes of change. It is concerned with a number of questions.

First, what is actually going on – what changes are actually occurring? Second, and more important, what is the significance of these changes, and in particular, to what extent do they represent a real and radical move away from some of the inherent difficulties and tensions of the original bureaucratic model? For obvious reasons those who design and launch programmes of organisational change are keen to assure us – and the employees and shareholders – that the change in question will solve current and historic difficulties and will open up a new phase for the business. But the selection contained in this section equips you to assess the merits of these claims.

SECTION 1: ORGANISATIONS AND WHY THEY MATTER

INTRODUCTION

The main objectives of this section are twofold. First, to discuss what the modern organisation is actually like: its size, structure, shape, scale, power, significance; how they are owned and controlled and how they impact on staff, customers, citizens, economies and societies. Chapters 1 and 2 are concerned with these objectives. Second we want to position the modern work organisation in its special, cultural and historical context and thus to 'problematise' it – i.e. to de-normalise it, to make it something remarkable that needs to be explained.

One way to do this is to explore the implications of the modern organisation for employees. For one of the key ways in which work differs is in the meaning it has for those who do it. And researching variations in the meanings of work is a powerful way of understanding how the nature of work has changed – and is still changing. What does it mean – what did it mean – to be employed by these organisations? And particularly what does it mean for the values and meanings used by employees? These questions are addressed by chapters three and four.

Chapter 1: Organisational aspects of business – David Needle

This reading establishes the basic underpinnings of the entire book. It offers a comprehensive summary of the main features of the modern organisation. It discusses the nature and origins of organisational goals; and organisational structures; it discusses the implications of organisational size and the role of the small business; and it addresses the contentious but potentially exciting issue of organisational cultures and their potential impact on performance. This first chapter is particularly important because it sets out some of the major features of the phenomenon we are addressing in this book.

Needle makes two important points about the dynamics and determinants of organisational structure and functioning: organisations are not simple unitary, consensual entities where everyone agrees on and focuses on shared organisational goals but where sectional, group interests and viewpoints exist and flourish. And although in many ways organisations are the most rational entities ever created where managers and employees strive to make sensible decisions about purposes and to design organisations and processes that efficiently achieve these purposes, in reality irrational forces also play a major role. These two features of organisations will be addressed throughout the book.

Chapter 2: The communications and financial revolution and the rise of the multinational corporation – Paul Kennedy

Organisations matter. They matter in all sorts of ways, which is one of the reasons we are studying them here. To managers they matter because they want to understand how they work in order to make them more efficient and effective. They matter to us as consumers – think of the benefits of their products and services, and also of GM foods and BSE. They matter to us as employees because they determine how we spend most of our waking time. And they matter to us as citizens. There isn't space to deal with all these forms of importance so here we focus on one major feature of modern organisations: the importance of the global organisation in global, economic and political terms.

Chapter 3: Work in traditional and modern societies – Craig R. Littler

A key objective of this first section is to locate or contextualise the modern work organisation historically and culturally and thus to 'problematise' it – i.e. to show that it is something remarkable that needs to be explained. One key way of doing this is by comparison – by comparison of work in the modern organisation with work in other contexts, periods and cultures. This sort of comparison is explored in this chapter. The author notes:

> Comparing types of economy and types of work organisation is important, especially to overcome the continual tendency to take Western capitalist society as the absolute centre of reference . . . comparison is intended to be a typological process in order to illuminate the particular mechanisms of modern industrial societies and to construct theories which have their roots in more than the quicksand of the present and the contemporary.

The purpose of this chapter is established in the first paragraph:

> This chapter explores some of the differences between work in traditional and modern societies. It does so by examining structures of production (economic structures) and the culture of "work". It is these frameworks of social organisation and social meaning that shape the nature of work experiences.

Chapter 4: Work – C. Wright Mills

The fourth chapter in this section is taken from Wright Mills' book *White Collar*. It is about the work of white collar workers. The expression 'white collar' is now rather dated – as are white collar workers themselves, thanks to various organisational changes which we will discuss later in the module. 'White collar' was used to refer to clerical workers, who proliferated enormously during the early part of this century.

Mills' argument is interesting not simply because he supplies a moving and almost poetic account of the decline of meaning in work but because he offers a causal explanation for this decline: essentially Mills argues that the nature of relations of production – 'For whom is work done and why?' – will establish how work is structured and organised and what it means to the workers.

1

ORGANIZATIONAL ASPECTS OF BUSINESS*

David Needle

[. . .] In this chapter we examine [. . .] the organization itself. We will consider five aspects in our model: goals, structures, size, ownership and organization culture.

As with other aspects of our model there is considerable interaction and overlap between these organizational issues. As well as pointing out the areas of overlap in each individual section, the way that issues relating to goals, ownership, structure and size come together is examined in more detail through the concept of organization culture. In addition, we highlight two specific issues, the public sector and small businesses, both of which illustrate the complex nature of these organizational relationships. The public sector has been chosen since it is a good illustration of the interaction and tensions both within the organizational elements, as well as those operating between the organization and its environment. In addition, government policy of privatization, deregulation and the commercialization of the public sector has meant that the distinction between public and private concerns is becoming increasingly blurred, further justifying our focus. The treatment of small businesses raises contemporary economic and political debates as well as highlighting the very specific nature of business problems found in this sector.

GOALS

In this section we shall examine the nature of goals, the purposes they serve and how they emerge. We shall also consider the potential problem arising from a number of different goals operating in the same organization. We often speak glibly of organizations like Marks & Spencer, British Rail, or even our own college as having goals. However, we ought not to ascribe behaviour to abstract entities such as organizations. Goals should always be attributable to some person or group. Case 1.1 illustrates the goals of three organizations, two explicitly stated (Sainsbury, the supermarket chain, and Rank Hovis McDougall, the food processors) and the third extracted from the Chairman's statement (Rhône-Poulenc, a French multinational with interests in chemicals, fertilizers, pharmaceuticals and computer tape and discs).

The renewal of interest in the role played by goals in influencing the behaviour of organization members has been highlighted through the concept of the 'excellent company' (see for example Peters and Waterman, 1982). In companies like IBM, Hewlett-Packard,

Key concept 1.1: Organizational goals

The stated goals of an organization exist to give direction to the activities of its members. In many companies, goals comprise both an overall statement of intent, sometimes referred to as a mission statement, and a set of more detailed objectives to guide strategic planning. Since many organizations are made up of different interest groups the formulation of goals can be a highly political process. This can cause conflict but the goals of most businesses are generally accepted as being those of the senior management team. There has been a renewal of interest in the role of goals to shape the culture of an organization. We deal with this aspect in our discussion of organizational culture (Key concept 1.5).

Case 1.1: Illustrations of company goals

A statement of company objectives by J. Sainsbury PLC

To discharge the responsibility as leaders in our trade by acting with compete integrity, by carrying out work to the highest standards, and by contributing to the public good and to the quality of life in the community.

To provide unrivalled value to our customers in the quality of the goods we sell, in the competitiveness of our prices and in the range of choice we offer.

In our stores to achieve the highest standards of cleanliness and hygiene, efficiency of operation, convenience and customer service, and thereby create as attractive and friendly a shopping environment as possible.

To offer our staff outstanding opportunities in terms of personal career development and in remuneration relative to other companies in the same market, practising always a concern for the welfare of every individual.

To generate sufficient profit to finance continual improvement and growth of the business whilst providing our shareholders with an excellent return on their investment.

(*Source*: Annual Report and Accounts 1988)

The stated aims of Rank Hovis McDougall

The business of the Rank Hovis McDougall Group of companies is to process and market a wide range of food products in the United Kingdom, Europe, the United States, the Far East and Australasia.

Our aims are:

- to provide attractive and wholesome food products at prices which represent good value for money;
- to provide our employees with worthwhile jobs in safe working conditions at fair levels of pay;
- to provide our shareholders with an acceptable return on the money they have invested in the Group;
- to provide for the long-term growth and stability of the Group in the interests of customers, employees, and shareholders alike.

(*Source*: Annual Report and Accounts, 1988)

Rhône-Poulenc: extracts from the Chairman's message, 1986

In this changing world our ambition is to lead the Rhône-Poulenc group along exceptionally vigorous lines to place it among the world leaders in each of the fields in which it excels. Our strategy can be summed up in three points. They are concomitant and complementary.

We must first increase the high-value added activities where Rhône-Poulenc already holds considerable know-how and strong markets . . . To succeed in these fields means continuing to pursue our capital expenditure program as well as continuing our substantial commitment to Research and Development . . . to sign research agreements . . . with the international academic world . . . seizing every opportunity for external expansion through acquisitions.

Secondly we reinforce our upstream activities . . . our chemical business in major intermediates, both organic and inorganic, areas in which we hold positions of leadership and where we have been able to set extremely competitive cost prices. To do this we must unceasingly pursue the improvement of our manufacturing processes. We must maintain here high levels of investments in productivity and capacity, and exercise a particularly rigorous industrial management policy.

Lastly we want to free ourselves from activities which are too far removed from our fundamental business or facing severe economic problems.

(*Source*: Company Report and Accounts, 1966)

---

and Boeing you will find clearly articulated goals which are so dominant that they appear to have a life of their own irrespective of the personnel involved. Closer examination will certainly reveal that such goals are carefully formulated by the chief executives of such companies as part of a policy of establishing a set of dominant values which guide the behaviour of every organization member. As with all organizations, the main purpose of goals is to give members a sense of direction and to reduce ambiguity and conflict.

Managers who use goals in this way make the assumption that the clear formulation of goals will influence performance. This assumption has been translated into a set of techniques aimed at influencing the behaviour of individual members, known as 'Management-by-Objectives' or MBO (Drucker, 1964). Where MBO is used, the goals for the organization as a whole are generally broken down into individual goals or targets for each manager, forming an entire network of inter-connected and internally consistent goals. The most effective MBO schemes tend to be those where there is some measure of negotiation between manager and subordinate over the precise nature of the goals to be achieved by the subordinate. This raises two points; that goal formulation is part of a political process and that goal achievement is undoubtedly related to the extent to which goals are shared by members of the organization.

However, the evidence on the influence of goals on performance is mixed, and even where such a relationship can be shown, it is unclear how it works. The use of goals to determine performance is easiest to understand where jobs are straightforward so that clear targets can be set and performance measured. Many jobs are more complex and performance measurement is difficult to achieve. Furthermore, employees may be expected to achieve a number of different goals which could conflict with one another or with those of other workers. We shall see that for some organizations internal consistency is difficult to achieve in the face of considerable inter-personal and inter-departmental conflict. The extent to which goals can be used to motivate performance is also a function of management behaviour and individual expectations.

[. . .]

The nature of goals

> We consider goals to be the ultimate, long-run, open-ended attributes or ends a person or organization seeks.
>
> (Hofer and Schendel, 1978, p. 20)

Allowing for the contention that organizations can engage in goal-seeking behaviour, this definition sees goals in terms of the future orientation of the company, but stated in rather loose, broad terms. The examples in our case illustrate this point. A popular notion is that business firms should possess some superordinate goal, namely the maximization of profit. This view has been challenged. Some, like Handy (1993), see profit as a by-product of other goals like survival, market expansion and enhancing reputation. Marris (1964) sees profit as less important than growth. In any case the profit notion is entirely inappropriate for those public-sector organizations where goals of service take precedence over all others.

Hofer and Schendel (1978) make the distinction between goals, objectives and strategies. Goals themselves are seen as being unbounded, generalized statements of intent, whereas objectives represent those intentions that can be measured within a certain time frame. Strategies are seen as the processes by which goals are determined through the adoption of certain courses of action and the allocation of resources.

Richards (1978) distinguishes between closed- and open-ended goals. Closed-ended goals are those which have clearly defined and measurable targets to be achieved within a stated time period. By contrast open-ended goals are the type which include some broad statement of intent such as the pursuit of excellence. This broader view of goals has sometimes been defined as a firm's 'mission', which would seem to equate with Hofer and Schendel's concept of a goal. A mission has been described as a master strategy which has a visionary content, and which overrides all other types of goal (Richards, 1978).

Despite the confusion over terminology we can therefore see a kind of hierarchy developing which comprises different types of goals, as follows:

Another classification made by Perrow (1961) distinguishes between 'official' and 'operative' goals. 'Official' goals are the statements of intent which occur in official documents and are the type illustrated by our case illustrations. 'Operative' goals on the other hand reflect the behaviour that is actually occurring, and which may in fact conflict with the official intention. To Perrow the development of a package of operative goals was the process of corporate strategy formulation. This process is developed in the following section.

How goals are developed

Our understanding of how goals develop owes much to the work of Cyert and March and their *A Behavioural Theory of the Firm* (1963). They see organizations as being formed around individuals and groups who combine to pursue mutual interests as coalitions. The interests need not be shared but the coalition is recognized by all participating interest groups as the most effective way of achieving their goals.

An interest group may be an entire department, such as marketing or research and development, or it might be a particular section within that department such as a project team. It may even be a less formal grouping of managers within a department who collectively wish to pursue a specific policy. The creation of such interest groups may be a deliberate structural device. [. . .]

Interest groups can emerge due to the complexity of the organization's task and/or its environment, requiring a degree of internal specialization, to deal with specific problems, such as product development, or external bodies such as banks. Interest groups may also develop informally, cutting across formal structures.

Each interest group will determine its goals by reference to the information it collects. Such information generally includes comparative data on other organizations on such issues as price, product design, and criteria for success. Many interest groups for example establish their goals in relation to competing groups in the same organization. The important point made by Cyert and March is that groups deliberately limit strategic choice by selecting information from the range available and having decided upon a course of action, often fail to consider alternative strategies. This is perfectly understandable given the range of information and the time available to make decisions. Such a process is sometimes referred to as bounded rationality.

Interest groups combine to form coalitions and in any one organization there will be a number of such coalitions. They are created by a process of influence, negotiation and bargaining between different interest groups. It is out of this process that the goals emerge which guide the behaviour of organization members. However in any one organization there is usually a group that may be identified as a dominant coalition. Once established, the dominant coalition will set up procedures to ensure that their goals are pursued by the organization as a whole. Such criteria will normally include establishing the procedures for staff selection, promotion, and reward as well as laying down the rules of operation. The dominant coalition usually comprises, therefore, the senior management of an enterprise. However, certain groups align themselves with top management to ensure their goals are well represented. Even in those organizations where decision-making proceeds along more democratic lines, as in institutions of higher education, the various coalitions will compete for membership of key committees at which decisions about such issues as resources are taken.

In short, the ability of groups to pursue their goals depends upon the power they wield in the organization, which may depend on a number of variables; such as their position in the hierarchy; the skills of group members; the resources they command; whether or not their role is seen as legitimate by the rest of the organization members.

It is inevitable that different coalitions will pursue different interests and that some will compete. The process of influence, negotiation and bargaining may be termed organizational politics. Such a concept tends to be viewed pejoratively and political activity in business firms is often seen as a problem. Yet if we subscribe to the views of Cyert and March the process is an inevitable prelude to goal-setting. None the less the potential problem of goal conflict will now be explored through the examination of multiple goals.

Multiple goals

In any organization made up of different interest groups some conflict over goals is inevitable. This has been illustrated by many writers. Marris (1964) speaks of the goal conflict emerging from the separation of ownership and control. He found that while shareholders were concerned primarily about profitability, the professional managers acting as the directors of companies were more concerned with growth. In this instance profitability is a by-product, for it is growth which expands the director's sphere of influence and hence his personal power and reward. Despite such potential conflict between director and shareholder goals, some compromise is usually made by directors to protect their own position. Handy (1993) presents several examples of goal conflict, including that between the sales and production departments. The goals of the sales department are normally measured by volume turnover, while those of the production department are measured by cost-efficiency. [. . .]

In some cases such conflict can be seen to operate against the best interests of the organization. [. . .] Burns and Stalker (1966) noted how a [. . .] conflict developed between the production and research and development departments in certain Scottish electronics firms with the subsequent decline in their competitive standing. In Pettigrew's (1973) study computer programmers saw their status threatened by an emerging group of systems analysts. In response they attempted to control information to preserve their exclusive position and prevent their work being downgraded.

In such cases, activities move away from dealing with customers or even coping with external changes in the market to focus on the resolution of internal tensions and management becomes the management of internal coalitions. [. . .] In many organizations conflict often remains hidden, emerging only when problems get out of hand. In most situations conflict can be contained and managed. A similar situation occurred within the BBC during the summer of 1993. Viewing figures revealed that BBC1 was achieving only 29% of the television audience against ITV's 41%. This created a much publicized debate about the future direction of BBC programming and there was a belief among senior managers at BBC1 that it was catering for an elite upper-income, middle-class audience and needed to widen its appeal. This debate led to further allegations of autocratic management and a stifling of creativity and positions were taken by different factions within the organization.

We can see that it is quite normal for multiple goals to exist in most organizations. Conflict does occur as can be seen by [. . .] the illustrations above. However, not all conflict of this kind is necessarily a problem. It would appear to be limited by four factors.

- Most groups in an organization will agree to those goals formulated by senior management as a means of achieving their own goals. This is the result of the bargaining and negotiating process between interest groups.
- Most organization members would appear to accept the goals of top management with little question. This would seem to be an implied element of the employment contract.
- The dominant coalition normally sets up a series of controls to ensure compliance to their goals. Such controls have been alluded to earlier and include selection procedures, induction and training to ensure that rules are followed. In addition, management can use technological controls in the form of work design and job allocation, and financial controls in the form of budgets and reward systems. In such ways as these, the management of organizations ensure at least a minimum level of compliance with their chosen goals.
- In many firms senior management acknowledge that different groups may have their own goals which need to be satisfied.

In this section we have depicted the formation of goals as a complex process involving the resolution of external influences and internal politics. As such, the system is highly dynamic and changes in the goals will occur with changes in the external environment, such as market demand, technology and government policy, as well as changes that take place between interest groups within the organization. A change in ownership or top management may lead to a shift in emphasis of the firm's operations. The acquisition of the department store chain Debenhams by the Burton Group led to a change in operation as well as image. More franchises were awarded to established retailers to operate within each Debenhams store and there was considerable investment on internal refurbishment in all locations.

Goals are not formalized, meaningless statements but the products of a highly interactive and dynamic process. The changing of goals in the face of external and even internal changes is seen to be a prerequisite for the survival of the organization. Those managers that cling to inappropriate goals would appear to place their companies at risk. However, simply changing goals may be an inadequate response by itself, since the relationship between goals and performance often demands some consideration of the organization structure. It is to this we now turn.

Key concept 1.2: Organization structure

An organization structure is a grouping of activities and people to achieve the goals of the organization. Considerable variation is possible in the type of structure employed and the influences at work include technology, size, the nature of the environment, management strategy, the behaviour of interest groups, the firm's history and wider cultural factors. In general terms a particular structure emerges to maximize the opportunities and solve the problems created by these various influences. In practice however the evidence concerning the influence of structure and performance is very patchy indeed.

STRUCTURE

A dominant theme in our discussion of goals was that organizations are made up of different interest groups formed as coalitions. One of the factors which may facilitate or inhibit the way these groups pursue their goals and whether such goals may be achieved is the structure of the organization. In this section we will examine how structures develop, the variations that occur in structural type, and their impact on performance. You should note however that any discussion of structure is biased towards the large firm, and most of the studies in this area are of large corporations. This is inevitable in that structural problems tend to be associated with size and complexity. The balance is redressed later in this chapter when we devote an entire section to the problems of small businesses.

A structure is concerned with the grouping of activities in the most suitable manner to achieve the goals of the dominant coalition. It is concerned with the organization of work around roles, the grouping of these roles to form teams or departments, and the allocation of differential amounts of power and authority to the various roles. It is associated with job descriptions, mechanisms for coordination and control, and management information systems.

In much of the writing there is an implicit assumption that senior management seek a structural elegance for their organizations to enhance performance. This in turn assumes that managers have a choice and that structures can be deliberately created to affect overall performance. We will now examine those factors which can influence a firm's structure to determine the extent to which structures can be manipulated by management.

The factors which influence structure

There are a number of factors which may influence the structure of an organization. We have identified them under six main headings, placed in no particular order of importance.

Technology

For some, technology is the most important, if not the sole, determinant of a firm's structure. This is part of the concept known as 'technological determinism'. Much of the work in this area is indebted to Joan Woodward's (1965) work on the impact of technology on 100 manufacturing firms in South-East Essex [. . .] She and her research team found that differences in manufacturing, from small batch to mass production to process technology, resulted in corresponding differences in such factors as the extent of the management hierarchy, the proportion of management to other employees, the proportion of direct to indirect labour, and the number of subordinates controlled by any one manager (the span of control).

Size

Other researchers find size to be a more significant variable in influencing structure than is technology. This was a particular theme of a group of academics at Aston University in the 1960s and '70s (see, for example, Pugh *et al.*, 1969). As firms increase in size, additional problems are created in terms of coordination and control often necessitating structural changes. For example, as the business expands, the owner of a small business often faces increasing pressures on his or her time. No longer is he or she able to maintain a close control of operations, act as the major representative to customers, as well as managing administration and wages. In such cases some formalization and delegation is inevitable and a stage is reached when small businesses take their first steps towards bureaucratization. Such changes in structure with increasing size can be viewed in large as well as in small firms. [. . .] The way firms respond to size may vary resulting in different types of structure, which we identify in the next section. While there are obvious connections between size and structure, Child (1984a) points out that the complexity of an organization's operations may have a more significant impact on its structure than sheer size.
[. . .]

Changes in the environment

[. . .] Burns and Stalker (1966) noted that technological and market changes in the post-war electronics industry were best served by a less bureaucratic, more flexible kind of organization. Such organic structures were an essential element in the firm's ability to cope with a highly changing environment, and firms which retained their traditional bureaucratic or mechanistic structures were much less successful. The IBM case at the end of this section illustrates the relationship between structure and a rapidly changing product market.

This theme of the structure fitting the dominant aspects of the firm's environment is the major plank in the work of Lawrence and Lorsch (1967). They believe that different tasks in the organization are confronted by different environmental problems and demands, differences which should be reflected in the structures of the departments carrying out those tasks. In their study of the plastics industry they found a highly uncertain technological environment which called for a flexible R&D function, while the demands imposed on the production department were more predictable, enabling a more traditional, bureaucratic structure to operate. The structural implications of Lawrence and Lorsch's analysis do not end with what they term the 'differentiation' of functions. In order to operate effectively all organizations so differentiated must establish integrative devices, which might include a committee structure or designing special coordinating roles.

An interesting illustration of a firm adapting to a predominant environmental condition is given by Child (1984a). He cites the example of the American multinational ITT operating in a highly volatile political environment in Chile in the 1970s. As part of its coping strategy, the firm set up a political intelligence unit.

Strategy

The influence of strategy on structure is related to the way management perceive their environment. A firm wishing to be a product leader in a technologically sophisticated product market will have a correspondingly large R&D department both in terms of investment and employees. A firm that places a great deal of emphasis on cost controls may have a larger than average accounting department.

The relationship of strategy to organizational structure owes much to the work of Alfred Chandler (1962, 1977). He based his first work around an in-depth case study of the development of four companies; DuPont, General Motors, Standard Oil and Sears Roebuck. His work, however, had a much broader perspective; that of charting the development of American capitalism and especially the role played by the professional manager. One of the major conclusions of his work is that structure is a product of managerial strategies. The relationship between the two is more complex than many summaries of Chandler acknowledge. He found that structure did not automatically follow strategy and that managements often needed a crisis before they would agree to structural change. This point emerges in Case 1.2 with IBM.

As might be expected of an economic historian, Chandler viewed the relationship between strategy and structure as dynamic and evolutionary. He identified several stages in the development of American capitalism. These were cycles of growth and consolidation, each with its own implications for the organizational structures of the emerging large corporations in his study. The growth of mass markets and the development of the techniques of mass production were accompanied by vertical integration to ensure the supply of materials and secure distribution channels, and horizontal integration through takeovers to maintain growth. Expansion brought its own problems of coordination and control and subsequent inefficiency. These were solved by the growth of professional management and the development of organizations structured around specialist functions, such as marketing and finance. As existing markets became saturated and the benefits accruing from organizational restructuring slowed down, new markets and products were vigorously pursued by overseas expansion and R&D respectively. Once again these developments brought their own problems of coordination and control. This time a new form of structure emerged. All four firms in Chandler's study had adopted a multi-divisional structure by 1929, with DuPont and General Motors leading the way. The essential qualities of this structure will be identified in the following section.

Similar cycles of expansion and consolidation through structural change can be found in studies of British companies (see for example Channon, 1973). While such works offer strong evidence for the influence of strategy over structure, we have already noted the complex nature of the relationship. Chandler noted that the motivation for structural change emerged not only from changes in strategy but that it needed the catalyst of an organizational crisis. We can see cases where structural change may be unnecessary or at least delayed by the sheer market power of the firm, as in the case of IBM. There may even be a case for arguing that structure can determine strategy. For example, once a company has adopted a multi-divisional structure, this could well give divisional managers the incentive, confidence and resources for even greater expansion. [. . .]

Culture

The influence of culture on structure should not be underestimated. There is evidence that different structural forms are favoured in different countries. For example, American firms developed initially through the adoption of divisional structures, while in Britain we favoured the holding company (Channon, 1973). Firms in different countries often reflect different emphases, so it has been noted that while American firms stress the finance and marketing

Case 1.2 IBM

In 1988 the senior management at IBM implemented significant structural changes, following the appointment of a new chairman in 1985. These changes were seen as a product of several interrelated factors not least of which was an unacceptable fall in profits since 1984.

Before 1988 the organization structure reflected a high degree of specialization between the various functional departments (known somewhat confusingly for our purposes as divisions). Clear distinctions were drawn between the technical division, which designed the computers, the manufacturing division, which made them, and the marketing division which was responsible for sales. In addition, IBM had no separate department concerned with software development. As a result of this type of structure management concluded that counter-productive internal conflicts were set up, new designs were delayed by as much as two years, and new models when they were introduced lacked supporting software, enabling competitors to increase their market share in key areas.

In a way IBM had been lulled by their dominant market position and early technical leadership in the field. The company firmly established its leading position throughout the 1960s and '70s. Current management thinking suggests that the company became complacent, highly bureaucratic, ultra-conservative and missed the essential entrepreneurial spirit associated with its early days.

While IBM still dominated the mainframe market, helped significantly by its US government contracts and supplies to many major companies throughout the world, it had not responded to important changes in other markets. The computer market has become technically very diverse and there have been many aggressive new entrants. Such new entrants have not been held back by a large bureaucracy, they have operated with flexible organization structures that have enabled them to respond more effectively to technological change and be sensitive to the needs of the customer. The resulting market has become highly fragmented and price-competitive. IBM mini-systems have been losing out to Digital and the personal computer market has been swamped by IBM compatibles like Amstrad, selling at considerably cheaper prices and offering a more comprehensive range of software.

The structural response of IBM has been divisionalization and decentralization. Five divisions have been created; mainframes, mini-computers, personal computers, telecommunications, and new technology. Each division is autonomous, and is responsible for its own product design, manufacture, sales and ultimately profits.

(*Source*: John Cassidy and David Holmes, IBM spreads workload for quicker pace, *Sunday Times*, 14 February 1988)

functions, those in Germany have a production orientation (Hayes and Wheelwright, 1984); industrial relations management plays a much more significant role in Britain than either of those two countries. Studies on such aspects as the shape and extent of the management hierarchy have also noted differences between countries (Brossard and Maurice, 1976; Trompenaars, 1993). For example the hierarchies in French firms tend to be steeper than those in the UK, and much steeper than those in Germany. Structure may also reflect specific organizational cultures; for example, those firms favouring the involvement of employees in decision-making may set up participative forums to facilitate this.

Interest groups

Although Chandler noted the resistance on the part of some managers to structural change, the whole issue of interest groups and organizational politics was largely overlooked. The preferences of the dominant coalition can exert considerable influence on the structure as can the demands of major stakeholders. Those firms where the owners play a major role in management tend to be highly centralized. In the public sector the pressure for accountability often results in elaborate financial control mechanisms and bureaucratic procedures. In some manufacturing firms the pressure from banks on lending may in times of recession lead to reductions in development activities, with a corresponding impact on the size of the R&D function.

[. . .] Case 1.2 shows structural changes following management changes. While size, market and other environmental influences inevitably played a major role in [. . .] IBM [. . .], the catalyst for new structures [. . .] would seem to be changes at the top.

Two important points emerge from our consideration of the six influences above. First, there is considerable overlap between the various factors. For example, the structural changes of firms like Dupont and General Motors link technology, size and strategy; the different structural routes taken by firms in different countries are both a function of cultural differences and variations in environmental factors. In short, the structure of an organization can only be explained by reference to a number of interrelated factors. Once again this is amply illustrated in [. . .] the [. . .] IBM case. Second, our analysis raises the issue of the extent of choice senior management have in determining the structure of their organization. Are structures creative innovations to implement changing strategies or are they the inevitable consequences of adaptation to prevailing influences? [. . .]

If managers do have a choice of structure for their organization, then it may include one of the following structural types.

Types of structure

In this section we present a brief review of the major structural types and examine some alternative structural forms as well as cover, albeit briefly, the debate on the flexible firm. Very few organizations conform precisely to a particular type. In some organizations a particular kind of structure predominates, while others display a variety of types. We will explain the basic characteristic of each type and present in Figure 1.5 a summary statement of the supposed advantages and problems associated with each one. In this summary we group the divisional and holding company types together, since each represents a different method of achieving decentralization. As we mentioned earlier, structure does not emerge as an issue until a firm reaches a certain size. Many small firms have no apparent structure at all, beyond a centralized control system, but even this is not inevitable as in the case of partnerships between professional people. We identify five main types of organization structure.

Functional

The main criteria guiding this type of organization is functional specialization. As we can see from the illustration in Figure 1.1 employees performing related specialist tasks are grouped together under a single management structure. Most firms as they develop adopt this form of structure and it is especially suited to single product firms. The structure was widely used by British firms, even very large companies, up to the 1960s, but became less common in larger firms especially, as it was superseded by divisionalization (Channon, 1973).

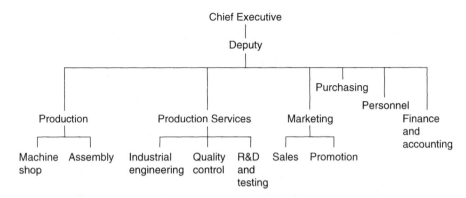

Figure 1.1 A functional structure: an engineering components business

---

Key concept 1.3: The multidivisional company

A multidivisional company comprises a number of different business units which may pursue markedly different types of business activity. The various business units operate as profit-centres and are centrally coordinated by a corporate headquarters, which may also control certain central services such as research and development and finance. This kind of structure developed in the USA in response to business growth. In Britain many large, diverse organizations have tended to favour a somewhat looser holding company structure with possibly less central coordination of strategic planning. In reality there is much overlap between the two kinds of structure.

Divisional

The development of the divisional or, as it is sometimes called, the multi-divisional company is associated with market expansion and product diversification. In both these cases traditional functional structures showed themselves to be inadequate in coordinating and controlling the firm's activities. Divisionalization was a particularly American development and is associated with 'pioneer' companies like General Motors and DuPont in the 1920s and with the multinational expansion of American firms in the 1930s (Chandler, 1962).

An illustration of a divisional structure is shown in Figure 1.2. Under such an organization structure each division is self-contained and operates as a profit centre. Divisions can be grouped around products or markets or a combination of the two, as in the case of Ford. The activities of the various divisions are directed by a central headquarters unit who take a global view of corporate strategy. Other central activities might include R&D and purchasing, to benefit from economies of scale. The dual existence of divisional profit centres and central units is a source of tension for many firms operating this structure, especially in the allocation of the costs of these central units to the individual divisions. In one case, a divisionalized engineering firm operated a central foundry, which also had to act as a profit centre in its own right. As well as serving the needs of its own organization, the foundry, having spare capacity, was encouraged to seek contracts outside the firm. This set up two sorts of tension: first, the various divisions complained about having to pay the 'going rate' for foundry products, and second, the divisions always demanded priority

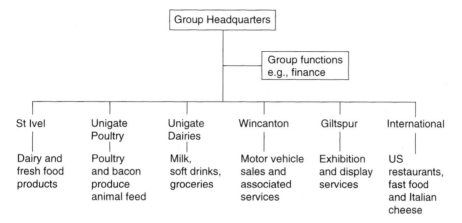

Figure 1.2 A divisional structure: Unigate – a divisionalized structure organized around product
   groupings
Source: *Company Reports and Accounts*, 1988

over external contracts, which hampered the foundry from achieving its own profit
objectives.

Once divisions have been established a decision still has to be made about grouping
within each division. In some cases this is done along traditional functional lines, whereas
in others staff are organized around products.

The holding company

This form of organization is associated with the growth of the firm by acquisitions and a
high degree of product diversification. It comprises, as we can see from the illustration in
Figure 1.3, a group of independent companies controlled by a coordinating group usually
made up of the chief executives of the constituent companies. At its extreme form, as
exemplified by a company such as Lonhro, this structural type represents as much a form
of ownership and investment as it does a kind of organization. Hanson Trust is one such
company that has been subjected to considerable criticism for pursuing policies of short-
term financial gain at the expense of company development through its selective policies of
corporate acquisition and sales. Hanson's attempt to buy ICI in 1991 generated considerable
speculation concerning major job losses and future investment in ICI. Amid growing
opposition the takeover was eventually thwarted by the ICI board (a fuller account of this
debate may be found in Adcroft *et al.*, 1991).

Holding companies can be highly diversified, as in the case of Trafalgar House, or built
around loosely related products as with the TI Group. Ultramar on the other hand
represents a holding company of highly related activities in oil and gas exploration and the
production, shipping and refining of crude oil and petroleum products.

As we saw in the previous chapter, the holding company is the prevalent structural form
for large Japanese companies. It has also been described as the peculiarly British route to
divisionalization (Channon, 1973). Although there are similarities between divisional and
holding company structures, Channon believed that the reluctance of British firms to adopt
divisionalization was a contributory factor in their relative failure in competitive world
economies; a case of structure influencing performance.

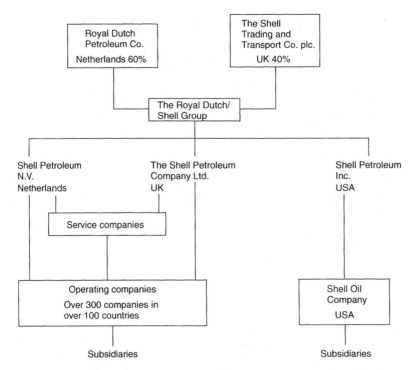

Figure 1.3 **A holding company: Royal Dutch Shell**
Source: *Company Reports and Accounts, 1988*

The project team

These comprise units specially created to cope with a highly unstable environment. In essence they are temporary structures formed around a particular task or problem and reflect technical expertise rather than any notion of management hierarchy. Such structures are commonly found in high-technology firms and some types of service organizations, especially consultancies. In advertising agencies, teams are usually created to deal with specific client accounts. In R&D departments the research work may be organized around several teams, each handling a different problem. In construction companies project teams may be created to deal with a particular job such as the building of a new office block. The membership of teams can be highly fluid; different specialists may be brought in at different times and one employee may be a member of several teams.

The approach reflects a close identification with the needs of the client and is an extension of the kind of client-based structure found in professional firms such as solicitors, accountants and the like. While focusing specifically on the needs of the client does have its advantages there can be some unnecessary duplication of resources and there can be scheduling and logistics problems. These become more severe as the organization gets larger and a stage may be reached where project teams need to be supported within a functional or divisional frame-work. The matrix structure was developed especially with such problems in mind and it is to this we now turn.

The matrix

Essentially the matrix is an attempt to combine the best of all worlds; the customer-orientation of the project team, the economies of scale and the specialist orientation of the functional organization, and the product or market focus of the divisional company. The matrix is an attempt to devise a structure that can effectively manage at least two different elements, be they size, products, markets or customers. [. . .] The illustration of a matrix in a university business school is presented in Figure 1.4.

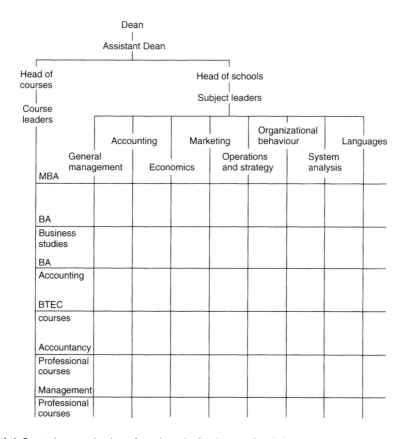

Figure 1.4 A matrix organization of a university business school

The matrix became very popular in the 1970s and owed much to the work of Lawrence and Lorsch (1967) and Galbraith (1971). It was embraced by companies such as Dow Corning [. . .], General Electric, Ciba Geigy and Citibank. The popularity was short-lived and of all the structural types the matrix has attracted most criticism. In a later work Paul Lawrence referred to the matrix as an 'unnecessary complexity', which was only justified in certain situations (Davis and Lawrence, 1977, p. 21): first, if two or more of a firm's dimensions, like products and markets, were especially critical to its performance; second, if employees needed to carry out highly complex, interdependent tasks in an uncertain environment; third, if economies of scale were needed especially in the use of scarce or expensive resources. Unless such conditions are present then the matrix can cause more problems than it solves. [. . .] Trompenaars (1993) has argued that the effectiveness of the

ADVANTAGES	*PROBLEMS*

1. Functional organization

❑ Specialization.	❑ Conflicting departmental objectives.
❑ The logic of custom and practice.	❑ Conflicting management values.
❑ A clear chain of command.	❑ A lack of coordination.
	❑ A lack of consumer orientation.

2. Divisional organization and holding company

❑ The operation of businesses as profit centres.	❑ Cooperation and interdependence.
❑ The encouragement of entrepreneurship.	❑ Accounting procedures, especially transfer pricing.
❑ Reduces upward dependency on top management.	❑ Increasing diversity of operations.
❑ Economies of scale by centralization of common functions like R&D.	❑ Overall management control.

3. Project teams

❑ The ability to cope with unstable environment.	❑ A costly duplication of resources.
❑ The use of individual expertise.	❑ Scheduling.
❑ The ability to cope with diverse problems	❑ The participants have no functional home.
❑ Deal directly with the customer.	❑ What happens when the project is finished?

4. Matrix organization

❑ Emphasizes the strengths of the functional and project types.	❑ Coordination and control.
❑ Flexibility of labour.	❑ A proliferation of committees and meetings.
❑ The ability to transfer expertise where it is most needed.	❑ Too many bosses.
❑ Dual control via function and project.	❑ Conflicting loyalties for staff.
❑ Closeness to the customer.	❑ Can be slow to adapt.

Figure 1.5 **A summary of advantages and problems associated with different types of organization structure**

matrix may be limited to specific cultures. Matrix organizations are not successful in Italy where, Trompenaars argues, bosses are seen as father figures. Since matrix organizations often require people to have two bosses, Italians find it difficult relating to two 'fathers'. It is interesting to note that at a time when most business organizations were finding the matrix wanting, it was emerging as perhaps the most popular structure in university business schools.

Students should always remember that the structural types identified above represent fairly broad categories. In reality a firm may display a mixture of structures. We have already seen how many divisionalized companies have functional specialisms within each division. In a functional organization we may find that different departments are organized along different lines; the operations department may well extend the functional structure, while the R&D staff may well be organized as project teams. New structural forms are emerging all the time, adapting the traditional approaches to suit their own needs. The Philips factory in South London was organized along functional lines but management redrew the organization chart to place the production function at the centre of a network of supporting activities, in an attempt to establish manufacture as the core activity.

Alternative forms of organization structure

A currently popular concept is that of networking. This type of structure has been made possible by developments in computer technology whereby computer systems can interact. Such a system enables people to operate from home and has been heralded as the organization structure of the future. Networking has attracted considerable publicity both in academic journals and the popular press. This attention however tends to exaggerate the real extent of networking. Even in pioneer networkers such as Rank Xerox, those employees operating under this system are but a very small percentage of the total employed. Of course, a form of networking has been around for some time in certain types of manufacturing industry in the form of homeworking. In this case individuals or even families engage in simple assembly work (as with electrical components) or in such activities as dressmaking and alteration. Homeworking has become a way of life in some countries such as Japan and is a particularly low-cost form of labour.

While the publicity surrounding networking outstrips the reality, this is not the case for franchising, an emerging form of organizational structure akin to the holding company. Under a franchise agreement a parent company will assist in the start-up of a new business enterprise. The terms of that agreement usually involve an initial investment on the part of the franchisee and an undertaking to deal exclusively with the franchisor in the marketing of his products. The purchase of the franchisor's products invariably involves the payment of a mark-up in return for the advertising and promotional support of a larger company. A good illustration of franchising is presented by the fast-food industry, such as Kentucky Fried Chicken although there are more than 300 different franchise operations in Britain including such diverse operations as the British School of Motoring, drain clearance and wedding-dress hire. A recent growth in franchise operations has taken place in the financial service sector, as in the case of insurance broking. In this case the franchisee, instead of buying goods from the franchisor, buys access to a computer database. The main advantage to both parties in a franchise agreement is the spread of risk. As such it has become a popular form of small business venture.

The two illustrations of networking and franchising focus on criteria of flexibility and cost. These are two major considerations in the debate about the concept of the 'flexible firm' and about the relationship between structure and performance. We end this section on structure by examining these two issues.

The flexible firm

The concept of the flexible firm emerged from work carried out by the Institute of Manpower Studies and associated largely with the writing of John Atkinson (his 1984 article offers an excellent summary). The main assumption is that new forms of organization are required as a strategic response to the combined effects of market stagnation, job losses, technological change, increased uncertainty, and reductions in the working week. The ideal strategic response to these forces involves some form of flexible manning. Atkinson identifies three types of flexibility.

- Functional flexibility is achieved when employees are able to perform a range of jobs and can move between them as the need arises. In many organizations this will see an end to demarcation between trades, the cause of many disputes and inefficiencies and lead to multi-skilling.

- Numerical flexibility is achieved through management's ability to make rapid alterations to the headcount of the firm to meet changes in demand. A growth in part-time and contract work was envisaged.
- Financial flexibility is required to reflect changes in the supply and demand of labour and to enhance the operation of functional and numerical flexibility. This can be achieved through the creation of differential rates of pay for full- and part-time workers and the use of incentives for workers to acquire more skills.

The ensuing 'flexible firm' will do much to break up traditional organization structures. For Atkinson, the key creation is that of the core and peripheral groups of employees. Core employees are those on permanent or long-term contracts and who hold the key skills in the organization. Accordingly they are well rewarded for their contribution. Peripheral workers comprise two groups. It is envisaged that there will be a group of full-time workers, who in general will be less skilled and not enjoy the security of the core employee. [. . .] The second group of peripheral workers will comprise part-time and contract workers hired in direct proportion to the demand or to deal with non-core business, such as catering and cleaning.

A superficial analysis of many large firms in the UK will reveal elements of the Institute of Manpower Studies' model. Many private-, and in particular, public-sector organizations have increased the use of part-time and contract workers. Major manufacturing firms such as Ford have introduced policies towards multiskilling and the end to demarcation, as in the creation of maintenance jobs that bridge the mechanical and electrical divide.

The model has also attracted its critics. Pollert (1987), in particular, accuses Atkinson and his team of offering vague concepts and of producing a model that is not supported by current evidence. She argues that elements of the flexible firm model can be seen in many organizations, but they have been introduced as cost-cutting exercises rather than a strategic response to a changing market environment. This is particularly true of local authorities and other public-sector organizations. She goes on to claim that many of the elements are far from new, citing multiskilling as a feature of 1960s productivity bargaining initiatives. In some industries, notably fast food, she cites core workers as anything but the skilled, highly paid élite of Atkinson's flexible firm. Finally she fears that the adoption of the flexible model could lead to more problems than it solves. Such problems as the growth of part-time employment have certainly attracted the interest of trade unions who view it as a part of the process of decreasing job security.

Clearly more evidence is required concerning the types and extent of flexibility and their relationship to overall management strategy.

Structure and performance

We can see from Figure 1.5 and our discussion of the various structural types that some structures are more suited to some situations than others. Conversely a firm that adheres stubbornly to a structure that is totally inappropriate to the contingencies that it faces may be creating problems for itself. However, the evidence on these matters is far from convincing. The major difficulties in establishing a correlation between structure and performance would appear to be first, identifying appropriate measures of performance and second, proving causality. We can make some general points.

- Whatever the relationship between structure and performance, Johnson and Scholes (1993) point out that once a structure has been installed, it is often very difficult to change it. Equally, frequent structural changes could be damaging in terms of the disruption that takes place and the requirement on the part of staff to learn new systems.

- It is extremely doubtful whether structure alone can lead to improvements in performance. However sound the structure may be, it is unlikely that it can totally overcome problems created by staff incompetence or even divisive internal politics. In some cases a high degree of specialization or divisionalization can lead to a worsening of relationships. We might even speculate that there is more evidence for suggesting that structure can affect performance in a negative way than there is for its having a positive impact. There is some evidence that structure in harness with other variables can lead to improvements in performance (Child, 1972). This point was taken up by Galbraith and Nathanson (1978), who argue that effective financial performance is obtained by achieving some kind of congruence between strategy, structure, processes, rewards and people.
- Child (1984a) also points out that performance can influence structure, citing the example that more successful companies financially tend to have fewer cost controls. This fits in with one of the key assumptions of our Business in Context model; that influences operate in more than one direction and while organizational factors such as structure can affect the outcome of a firm's activities, that outcome in turn affects the organization.

OWNERSHIP

We might assume quite logically that ownership is an important variable in that the owners of a business will wish to determine the goals and the way that business operates. In support of our assumption we could cite illustrations of influential founders such as Henry Ford, Thomas J. Watson of IBM, and the Sainsbury family of supermarket fame. We could also refer to numerous cases of small firms where the owner, often single-handedly, controls the destiny of the business. In the case of the small firm the owners can be clearly defined and their impact easily assessed. Discovering who actually owns and controls businesses becomes much more difficult with large corporations like the major oil companies, or even an organization like British Airways, where privatization has been accompanied by widespread share issue, at least, in the first instance. It would appear that the greater the size of the organization and the greater the dispersal of share ownership then the more we can question our original assumptions and need to examine the relationship between the ownership and the control of businesses.

The degree of private and public ownership is another issue which holds significant interest for students of business in this country. Organizations that are wholly or partly state-owned, like the coal mines or the local hospital, raise important issues of management control and public accountability.

In this section we will focus on these two aspects of ownership and examine the implications for the way businesses operate. We deal first with the traditional debate surrounding ownership and control. Second, we examine the issue of the public ownership of organizations and the trend of privatization. The two elements were brought much closer together in the latter half of the 1980s in Britain. Traditional public-sector concerns such as hospitals and local authorities have been urged to take a more commercial approach. Since 1983, many organizations like British Telecom, Jaguar, British Aerospace, and utilities such as gas, electricity and water have passed from public to private ownership or to a mixture of public and private ownership. This has been accompanied by a massive increase in the proportion of the population owning shares and a highly dispersed ownership pattern for those concerns. It is this dispersal that is at the heart of the ownership and control debate.

Ownership and control

The issue of ownership and control is one of continuing interest for academics, more especially among economists and sociologists. It is also a debate which raises significant questions for businesses in practice. How committed to the future of an enterprise are managers who have no stake in its ownership, or shareholders who have no interest beyond a return on investment? Are the resulting strategies in the best interests of all concerned; owners, managers, employees, the state, the public at large? How much freedom do managers have in developing business strategies?

The debate around these issues originates from the separation of ownership and control through the creation of the joint stock company and the subsequent dispersal of share ownership. With increased investment businesses grew in size and complexity and control by professional managers became a necessity. The complexity of such growing businesses led to a specialization within the management group and the separation of the firm into different specialist functions and activities. Bureaucratic rules and procedures were developed to coordinate and control such activities. Both the specialization and bureau-cratization reinforced the control of the management group with a supposed weakening in the power of the owner to influence decisions. The owner's main source of control was through the possession of capital stock.

This phenomenon was highlighted in the seminal study of Berle and Means (1932) and developed in later work by Berle (1954). Berle and Means in a study of the 200 largest non-financial corporations in the USA classified the firms by their mode of control. They concluded that 44% of the firms were management controlled and that this trend was increasing. The Berle and Means study has been replicated in both the USA and Britain with similar results, although both the data and conclusions of such studies have been the subject of significant controversy (Scott, 1979 has a reasonable summary of these studies).

Berle and Means used their data to develop and support their own view of a 'managerial revolution'. To them management control was 'better' in that it resulted in more effective decisions both for the profitability of the firm and for the general good of society; it was more professional and more socially responsible. The concepts of a 'neutral technocracy' and a 'soulful corporation' have stemmed from such value assessments of management control. We can see a clear link between Berle and Means's notion of 'managerialism' and the earlier work of F. W. Taylor on 'scientific management' (published in 1947). For both Taylor and Berle and Means, management should use a professional approach based on the application of science to solve the problems facing the firm. According to Berle and Means, management control would be truly professional in that strategies would be guided more by scientific analysis and be more answerable to society than the potentially narrow self-interest of the owner-manager. This concept of a managerial revolution was popularly espoused by Burnham (1941), whose ideas have attracted perhaps more attention than his analysis deserves. Burnham, writing at the time of Roosevelt's 'New Deal' saw similarities in many nations through the increased state control of the economy. He believed that through this managers, as the controllers of capital, would be able to assume a powerful role in society and direct businesses to serve their own ends.

There is a tendency to view such debates as purely academic. This would be wrong since the questions that emerge are central to the way businesses operate and the control of organizations has implications not only for the survival and prosperity of the organization itself, but also for the people who work for it, firms who deal with it, and society at large. We therefore examine some key issues in the ownership and control debate and raise a number of questions around the conclusions drawn by Berle and Means.

- Do managers really have more power and control than shareholders? Even with a dispersal of share ownership shareholders' needs still have to be satisfied, which may place constraints on management decisions. There is always a danger that shareholders, in the face of what they perceive as unpopular management decisions will sell their shares creating instability in the firm's stock market position.

In any case the distinction between managers and shareholders has become increasingly blurred. While in many companies there clearly has been a separation of ownership and control, there is an increasing tendency, especially in the larger firms, to offer senior management shares in the company as part of their annual remuneration deal. In this way, managers may well identify with shareholders' own aspirations. This argument has been extended by the Marxist analysis of ownership and control, which views shareholders and managers not as being separate but as different forms of the same animal; no real distinction is drawn between managers and capitalist owners. In addition to such arguments we can see that management freedom to make decisions is often held in check by banks, governments and trade unions. This complicates the ownership and control debate and we return to the role of the financial institutions later.

- In addition to the above arguments it has often been pointed out that many large and influential companies are both family-owned and controlled and no separation has in fact occurred. In the retail trade in Britain such family-run businesses as Sainsbury, Asda and Dixons have grown and prospered in relatively recent times. Empirical work from the USA suggests that family ownership and control of major businesses is still a significant feature; Sheehan (1967) found of the largest 500 American firms, 150 could be designated as having a significant family interest in terms of management and control.

- Has the ownership of shares really been dispersed? The data presented by Berle and Means (1932) showed that 86% of the largest 200 US companies had a minimum of 5000 shareholders, with 22% having over 50 000. Putting such data in perspective Miliband (1969) cites evidence which reveals that in Britain in 1961 only 4% of the population owned shares and 1% of the population owned 81% of all shares. Others, notably Child (1969), interpret the evidence that while there may be some evidence of share dispersal, the majority of shareholders own relatively small numbers of shares and tend to be extremely passive. This can result in minority shareholders owning a substantial proportion of all shares with considerably more interest and potential influence in management decision-making. It is not just the dispersal of shares which should concern us, but the pattern of that dispersal.

   Most of these data are of course fairly old, and the entire pattern of share ownership, in Britain at least, has been confused by the large number of share issues in the 1980s and 1990s resulting from the government's policy of privatization. Many of the earlier share issues, such as British Telecom, were oversubscribed to a significant extent. While it is undeniable that large numbers have been brought into share ownership for the first time, it is however much too early to assess the situation. Many of those who have bought shares have done so with the prime intention of a quick sale for profit.
   [. . .]
   The shares of such public sales may well find themselves consolidated among a much smaller group of traditional shareholders within a relatively short space of time.

- Are professional managers more effective and more socially responsible than the traditional owner-manager? Recent assessments of management in Britain have raised serious doubts about the competence of those managers. Degrees of social responsibility are particularly difficult to gauge. In any case there is some logic in suggesting that the career-motivated professional manager would show less, not more, paternalism towards staff and less concern for social issues in general than the traditional entrepreneur, who would often have strong connections with the local community.

The contemporary plausible interpretation of the ownership and control debate focuses on the role of financial institutions. We can always cite the case of small firms and even large corporations where owner control is the norm. However, in both Britain and America a substantial shareholding of many of the major firms has passed to the hands of financial institutions, including banks, insurance and pension companies (Scott, 1979 provides an excellent summary of the supporting evidence). Their presence changes the nature of the Berle and Means debate. There is an acknowledgement of a separation between shareholders and managers, but a serious challenge to the concept of the passive shareholder. Such financial intermediaries not only tend to hold a significant minority stockholding, which gives them both power and influence, but they also take an active interest in important strategic decisions. Their credibility with their current clients and their ability to attract future investors rests upon the ability of their investment managers to ensure that yields are both attractive and secure. The sale of large numbers of shares by a bank or pension fund could well undermine the confidence of the stock market in a particular firm. Scott (1979) argues that large financial investors have become the dominant form of strategic control in British companies. They possess the mechanisms to be well informed and the power to make their views known to management. They become particularly active in crises and may be instrumental in not just dictating the policy of top management, but determining the composition of that group.

The clear inference from such an examination of the stockholding role of financial institutions is that the envisaged separation of ownership and control has not taken place. However, as Scott points out, the influence of financial institutions on business is far from being just financial. He propounds the notion of a 'constellation of interests', whereby the representatives of financial institutions are elected or appointed to the boards of directors of those companies where they hold a substantial minority interest. The senior officials of a bank may each hold a number of such directorships, as do the senior officials of other financial institutions. A pattern is thus built up of interlocking directorships representing a very important network of information, which supersedes finance as an instrument of power. Such directors will influence the recruitment of other directors and will inevitably favour those with access to vital information.

We can see that management decisions in a single firm may be influenced and even significantly constrained by directors representing the interests of other institutions altogether. A similar pattern of influence and constraint occurs in the management of public-sector organizations and it is to this we now turn.

Key concept 1.4: The public sector

This is a broad term covering a range of organizations in both the manufacturing and service sectors. Despite the differences, public-sector organizations share many problems. These include the extent of State control over management decisions, the public accountability of management decisions, levels of government spending and conflict over goals. The Government in Britain since 1979 has attempted to solve such problems by taking organizations out of the public domain and establishing them as private enterprises.

Management and control in the public sector

We often refer to the public sector as if it were a homogeneous group of organizations. This is highly misleading, for the public sector encompasses a wide range of institutions. At least three broad types may be identified. First, we have the nationalized industries; these are wholly owned and controlled by the state and include such organizations as the National Coal Board and the Post Office. Second, we have those companies which are controlled by the state acting as a majority shareholder and holding company; currently this operates through the British Technology Group (incorporating the National Enterprise Board). Both these types of enterprise have business objectives in that they sell their goods and services in the marketplace, in many cases with the profit motive in mind (although nationalized industries are theoretically bound by statute to break even). The third type of public-sector organization, such as the health, education and social services, offers its services to the population and is funded indirectly through the taxation system.

The rationale for a public sector can be explained in political, economic and social terms, although we can make a broad distinction here between the business and non-business institution. In terms of the provision for health, education, social services, and especially the police and armed forces, there is a broad consensus that public ownership and control is socially and indeed politically desirable, but even here there is fierce political debate on the extent of public provision in areas such as health and education. The major political contention concerns a public-sector business presence, brought sharply into focus by the privatization of many public-sector concerns in the 1980s. The commitment to public ownership has been a major ideological strand in the constitution of the Labour party enshrined in Clause 4. Indeed the nationalized industries have their goals defined by statute; to provide a specific service, to break even and to operate in the interests of employees and the public at large. Other arguments are made in support of the business public sector; that it supports the growth of other industries by providing such needs as energy; that it can both prevent and ease the decline of industries, significant either for the product or numbers employed or both, as in the case of British Leyland; that the state is in an ideal position to develop new technology. [. . .]

Traditionally the public sector has always faced a number of serious problems arising from the tensions between public ownership, political control and day-to-day management. These tensions may be viewed in terms of goals and objectives, finance and control.

Despite the statutory responsibilities of nationalized industries, the goals of public-sector organizations have often been ill-defined and conflicting. For example, there was never a clear policy coordinating the activities of the coal, gas and electricity industries, when all three were under public ownership. Moreover, many public-sector operations have found conflict between the provision of a service and the necessity to break even, the railways being a good illustration. Such confusion over the goals led Sir Peter Parker to comment on his time as Head of British Rail,

I'd never before been in a job where no-one could tell me what winning means.

(quoted in Foy 1983, p. 68)

The superordinate goal of the public sector to operate in the public interest is itself open to question. Who defines the public interest and is it possible to satisfy all elements of the public at the same time? The National Coal Board, British Steel and British Rail have suffered possibly the greatest losses of any public-sector industry, but would the public be best served by making reductions in the services they provide? In the 1990s the government clearly thought just that, with a radical pruning of the coal industry and the wholesale closure of collieries.

Financially the public sector operates under considerable constraints. Pricing policies are often dictated by government in attempts to tackle inflation, as under an incomes policy, or to direct consumption, as in the case of energy use. Public-sector enterprises often find investment difficult; they are often prevented from borrowing from the government to hold down the public-sector borrowing requirement (PSBR), and the sources of external funding are severely restricted. As we have seen, many public-sector enterprises are required only to break even, yet there remains a strong belief among senior management that the greater the profit, then the greater the freedom to operate free of government interference.

Variations in profit margins have certainly led to inconsistencies in the treatment of public-sector concerns by successive governments, the relatively prosperous gas-supply industry enjoying considerably more policy-making freedom than the coal industry.

Excessive intervention has been a frequent complaint among public-sector managers. The very structure of the public sector demands answerability to different groups within government itself, to politicians, civil servants, appointed governing bodies, and to various consumer groups, all of whom may have differing expectations and impose conflicting demands upon management. The whole issue is invariably complicated by the organizational politics that develop in the relationship between the heads of public-sector organizations and their respective government masters.

The response to these problems by the Conservative Government since 1979 has been to embark upon a policy of privatization, deregulation and the introduction of a commercial approach in the public sector that remains. It is to these issues we now turn.

Privatization

The privatization policy vigorously pursued by the Conservative Government has its roots, as we have indicated, in an ideological commitment to the free market, and a belief in the inherent inefficiency of the public sector. This has not only resulted in the selling of entire industries, but in the privatization of certain services within the public sector, such as the laundry in hospitals and rubbish collection in some local authorities. [. . .]
[. . .]

The Government's opposition to the public sector and its belief in the private sector focuses on issues of efficiency and effectiveness, as well as control. Heald (1985) sensed that the pro-privatization lobby viewed the public-sector organization as inherently flawed, which no amount of attention paid to efficiency and control can cure. According to Heald, the privatization enthusiast's case rests upon two major assumptions. First, public-sector organizations are seen as less effective instruments of public policy than those of the private sector and second, the political objectives of public ownership are seen as less valid than the market criteria of private enterprise. The public sector was seen by the New Right Tories as a group of organizations with confused goals and inefficient operations dogged by industrial-relations problems. The service they provided was considered poor, leaving its customers dissatisfied and creating a burden for the taxpayer.

The alternative, privatization, offered a number of advantages to different groups. It was envisaged that competition would be stimulated with an accompanying increase in efficiency and effectiveness. For the general public it was an opportunity to widen share ownership and to benefit from an improved service with a greater responsiveness to customer needs. For the newly privatized organizations there would be greatly increased opportunity for raising revenue which could be reinvested in the operation. It was assumed this would stimulate innovation to the benefit of all. For the government, public spending would be reduced and the sales would raise much needed revenue. Furthermore the policy was seen by some Conservatives as a further erosion of the power of trade unions and an ideological victory over the Labour Party opposition.
[. . .]

Almost certainly it is too early to assess fully the impact of such measures and there is considerable difficulty in disentangling the ideological, political and economic aspects of the argument. Apart from the social issues at stake there is at the moment mixed evidence to suggest that the private sector is any more or less efficient or effective than the public sector.

SIZE

The influence of size as an organizational variable interacts across all levels of our Business in Context model. Many of the issues relating to size are dealt with elsewhere in this book and in this section we simply present a summary of those issues. We do however develop the concept further by examining the issues relating to small businesses.

We have already seen earlier in this chapter how size is an important determinant of structure. Hickson *et al.* (1969) noted that with increasing size the technological imperative gives way to the size imperative. Increasing formalization and bureaucratization are inevitable consequences of the growing firm, and the organization structure and management procedures are shaped by the need to coordinate and control large numbers of people. In our earlier discussion we saw how the growth of firms, especially through diversification, was an important element in companies such as General Motors adopting a divisional structure.

With size comes the development of specialist activities. [. . .]. The employment of large numbers of people invariably calls for specialist expertise in the areas of recruitment, training, job evaluation, payment systems and industrial relations. [There is also] a relationship between size and the R&D function. In this case it is not simply a matter of the numbers employed, but also a function of the need to maintain a powerful market position through investment in both product and process development and, of course, the ability to attract that investment.

Size is also related to dominance in the marketplace, as illustrated by the brewing industry in Britain. The industry is dominated by a handful of very large firms who maintain their market position not just by their ability to invest in product and process development, but also by the amount they are able to spend on nationwide advertising campaigns. Their position is further strengthened by their strategy of acquiring smaller independent breweries who find themselves unable to compete. The growth of lager sales at the expense of the traditional bitter beers has attracted the attention of the international brewing industry who are investing heavily in the British market. A similar pattern can be found in the record and music industry. By 1993, the industry was dominated by four companies controlling over 70% of the market. These were Warner, Thorn EMI, Sony and PolyGram. In almost every case they had grown by acquisition. A key element in concentration in the music industry has been the growth of sales in compact discs. Not only do these require considerable investment in technology for their manufacture, favouring the big firm, but also the public demand for reissues of old vinyl records in CD format has led to the larger firms buying up smaller independent producers to acquire their catalogues.

The big four record and CD producers dominate the sector, not just in terms of market share. There is a clear correlation in this industry between size and profitability. The biggest companies announce the biggest profit margins. There is a view that, in some industries, as with the illustration of the CD market, size is important. There is a considerable fear that the decline of the UK manufacturing industry in the 1980s has resulted in a lack of critical mass that is unable to compete in world terms. [. . .]

The ability of the large firm to dominate the marketplace is only part of its relationship with its environment. The size of a firm may be an important buffer in dealing with the demands imposed by its environment. [. . .] The multinational corporation is able to dominate its environment, including influencing and in some cases overriding the policies of nation states. Size has also been a factor in attracting government support, not only in terms of R&D investment; the numbers employed by such firms as British Leyland have necessitated government rescue attempts during financial crises for political and social reasons as much as for economic ones. In the 1970s in particular, size was often a vital protection against enforced closure. Size, structure and market position are themselves important variables in the determination of organization culture, which we deal with in the next section. At the micro-level there has been a great deal written about the impact of organizational size on the individual by focusing on the concepts of bureaucracy and alienation. Large organizations can undoubtedly present behavioural problems in terms of both management control and individual motivation. Such problems have been tackled by a range of devices including the creation of autonomous work groups in an attempt to break up the organization into more easily managed units. Despite such behavioural problems it should not be forgotten that, at the management level at least, many employees actively seek out large firms for the career opportunities they offer.

While there is considerable evidence supporting the dominant position of the large firm, the problem of control in particular questions whether large firms actually make the best use of their resources. The relationship between size and performance has been challenged by the small firms' lobby, elevated from a 'small is beautiful' campaign in the early 1970s to a near-political crusade for the future of Western capitalism in the 1980s. We now deal with the issues and arguments surrounding small firms.

SMALL BUSINESSES

The small firm has played a key role in the development of the business enterprise, particularly in the nineteenth century when economic growth owed much to the activities of individual entrepreneurs. The role of the small firm was overtaken by the development of mass production, mass markets, and above all the creation of the joint stock company which created investment and effectively removed a major constraint to the growth of businesses. Throughout this century the focus has been on the increasing size of businesses and the market domination by big business and the multinationals in particular.

The watershed came in 1971 with the publication of the Report of the Committee of Inquiry on Small Firms, generally referred to as the Bolton Report, after the Committee's chairman. The Committee's investigation was born out of a concern that the small firms' sector was being neglected, but also out of a disillusionment and fear of the economic and social consequences of domination by big business. The conclusion of Bolton and his colleagues was that the small firms' sector in Britain was in decline, both in terms of it size and its contribution to the nation's economy and that the decline was more marked in the United Kingdom than in its major economic rivals. The report concluded that despite the decline the small firm sector 'remains one of substantial importance to the United Kingdom economy' and that 'the contribution of small businessmen to the vitality of society is inestimable' (Bolton, 1971, p. 342).

The Report's importance lay not just in its conclusions, but as the first serious and subsequently influential attempt to define the small firm and in its stimulus to later research, much of which takes Bolton as its base point. The stimulus of the 1970s became the academic growth area of the 1980s, with many business schools setting up special small firms' units, both for the purposes of academic research and to provide support for the regeneration of the small firms' sector. The stimulus was fuelled in the 1980s by a government increasingly determined to publicize the small business as the key element in the nation's economic revival. A report published in 1983 by a group of conservative MPs and researchers stated,

> A high small firms ratio is consistent with high levels of growth and output. The malaise of our small business sector is a symptom and a cause of our comparative decline as an industrial nation.
>
> (Bright et al., 1983, p. 15)

Such statements were reinforced by a host of measures aimed at supporting the small businessman including special loans for business start-ups and special extension of welfare benefits to stimulate self-employment. In addition changes were made in the stock market through the creation of the Unlisted Securities Market whereby small firms could raise investment capital. The entrepreneur became the hero figure for the 1980s and people such as Clive Sinclair and Eddy Shah became household names. The rationale for government support was more than a belief in the economic importance of the small firm. At a time of high unemployment the small business start-up offered a practical, and to some, a highly attractive solution. Moreover it was a solution that was ideologically compatible with the Government's views on economic management, welfare, and self-help. It would be wrong of us to view the support of the small firm as the sole prerogative of the 'New Right' in British politics. Support for the small-firms sector has come from all sides of the political spectrum and it is one area where a Conservative government has met with agreement in many Labour controlled urban areas (with the notable exception of the now defunct Greater London Council, of which more later).

In this section we will look at the extent and nature of the small businesses in this country and assess their value, focusing particularly on the economic arguments for continued state support. [. . .]

The extent of the small firms' sector

[. . .]

Table 1.1 The Bolton Report definition of the small firm

Industry	Statistical definition of small firms
Manufacturing	200 employees or less
Retailing	Turnover £50 000 p.a. or less
Wholesale trades	Turnover £200 000 p.a. or less
Construction	25 employees or less
Mining/Quarrying	25 employees or less
Motor trades	Turnover £100 000 or less
Miscellaneous services	Turnover £50 000 or less
Road transport	5 vehicles or less
Catering	All excluding multiples and brewery managed houses

Source: Bolton Report 1.9, p. 3

[. . .] By 1986 it was estimated that 10% of the population worked for themselves and there was an increase in the number of small firms in all sectors, with the exception of retailing, where small businesses have declined. In addition, new types of small firm have emerged such as producer cooperatives and franchise operations (Curran, 1986). All these developments led Curran to conclude:

the official data does indicate that, for a wide variety of small enterprise, there has been a remarkable increase since 1970 so that the overall total and proportion of small scale activity in the economy has increased.

(Curran, 1986, p. 15)

Small businesses still predominate in the distribution, hotel and catering, repair and construction sectors, but between 1963 and 1980 there was a 25% increase in the numbers of small manufacturing concerns (Department of Employment, quoted in *New Society*, March 1986). The same source points to an increase in the numbers of ethnic minorities setting up small firms.

In addition to the increase in the number of firms, the survival chances of small firms appear to have improved. Although the problems of data accuracy are as acute here as elsewhere, estimates of the failure rate of business start-ups in the 1970s ranged from 50 to 75% within the first two years (Bannock, 1981). More recent and perhaps more reliable data suggest a figure of around 50% for the first two years, but that the chances of survival over ten years are 40–45% (Ganguly and Bannock, 1985). More significantly it has been found that the death rate of small firms actually slowed down during one of the worst periods of the recession in the early 1980s, although it is felt that business owners are intent on survival only in the absence of other opportunities (Stewart and Gallagher, 1985 have a fuller explanation). Other studies, however, remain more sceptical (Binks and Jennings, 1986 [. . .]).

More recent international figures confirm the view that the small business start-up is still a risky venture. A survey of small firms across the world from 1980 to 1990 revealed that, on average, 50–60% of startups fail within the first five years. The same report highlighted that in some countries, notably Singapore, the failure rate was as high as 70% (El-Namaki, 1993).

However incomplete the database on small firms may be, there is considerable evidence that the United Kingdom has fewer self-employed than many other comparable industrial nations, and it has fewer small firms making far less of a contribution to the economy. The small-firms sector here is smaller than that in the United States and West Germany, and significantly smaller than that in Japan (Ganguly and Bannock, 1985).

The value of small businesses

The value of small businesses may be viewed in terms of the benefits to the owners, their impact on economic growth, the number of jobs they provide, and their service to the consumer. We will deal with each of these aspects in turn.

In terms of the individual, the small firm offers a number of assumed advantages. A Gallup Poll finding in 1986 cited the desire to 'be your own boss' was the main motivation behind small business start-ups, and more significant than unemployment (*New Society*, March 1986). Certainly self-employment offers the individual far greater opportunities for control, and perhaps greater satisfaction through direct involvement, than working for someone else. The small business has for many been the pathway to real wealth, social mobility and perhaps political power in the local community. Some owners doubtless see their own business as a source of security for their family and as a kind of immortality via family succession. Against such values is the very real risk of failure, and serious financial loss for the owner and their family, and romantic tales of individualism, wealth and job satisfaction should be set alongside the long working week, the frustration and the stress that many small-business owners inevitably experience. The reality for many is that self-employment is less lucrative than working for someone else (*New Society*, March 1986), and those that are successful either become prime candidates for a takeover bid by a larger firm or fear a loss of control that inevitably comes with growth.

We have already noted that the Conservative Government of the 1980s saw the small firm as an essential ingredient of a healthy economy. The most obvious role for the small firm in this respect is to act as a 'seedbed' for future big business and in so doing secure the future of the economy. In addition, the small firm is seen as filling gaps in the marketplace by offering specialist products that would be uneconomic for the large firm to offer. More significantly the small firm is seen as a force for change by being inherently more flexible and innovative than the larger business. This image of the small firm was strengthened in the 1980s by the publicity given to the success and growth of certain small firms in the computer industry, although the majority of small businesses are decidedly 'low-' rather then 'high-' tech. In particular the small firm is seen as a useful vehicle in a recession; small firms are seen as price-takers and therefore offer no threat to inflation rates, and are able to plug the gaps left after larger firms have rationalized their operations. The rationalization of bus routes by the major companies, together with the government deregulation of bus services, paved the way for a number of smaller companies to enter the market, especially in rural areas and on the larger housing estates. These bus companies were able to operate routes that were uneconomic for the larger companies.

Many writers (for example, Scase and Goffee, 1980; Rainnie, 1985) are more sceptical of the economic contribution of the small-firms' sector, feeling that the small firm is exploited by big business and the main economic advantages of a small-business presence accrue to the larger company. Certainly large manufacturing concerns could not survive without the components supplied by a host of smaller companies, but this could be seen as a symbiotic rather than an exploitative relationship. However, the purchasing power of the large firm can have a significant impact on the profit margins of smaller companies. Certainly there is evidence of larger firms taking over markets created by smaller companies when those markets prove successful, the activity of IBM in the personal computer market being a case in point.

There is an assumption that small firms are first to the marketplace because they are inherently more innovative. Supporters of this view cite inventions such as air-conditioning and cellophane that originated from individual entrepreneurs and that small businesses often emerge from ideas for new products or clever adaptations of existing products. Big business on the other hand is often accused of channelling R&D along predictable lines and being less cost-effective in its use of R&D expenditure. Apart from the difficulties of measuring such things, the evidence for these claims is very mixed (Rothwell and Zegveld, 1981 have a good summary of the research). More recent research suggests that even if small firms are inventive they often lack the development capital for successful innovation. Moreover there is evidence to suggest that a high proportion of small business start-ups do not involve new products but involve the owner in replicating his previous employment (Binks and Jennings, 1986). This trend becomes especially critical where buy-outs are concerned and may be a primary cause of small-business failure among buy-outs. In this case an ailing firm either sells out or divests part of its operation to a group of existing employees, usually management. Their experience and skills give them the optimism to continue operations in the same product market, perhaps ignoring the lack of demand or excessive competition operating in that same market, and they merely repeat the failure of the original firm.

There are obvious benefits of a thriving small-firms sector for the labour market. [. . .] Redundancy and unemployment are big push factors towards self-employment. Small firms have been started and operate successfully in growth areas of the economy such as computer software and consultancy and the service sector in general. Moreover, self-employment is a valuable source of work for those groups, such as ethnic minorities who are discriminated against in the labour market. In certain communities an overdependence on a few large firms for employment can have serious consequences when those firms close, as the people of the Lancashire town of Skelmersdale found when Courtaulds decided to cease trading in the town. Under such circumstances a healthy small business presence may provide employment diversity and help counter the worst effects of mass redundancy. This view was taken by the government with the experience of mass redundancies at the nationalized

British Steel Corporation in the Sheffield area. The company took advantage of tax advantages by providing venture capital to business start-ups in the area.

However, the small firm is hardly a great provider of employment. A study of the hi-tech industry, one of the flagships of the small-firms lobby, in the Cambridge area from 1971 to 1981 concluded that only 800 new jobs had been created during the entire period (Gould and Keeble, 1984). Rainnie (1985) points out that whatever new jobs are created, they can easily be overshadowed by job losses in a large organization and cites a report of 10,000 redundancies at Britain's largest computer firm, ICL, in 1984. Moreover we have already seen from the high proportion of start-up failures that small firms are a source of job losses too. Outside the arguments about the small firm as a source of employment, the Greater London Council was especially critical of the small firm as an employer citing exploitation through low wages, long hours and an absence of trade-union recognition as the main reason for their lack of support for small business development (GLC, 1983). This view of small firms was also taken by Scase and Goffee (1980) who saw their main contribution to employment as solving the problems as defined by employers. Obviously not all small firms exploit their workforce, and many employees prefer the informal working environment that the small firm can provide.

[. . .] The small firm can benefit the consumer by filling the gaps left by the larger company. There is also the argument that the smaller firm is also closer to its customers and can provide them with a more personalized, responsive and specialized service. There are certain highly specialized product markets, such as precision scientific instrumentation which tend to favour the smaller concern. Whether the smaller firm offers a 'better' service to the consumer is impossible to generalize or even judge. When buying expensive wine for keeping several years, a small specialist firm may be the most appropriate consumer choice, while a supermarket chain may offer the best value on less expensive purchases. The situation becomes particularly blurred when you consider that a number of larger firms of all types pay particular attention to customer sales and after-sales service. At a broader level a small firms' sector may be of considerable benefit to the consumer in challenging the power of monopolies.
[. . .]

Concern for the small firm may well be, like the interest in Japanese management, a fashion born out of recession. Certainly small business development is important in the future of any economy, but current political interest owes as much to ideology as it does to sound economic argument. For our purposes the case of the small firm is again an excellent illustration of the interplay between the various elements of our business in context model.

Key concept 1.5: Organizational culture

In general terms the culture of an organization refers to those factors which enable us to distinguish one organization from another and are the product of its history, management, operating environment, technology, goals and so on. More recently the notion of organizational culture has been used in a more positive way and a set of principles have been developed which mark out the culture of a successful company from that of an unsuccessful one. As with all such universal principles, such claims have aroused considerable debate.

ORGANIZATIONAL CULTURE

[. . .] In this section we focus upon culture in a more localized setting, that of the organization itself. The goals, structure, patterns of ownership and size of an organization both reflect and are reflected in its culture. [. . .] The importance of the organizational culture is that it sets the scene for the determination of strategy and hence the operational aspects of organizational life. The concept assumes therefore a central position in our model of business.

Interest in the workings of an organizational culture were heightened in the USA during the 1970s as American companies searching for a solution to the problems of the economic recession looked to the role models of Japanese firms and the more successful firms within their own country. In turn, academic research in business shifted its focus away from individual management techniques to examining the business as a complete entity and viewing the way people responded to their own organization. A more subjective view of organizations began to emerge. Some would differentiate between the term organizational culture and that of corporate culture, the latter sometimes being associated with specific management initiatives to achieve corporate ends. Increasingly, however, the two terms are used interchangeably, and this text is no exception.

In this section we will examine the precise nature of organizational or corporate culture, attempt a classification of different types, examine its relationship to the concept of the 'excellent company', and assess its value as a business tool. We will illustrate these points by reference to Hewlett-Packard, the American computer and electronic instrument firm, presented as Case 1.3.

Case 1.3: Hewlett-Packard

Hewlett-Packard is an American multinational operating in most major countries of the world. It was founded in the late 1930s in Palo Alto, California by Bill Hewlett and Dave Packard, both of whom still have considerable influence on company philosophy. The firm operates in four main divisions each representing different product groupings. The divisions are: the Computer Systems group, the Measurement Systems group, the Medical Products group and the Analytical Instrumentation group.

The central element in all their activities is the 'HP Way', a set of beliefs, objectives and guiding principles, and described by Bill Hewlett as follows.

the policies and actions that flow from the belief that men and women want to do a good job, a creative job, and that if they are provided with the proper environment they will do so. It is the tradition of treating every individual with respect and recognising personal achievements . . . You can't describe it in numbers or statistics. In the last analysis it is a spirit, a point of view. There is a feeling that everyone is part of a team and that team is HP. As I said at the beginning it is an idea that is based on the individual. It exists because people have seen that it works, and they believe that this feeling makes HP what it is.

(quoted in Peters and Waterman, 1982, p. 244)

The HP Way is probably best illustrated from a number of words and concepts extracted from Hewlett-Packard's own publications. These are love of the product, love of the customer, innovation, quality, open communication, commitment to people, trust, confidence, informality, teamwork, sharing, openness, autonomy, responsibility.

continued

It is not just the communication of such sentiments that appears to be important in Hewlett-Packard but that such sentiments appear to be shared by a majority of employees and felt with a certain intensity.

The sentiments are reinforced by a series of processes and procedures which we identify below.

- Communication is the key underlying theme behind all activities in Hewlett-Packard and is an important ingredient of the company's attitude towards innovation and quality. Informal communication is encouraged between all employees of different levels and functions. The physical lay out of the offices and work stations has been deliberately created to encourage *ad hoc* meetings and brainstorming. The use of first names is almost obligatory and is the norm even in the West German operations, where employees are used to a much greater degree of formality in personal relationships. Management assists the informal processes by engaging in what Hewlett-Packard term MBWA ('management by wandering around'). At a more formal level there are frequent announcements to the workforce on such matters as company performance and all employees are given a written statement of the company goals, stressing as they do the contribution which individuals can make. The communication policy is assisted by the company's commitment to decentralization.

  An important aspect of communication in Hewlett-Packard is the various stories and myths that are a continual feature of management training, retirement parties, company speeches and in-house journals. These stories generally tell of key moments in the company's history, or recount the exploits of the corporate heroes, usually Bill Hewlett and Dave Packard. These stories serve an important purpose of stressing a collective identity and underlining the goals of the founders.

- Quality, according to Peters and Waterman, is pursued with zealotry. The company certainly sees its prime objective as a commitment to the design, manufacture and marketing of high-quality goods. Commitment to quality is viewed as ongoing with continual product improvement as a major goal. All employees are involved in the definition and monitoring of quality, a process reinforced by procedures such as MBWA and ceremonies to recognize, reward and publicize good work.

- Innovation, like quality; is regarded as the responsibility of all employees. Following the espousal to 'stick to the knitting' there is a clear commitment to products related to electrical engineering and the company's existing product portfolio. Openness is encouraged and prototypes are often left for other employees to test and criticize. Employees are free to take company equipment home with them. In relations with their customers the company is guided by yet another principle and mnemonic, that of LACE ('laboratory awareness of customer environment'). A central strategy in R&D is the design of products to customer specifications and the LACE programme gives customers the opportunity to make presentations to the company. Such procedures stress the strong emphasis on customer service.

- Personnel policies are carefully designed to reinforce the HP Way as well as ensuring that it works. Most HP employees have no requirement for clocking-on and many operate on flexible working hours. All employees attend a detailed induction programme with communication of the HP Way as a key ingredient. In terms of selection care is taken to select only those who meet the criteria of being high calibre and possessing flair, adaptability and openness. Most recruits are young. As we have seen, considerable attention is paid to the environment and the general well-being of employees is a major consideration.

- There is a somewhat traditional and conservative approach to finance and accounting. There is an emphasis on careful management of assets, self-financing investment, and minimal long-term borrowing.

The overall impression is often that Hewlett-Packard is too good to be true.

We tried to remain sober, not to become fans. But it proved impossible.

(Peters and Waterman, 1982, p. 246)

Certainly on most measures of performance and employee satisfaction, Hewlett-Packard emerges as a highly successful company. A measure of the employees' commitment occurred in 1970 when in the middle of a recession and bad time for the company financially, a 10% pay cut was agreed rather than lay people off.

(*Sources*: Peters and Waterman, 1982; Beer *et al.*, 1985; Needle, 1984)

The nature of organizational or corporate culture

Judging by the growing literature on the subject, corporate culture appears to have replaced Japanese management at the top of the management best-seller lists. If we add specific references on Total Quality Management (TQM), a technique which espouses a culture change approach to quality improvement, then we might assume that modern management is preoccupied with the notion of corporate culture.

Deal and Kennedy (1982) refer to corporate culture as the 'way we do things around here'. However, the concept appears to be used in two different ways as follows.

- First, it is used as a basic concept to understand social phenomena in organizations and to explain differences between companies, particularly those operating in the same product market. Pettigrew describes corporate culture as 'an amalgam of beliefs, ideology, language, ritual and myth' (Pettigrew, 1979, p. 572), which enables people to function in a given setting. That amalgam differs from one firm to the next as a result of the different forces operating upon them. Such forces have been listed by Handy (1993) as history and ownership, size, technology, goals and objectives, environment and people. The Business in Context model would be another appropriate model to analyse differences between companies.
- Second, it is used as a device by management to achieve certain strategic ends that could incorporate improved performance or the control of labour, or both. Management in several firms look to culture change, not only as a mechanism for greater profitability, but also as a mechanism for greater cooperation between management and worker and an end to industrial-relations conflict.

The main difference between the two treatments is the more specific context of the latter approach. This approach is typified by the work of such as Deal and Kennedy (1982) where organizational culture has the function of establishing values and creating a cohesive unit. There is a clear link between Deal and Kennedy's analysis and the notion of the 'excellent company' attributed to Peters and Waterman (1982). In this way the concept of organizational culture becomes a much more normative and prescriptive tool that can create and fashion increased productivity, profitability and compliance. Writers like Peters and Waterman and Ouchi believe they have discovered those elements of culture which contribute towards success in business which management can then develop in their own organizations.

In short, organizational culture is both a set of distinguishing features that mark off one organization from another, and more popularly used has become a set of universal principles guiding best practice. The concept has both descriptive and normative elements. A definition which can embrace both perspectives is offered by Gordan and Ditomaso,

> A pattern of shared and stable beliefs and values that are developed within a company across time.
>
> (Gordan and Ditomaso, 1992, p. 784)

Types of corporate culture

A well-known classification of corporate culture has been offered by Handy (1993). A similar model has been developed by Trompenaars (1993), who feels that different types of corporate culture fit more easily with some types of national culture than others. We will use Handy's classification as a base and offer additional comments from Trompenaars as appropriate. The Handy approach would not be out of place in a discussion of organization structure. He identifies four types of culture as follows.

Power culture

Handy uses the analogy of a spider's web to depict a power culture. It is typified by an absence of bureaucracy and control is exercised from a central power base through key individuals. Such cultures are found in small entrepreneurial firms and certain smaller financial institutions. Power cultures are threatened by the increasing size of the firm and the death or departure of the central figure. Trompenaars refers to the power culture as the '**Family**', with the head as a father figure achieving moral compliance from 'family' members. Such cultures are associated by Trompenaars with late industrialized nations such as Japan, Italy and Singapore. Firms in such countries are more comfortable with power cultures and find project teams and matrix management difficult, since, in such structures, employees must often divide their loyalty.

Role culture

Handy sees this as a Greek temple representative of a classic bureaucracy that acquires its strength through functions, specialities, rules and procedures. It is found in many organizations, more especially when economies of scale are important. A major drawback is its slowness in responding to change. Trompenaars's role culture is depicted by the '**Eiffel Tower**'. It operates in most national cultures, but with different degrees of formality.

Task culture

Here the analogy used is that of a net, and task cultures are typified by matrix organizations. The focus is on getting the job done and such cultures are appropriate when flexibility and responsiveness to market changes are needed. Task cultures are found in advertising agencies, research groups, and Grand Prix racing teams. The difficulties with task cultures are the same as those with matrix structures, discussed earlier in this chapter. Trompenaars refers to this culture as a '**Guided Missile**'. He and his associates have devised a questionnaire to determine the kind of culture employees would favour. Most people, when given such a choice, opt for the 'Guided Missile', although the majority claim to be working in a role culture.

Person culture

Such cultures, viewed by Handy as clusters, focus on individuals. The main purpose of the organization is to satisfy the needs of individuals and the organization itself is secondary to individual self-fulfilment. A group medical practice or a barrister's chambers are examples of a person culture. Such a culture is attractive to many people who would like to operate as freeholders within the security of an organization. This is not always possible and conflict often arises when individuals attempt to operate according to a person culture within an organization that is essentially a role culture. A good illustration of this would be that of an academic focusing on goals of personal research within a university, increasingly operating as a classic role culture. Trompenaars refers to such cultures as '**Incubators**'.

In Figure 1.6 we may view Trompenaars model of corporate culture. The model shows the importance of two sets of variables. The first relates to whether the culture is person- or task-oriented, and the second focuses on the extent to which the culture is hierarchical or egalitarian.

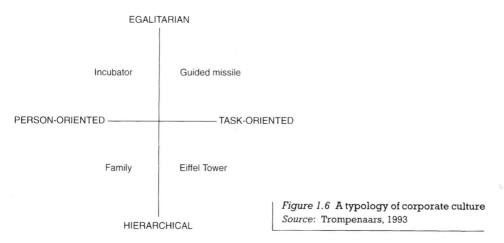

Figure 1.6 A typology of corporate culture
Source: Trompenaars, 1993

We noted in our introduction to this section that organization culture could be viewed descriptively or normatively. The models of Handy and Trompenaars are attempts to describe and analyse different cultural types. Such models are, however, simplistic and highly generalized. [. . .] There is, however, a popular belief that there is an ideal type of culture that holds the key to improved corporate performance. It is to this notion we now turn.

The concept of strong cultures

Strong cultures are associated with those organizations where the guiding values of top management are clear and consistent and are widely shared by the employees. Such cultures are typified by a set of strong values passed down by senior management. The values are strengthened by rituals which emphasize and reward appropriate behaviour and a cultural network, comprising a system of communication to spread the values and create corporate heroes. A feature of strong cultures is their association with hero figures, who exemplify the key values. Ray Kroc of McDonald's, Bill Hewlett and Dave Packard of Hewlett-Packard, and Anita Roddick of the Body Shop are examples of such corporate heroes.

The processes of creating such a 'positive' organizational culture would appear to operate as follows. The senior management of a company set goals and issue guidelines which promote strongly held shared values; there is normally an emphasis upon enthusiasm, diligence, loyalty and service to the customer. To ensure that such guidelines are passed on to all employees there is usually a high investment in the procedures of communication and integration. A number of techniques are commonly used to create and maintain a specific corporate culture. Some firms pay particular attention to the physical environment; the layout in Hewlett-Packard is designed to encourage communication and they try to maintain the same layout in all their establishments throughout the world; in IBM layout is equally important as is the use of a corporate colour, blue. The goals of the company are invariably written, explicit, communicated to all employees and tend to stress the contribution that employees can make to the firm. Heroes and myths play an important role in communicating the core values as illustrated by the 'Bill and Dave stories' in Case 1.3. The same role is ascribed to important rituals such as presentations to successful employees and social gatherings; in companies such as IBM, employees are encouraged to participate in out-of-work activities, with non-participation being frowned upon.

The culture is also strengthened by more formal procedures such as training and induction and the design of the organization structure. There is usually a deliberate attempt to create clearly defined autonomous units to enhance group identity and loyalty, together with an emphasis upon informality and avoidance of bureaucratic controls. In recruitment and selection procedures a great deal of care is usually taken to select only those individuals who would fit in with the prevailing culture.

At its most influential the corporate culture is seen as having replaced organized religion and the family as the most important focus in a person's life (Ray, 1986). In a recent television documentary about the establishment of the Japanese firm Komatsu in Britain, one of its senior Japanese employees listed his priorities in order as the firm, the state, and finally his family. Not surprisingly the Japanese firm is often held as the prime example of a strong corporate culture.

Those who subscribe to this view of organizations claim that firms which have such strong cultures are more successful than those that do not. This was the notion behind Peters and Waterman's study of 'Excellent Companies' and has been the subject of recent research. Unfortunately, much of the evidence remains inconclusive. For example, a study by Gordan and Ditomaso (1992) of 11 insurance companies over a six-year period found some correlation between the strength of a widely shared culture and short-term financial performance. The same study also pointed to the significant problems inherent in proving connections given the large number of variables involved. Nevertheless there is a belief that the ideas constitute a new management theory and a return to the universal principles approach which typified the earlier but essentially different theories of people such as Fayol and Taylor. The type of firms which embody such principles better than most are the so-called 'excellent companies'.

The notion of the excellent company

Peters and Waterman (1982) may not be the only writers to attempt to identify the features of the excellent company (Ouchi attempted much the same a year earlier), but their attempt proved to be the most successful by far with their book *In Search of Excellence* selling several million copies since its publication in 1982. It arguably ranks alongside Taylor's *Scientific Management* as one of the most influential management texts of all time. Peters and Waterman carried out an investigation of 62 top performing American companies. Six measures of long-term productivity were devised and only those firms which ranked in the top 20 of their industry on four out of the six criteria were included in their in-depth study.

Their final sample numbered 43 firms including IBM, Hewlett-Packard, Boeing, Digital, Caterpillar, Eastman Kodak, Walt Disney, and 3M. The sample was not intended to be representative of all types of firm and banks are notable by their exclusion.

In all eight attributes of excellence were identified. These were, using Peters and Waterman's own terminology, as follows:

- '**bias for action**', being typified by clear objectives and a marked absence of committee procedures;
- '**closeness to the customer**', typified by processes and procedures aimed at identifying and serving the customers' needs;
- '**autonomy and entrepreneurship**', which are best achieved through the creation of small cohesive teams;
- '**productivity through people**', with workforce involvement at all times;
- '**hands on; value driven**', involving the fostering of a strong corporate culture by top management who are seen to be in touch with all employees;
- '**stick to the knitting**', which involves limiting activities to what the firm does best and avoiding diversification into unknown territory;
- '**simple form, lean staff**', avoiding complex hierarchies and large administration sections;
- '**simultaneous loose–tight properties**', which means that organization structure should display a combination of strong central direction with work-group autonomy.

Throughout their work Peters and Waterman stressed the importance of excellent companies socializing and integrating individuals into a clearly defined corporate culture. The firm becomes much more than a place of work,

by offering meaning as well as money, the excellent companies give their employees a mission as well as a sense of feeling great.

(Peters and Waterman, 1982, p. 323)

How useful is organizational culture as a concept?

We need to distinguish between organizational culture as a means of differentiating between companies and organizational culture as a set of principles which shape 'excellent' companies.

The development of organizational culture as an analytical device leaves much to be desired. There are problems of defining the elements which comprise organizational culture, and, in a review of the literature, Hofstede (1986) is disappointed by the apparent lack of empirical research. Until we develop some systematic measures of organizational concept then its utility as an analytical tool must be limited. Even then, culture is much more complex than many credit. It is dynamic, in that the behaviour and expressed feelings of staff can modify a culture over time. Many organizations are also multicultural. Furthermore it is very difficult to observe and measure something that is implicit, informal and very often invisible. Given such problems it is difficult to prove consistent links between culture and performance, let alone understand how such a relationship operates.

The major controversy concerns the concept as a set of principles to guide 'good' management practice. Advocates argue that they have analysed successful companies and found links between organizational culture and performance. There are a number of difficulties with this approach which we identify below.

- Several writers feel that the importance of culture has been overstated. Carroll (1983) considers that the important effects of technology, market dominance, the influence of the state and the control of critical raw materials have all been ignored in the analysis. Dawson (1986) takes this a stage further. She feels that what people such as Peters and Waterman have uncovered is not a set of universal principles of management, but strategies that only work in certain types of company. She writes,

> Their 'slim consensual organizations' of the future are probably applicable to firms employing professionals and technicians from the primary labour market in the development and operation of new technology or highly fashionable products and processes. They may however be less successful in other technological, product and labour market conditions.
>
> (Dawson, 1986, p. 137)

- It is interesting to speculate whether the kind of processes and procedures illustrated in our Hewlett-Packard case would have any relevance for an inner-city local authority or the health service, or assist management in older industries such as British Steel. While strong cultures may be feasible in organizations such as hospitals or universities where shared goals are common, problems can and do arise when such institutions attempt to modify those goals. In addition, there are undoubted limitations of imposing or changing a culture in certain types of work, as with boring or unglamorous jobs, and with certain types of worker, such as contract staff or part-timers.

- Anthony (1990) feels that there is a misguided assumption that organizational cultures are relatively easy to change. Such assumptions are often held by managers, who see culture change as the panacea for all the ills facing their companies. Since cultures are built upon deep-rooted values developed over time, it is not surprising that exhortations to change the culture never progress beyond the exhortation stage. Given this difficulty it is hardly surprising that the focus is often upon behaviour change, rather than value change. In a study of culture change in British Airways there was evidence that cabin crew had changed their behaviour, but it was equally clear that they have not taken on board changed values and attitudes (Höpfl et al., 1992). In such circumstances staff are acting roles.

- The focus of research has been on 'excellent' companies. Child (1984a) speculates what would happen if the very same attributes were found in less than excellent companies. There has been little or no comparison with the cultural characteristics of poor performers. In fact, immediately following Peters and Waterman's study, three of their excellent companies, including Texas Instruments and National Semiconductors, suffered serious setbacks in their performance and there was evidence of a reversion to more bureaucratic types of control.

- The above paragraphs may be summed up by the difficulty of proving a relationship between the features of excellence and company performance. More significantly, we could argue that the features displayed by these excellent companies are a direct result rather than a cause of company performance. It is much easier to gain employee consensus and focus on customer needs when profits are healthy.

- Situations might be envisaged where a strong commitment to a corporate culture could lead to resistance to change, when major reorganization is called for in response to market, technological or other changes. If all employees are selected in the same image, where will the organizations find the 'deviants' to initiate change? This view would doubtless be challenged by representatives of such as Hewlett-Packard who would point to the emphasis placed in their organization on innovation. Moreover, given the commitment to corporate values in such 'value-driven' firms, change could well be initiated through a series of top management exhortations.

- The type of processes and procedures used by 'excellent' companies do have certain similarities with techniques of conditioning and even brainwashing and may be morally unacceptable to some. Nevertheless, while there are personality types who would find working for such companies difficult, there are countless others who enjoy their association with them.

- There may also be problems for managers. They may become so that they become isolated and fail to know what is really happening. In addition, middle management can feel threatened in that their roles for directing and controlling are usurped by centralized control.

Despite such criticisms the development of an organization culture to enhance performance can be appealing to management and workforce alike. For management it is an important source of control through the moral involvement of the workforce (Ray, 1986). In this respect there is a similarity with the techniques associated with the 'human relations' and 'organizational development' schools of management thinking. Moreover the popularity of *In Search of Excellence* is in part testimony to the optimism it portrays and its morale-boosting effects on managers. As far as employees are concerned, they are given clear guidelines about the kind of behaviour expected of them, which has been estimated as saving up to two hours a day (Deal and Kennedy, 1982). In addition there is no doubt that many employees enjoy working in the deliberately created integrated atmospheres of the IBMs and the Hewlett-Packards, and successful, 'excellent' companies do tend to pay well!

SUMMARY

In this chapter we focused our attention on the organizational elements of business which we identified as goals, structure, ownership, size and organizational culture. As befits our model, all elements interact not just with each other but with aspects of the environment, business strategy and operations.

We view goals as the products of a highly interactive and dynamic process such that changing goals may well be a prerequisite for business survival. Goals give a sense of direction to a firm's activities and may be presented in a hierarchy involving a mission, objectives and strategies. The formulation of goals is closely related to the way power relations are worked out in organizations, and often involve highly political processes of influence, conflict and compromise between different interest groups. A number of goals may operate at any one time. These may conflict, but in general the goals of a business follow closely those of the dominant coalition.

The factors which influence *structure* are identified as technology, size, environmental changes, strategy, culture and the behaviour of interest groups. We identify various models of organizational structure including, functional, divisional and matrix, but acknowledge that very few firms conform to such ideal types. Many firms have mixed structures and new variations are emerging all the time with recent attention being given to flexible structures. The relationship between structure and performance is of obvious interest to businessmen, but as yet the evidence is inconclusive.

Ownership is important because of its potential impact on the way businesses are managed. We examine this relationship by focusing on the traditional debate of ownership versus control and the freedom of managers to make decisions in the face of the growing influence of institutional shareholders and the power of interlocking directorships. The dilemmas that can arise in the relationship between ownership and control are examined with reference to the public sector, and, in particular, the growing trend in many countries of the privatization of public companies.

We examine the influence of *size* on such factors as structure, market power, relationship with the state, and the impact on the individual. The main focus of this section is the small firm. The case for government support of the small firm is examined in light of the potential contribution of small businesses to the economy and society. We conclude that the current enthusiasm for small firms owes more to ideology than it does to economic analysis.

Organizational culture is viewed as the product of goals, structure, ownership and size, as well as company history, technology, its product-market environment and several other variables as well. The sum total of those influences distinguish organizations from one another. The main argument surrounding organizational culture is that a particular culture can be created to enhance performance and the debate has focused on the notion of 'excellent' companies. Despite the enthusiasm for 'excellence', the research is inconclusive and culture may be less important than technology or the product-market.

NOTE

* This chapter has been adapted from, Needle, D. (1989) *Business in Context*, International Thompson Business Press.

REFERENCES

Adcroft, A., Cutler, T., Haslam, C., Williams, J. and Williams, K. (1991) Hanson and ICI: the consequences of financial engineering, *University of East London, Occasional Papers in Business, Economy and Society* No. 2.

Anthony, P. D. (1990) The paradox of management culture or 'He who leads is lost', *Personnel Review*, 19(4), pp. 3–8.

Atkinson, J. (1984) Manpower strategies for flexible organizations, *Personnel Management*, Aug. pp. 28–31.

Bannock, G. (1981) *The Economics of Small Firms: Return from the Wilderness*, Basil Blackwell, Oxford.

Beer, M., Spector, B., Lawrence, P., Quinn Mills, D. and Walton, R. E. (1985) *Human Resource Management, The General Managers Perspective Text and Cases*, Free Press, New York.

Berle, A. A. (1954) *The Twentieth Century Capitalist Revolution*, Harcourt Brace, New York.

Berle, A. A. and Means, G. C. (1932) *The Modern Corporation and Private Property*, Macmillan, New York.

Binks, M. and Jennings, A. (1986) New firms as a source of industrial regeneration, in M. Scott (ed.), *Small Firms Growth and Development*, Gower, Aldershot.

Bolton, J. (1971) *Small Firms: The Report of the Committee of Inquiry on Small Firms*, HMSO, Cmd 4811, London.

Bright, C., Colvin, M., Loveridge, J., Page, R. and Thompson, C. (1983) *Moving Forward: Small Business and the Economy*, Conservative Political Centre, London.

Brossard, M. and Maurice, M. (1976) Is there a universal model of organisational structure? *International Studies of Management and Organization*, 6, pp. 11–45.

Burnham, J. (1941) *The Management Revolution*, Day, New York.

Burns, T. and Stalker, G. M. (1966) *The Management of Innovation*, Tavistock, London.

Carroll, D. T. (1983) A disappointing search for excellence, *Harvard Business Review*, 63, Nov.–Dec., pp. 78–88.

Chandler, A. D. (1962) *Strategy and Structure: Chapters in the History of American Capitalism*, MIT Press, Cambridge, Mass.

Chandler, A. D. (1977) *The Visible Hand: The Managerial Revolution in American Business*, Harvard University Press, Cambridge, Mass.

Channon, D. F. (1973) *The Strategy and Structure of British Enterprise*, Macmillan, London.

Child, J. (1969) *The Business Enterprise in Modern Industrial Society*, Collier-Macmillan, London.

Child, J. (1972) Organisational structure, environment and performance: the role of strategic choice, *Sociology*, 6, pp. 1–21.

Child, J. (1984a) *Organizations: A Guide to Problems and Practice*, 2nd edn, Harper & Row, London.

Child, J. (1984b) New technology and developments in management organization, *OMEGA*, 12, 3, pp. 211–23.

Curran, J. (1986) *Bolton Fifteen Years On: A Review and Analysis of Small Business Research in Britain, 1971–86*, Small Business Trust, London.

Cyert, R. M. and March, J. C. (1963) *A Behavioral Theory of the Firm*, Prentice Hall, Englewood Cliffs, N. J.

Davis, S. M. and Lawrence, P. R. (eds) (1977) *Matrix*, Addison-Wesley, Reading, Mass.

Dawson, S. (1986) *Analysing Organizations*, Macmillan, London.

Deal, T. E. and Kennedy, A. A. (1982) *Corporate Cultures*, Addison-Wesley, Reading, Mass.

Drucker, P. F. (1964) *Managing for Results*, Harper & Row, New York.

El-Namaki, M. (1993) *Contemporary Dynamics of Entrepreneurship*, Netherlands International Institute for Management, Netherlands.

Foy, N. (1983) The public productivity poser, *Management Today*, July, pp. 67–71.

Galbraith, J. R. (1971) Matrix organization designs, *Business Horizons*, 14, pp. 29–40.

Galbraith, J. R. and Nathanson, D. A. (1978) *Strategy Implementation: The Role of Structure and Process*, West Publishing Co., St Paul, Minnesota.

Ganguly, P. and Bannock, G. (1985) *UK Small Business Statistics and International Comparisons*, Harper & Row, London.

Gordan, G. G. and Ditomaso, N. (1992) Predicting corporate performance from organizational culture, *Journal of Management Studies*, 29, 6, pp. 783–98.

Gould, A. and Keeble, D. (1984) New firms and rural industrialization in East Anglia, *Regional Studies*, 18, 3, pp. 189–201.

Greater London Council (GLC) (1983) *Small Firms and the London Industrial Strategy*, Economic Policy Group Strategy Document, No. 4, GLC, London.

Handy, C. (1993) *Understanding Organizations*, 4th edn, Harmondsworth, Penguin.

Hayes, R. H. and Wheelwright, S. C. (1984) *Restoring our Competitive Edge: Competing Through Manufacturing*, John Wiley, New York.

Heald, D. (1985) Will privatisation of public enterprises solve the problems of control?, *Public Administration*, 63, Spring, pp. 7–22.

Hickson, D. J., Pugh, D. S. and Pheysey, D. C. (1969) Operation technology and organization structure: an empirical appraisal, *Administrative Quarterly*, 14, pp. 378–97.

Hofer, C. W. and Schendel, D. (1978) *Strategy Formulation: Analytical Concepts*, West Publishing, St Paul, Minnesota.

Hofstede, G. H. (1986) The usefulness of the organizational culture concept, *Journal of Management Studies*, 23, 3, May, pp. 253–7.

Höpfl, H., Smith, S. and Spencer, S. (1992) Values and valuations: The conflict between culture change and job cuts, *Personnel Review*, 21, 1, pp. 24–37.

Johnson, G. and Scholes, K. (1993) *Exploring Corporate Strategy: Text and Cases*, 3rd edn, Prentice Hall, London.

Lawrence, P. R. and Lorsch, J. (1967) *Organization and Environment*, Harvard University Press, Cambridge, Mass.

Marris, R. L. (1964) *The Economic Theory of Managerial Capitalism*, Macmillan, London.

Needle, D. (1984) The selection process in Britain and West Germany: a cross-national study, unpublished MSc thesis, London School of Economics.

Perrow, C. (1961) The analysis of goals in complex organizations, *American Sociological Review*, 26, pp. 854–66.

Peters, T. J. and Waterman, R. H. (1982) *In Search of Excellence: Lessons from America's Best Run Companies*, Harper & Row, London.

Pettigrew, A. M. (1973) *The Politics of Organizational Decision Making*, Tavistock, London.

Pettigrew, A. M. (1979) On studying organizational cultures, *Administrative Science Quarterly*, Dec., 24, pp. 570–81.

Pollert, A. (1987) The flexible firm: a model in search of reality (or a policy in search of a practice)?, *Warwick Papers in Industrial Relations*, No 19.

Pugh, D. S., Hickson, D. J. and Hinings, C. R. (1969) The context of organization structures, *Administrative Science Quarterly*, 14, pp. 115–26.

Rainnie, A. (1985) Small firms, big problems: the political economy of small business, *Capital and Class*, 25, Spring, pp. 140–68.

Ray, C. A. (1986) Corporate culture: the last frontier of control, *Journal of Management Studies*, 23, 3, May, pp. 287–97.

Richards, M. D. (1978) *Organizational Goal Structures*, West Publishing, St. Paul, Minnesota.

Rothwell, R. and Zegveld (1981) *Industrial Innovation and Public Policy*, Frances Pinter, London.

Scase, R. and Goffee, R. (1980) *The Real World of the Small Business Owner*, Croom Helm, London.

Scott, J. P. (1979) *Corporations, Classes and Capitalism*, Hutchinson, London.

Sheehan, R. (1967) Proprietors in the world of big business, *Fortune*, 15 June.

Stewart, H. and Gallagher, C. C. (1985) Business death and firm size in the U.K., *International Small Business Journal*, 4, 1.

Taylor, F. W. (1947) *Scientific Management*, Harper & Row, New York.

Trompenaars, F. (1993) *Riding the Waves of Culture: Understanding Cultural Diversity in Business*, The Economist Books, London.

Woodward, J. (1965) *Industrial Organization: Theory and Practice*, Oxford University Press, London.

2

THE COMMUNICATIONS AND FINANCIAL REVOLUTION AND THE RISE OF THE MULTINATIONAL CORPORATION*

Paul Kennedy

[. . .]

[G]lobal prosperity has occurred at the same time as – and has interacted with – the emergence of large multinational companies which are increasingly less attached to the particular interests and values of their country of origin. As they compete against rival firms for world market shares, they have developed a strategy of directing investment and production from one part of the earth to another, with the help of revolutionary communications and financial technologies that have created a global marketplace for goods and services. Already important in today's world, these corporations will be even more significant in the future, as Cold War trading barriers break down and the global economy becomes increasingly integrated.

Companies with international rather than national interests are not new. They existed, in embryonic form, in the cosmopolitan private banks of the late nineteenth and early twentieth centuries, whose growth was assisted by the earlier "communications revolution" of the telegraph and by the absence of major Great Power coalition wars. The House of Rothschild in 1900, for example, had branches in Frankfurt, Vienna, Paris, and London in daily contact with one another. Lloyds of London before 1914 insured most of the German shipping industry and was prepared to pay out compensation for losses even in the event of an Anglo-German war. Again, earlier examples abound of multinational companies such as Lever Bros (the forerunners of Unilever), with production facilities ranging from West Africa to India; or of major oil companies, scouring the globe for fresh sources of petroleum and switching the refined products from one market to another. Ford also went "global" when it decided to manufacture cars and trucks on both sides of the Atlantic.

But today's globalization is distinguished from those earlier examples by the sheer quantity and extent of the multinational firms in our expanded and integrated global economy. As noted above, they emerged in a postwar international economic order that reduced protectionism and encouraged a recovery of world trade, and were further stimulated in the 1970s by the United States' decision to abandon the gold standard, followed by a general liberalization of exchange controls, at first only in a few countries, later in many others. This not only provided more liquidity for world trade, but increased the flow of transnational capital investments, as companies invested abroad without constraints imposed by central banks.

Although this financial liberalization helped to expand world commerce, it also produced another effect: the increasing separation of financial flows from trade in manufactures and services. More and more, foreign-currency transactions took place not because a company was paying for foreign goods or investing in foreign assembly, but because investors were speculating in a particular currency or other financial instruments. This surge in global capital flows beyond those required to finance the boom in world industry and commerce is intimately connected with two further occurrences: the deregulation of world money markets, and the revolution in global communications as a result of new technologies. Without the vast increase in the power of computers, computer software, satellites, fiber-optic cables, and high-speed electronic transfers, global markets could not act as one, and economic and other information – politics, ideas, culture, revolutions, consumer trends – could not be delivered instantaneously to the more than 200,000 monitors connected into this global communications system. And all this, according to some pundits, may be only the initial phase.

[. . .]

Within this system, and largely because of it, many successful companies are internationalizing themselves. Given a global market, competition among firms – whether automobile producers, aircraft manufacturers, pharmaceutical companies, makers of computer hardware, or publishing houses – is driving them to sell and produce in all of the major economic regions of the world. Not only does the company benefit from economies of scale, but it hopes to protect itself from the vagaries of currency fluctuations, differentiated economic growth, and political interference. A recession in Europe will be of less concern to a firm which also operates in booming East Asian markets than to one exclusively dependent upon European sales. A company interested in developing goods banned by certain bureaucracies (in the biotech industry especially) can switch its manufacture to parts of the world lacking such regulations. A multinational corporation, fretting at the "voluntary controls" imposed by governments to protect indigenous firms from open competition, can often get around those barriers by setting up plants inside the protected territory. Once a multinational breaches protectionist obstacles, it is likely to enjoy handsome profit opportunities, at least in the early years, in the newly accessible market. Even research and product development is being shifted – from the United States to Switzerland, from Germany to California – when it suits a company's needs. For the same motives, large companies rush in to acquire small, innovative firms on the other side of the globe, to forestall preemption by their competitors.

A popular and somewhat shallow interpretation of these trends – put forward not coincidentally by people involved in international consulting and banking – is that the economic consequences of globalization can only be beneficial. In this interpretation, whereas government restrictions previously prevented the consumer from purchasing the best goods, free trade now permits individuals and companies to buy and sell on a world market. [. . .]

This optimistic interpretation also applauds the way in which the revolution in communications is influencing politics and society. In a world with more than 600 million television sets, viewers are as much consumers of news and ideas as they are of commercial goods. Thus governments of authoritarian states find it increasingly difficult to keep their people in ignorance. [. . .] Knowledge and openness, it is assumed, brings with it truth, honesty, fairness, and democracy.

Such a vision of a prosperous and harmonious world economic order, founded upon laissez-faire, twenty-four-hour-a-day trading, and all-pervasive television, seems breathtakingly naive in the light of this planet's demographic, environmental, and regional problems. Cheering references to the way in which the "discriminating consumer" can nowadays buy a Mont Blanc pen or a Vuitton suitcase without regard to that product's country of origin (Ohmae, 1990, p. 3) recall Jevons's enthusiasm a century ago about the easy purchase of Argentine beef and Chinese tea. In both cases, there is a failure to recognize that newer technologies may not benefit all, that the vast majority of the world's population may not be able to purchase the goods in question, and that profound changes both in economic production and in communications can bring disadvantages as well as advantages in their wake.

Since globalization has recently attracted immense publicity, it has become easier to identify which groups and interests are already being hurt by the process or are likely to be affected in the future: economic nationalists, interest groups and companies that wish to protect their domestic markets, workers whose jobs are made redundant when a multinational company moves its assembly and manufacturing elsewhere, and localities in which employment (especially of skilled labor) shrinks. There is, in addition, reason for concern about the volatility of the vast, computer-driven system of financial trading. Finally, since enthusiasts of globalization seem to focus overwhelmingly upon what it means for the "triad" of prosperous societies in North America, Europe, and Japan, they devote less attention to the prospect of a further marginalization of four-fifths of the earth's population not well prepared for these new commercial and financial trends.

To today's economic nationalists, globalization threatens to undermine the assumed integrity of the nation-state as the central organizing unit of domestic and external affairs. [. . .] [T]he general reason for this unease is clear: like illegal migration or global warming, the internationalization of manufacturing and finance erodes a people's capacity to control its own affairs. The idea that we are entering an era in which there will be no national products or technologies, no national corporations, and no national industries is bewildering to all who think in traditional terms. In the United States in particular, which for so long has possessed much more of a self-contained economy than, for example, the Netherlands or Britain, it must be unsettling to hear that "as almost every factor of production – money, technology, factories, and equipment – moves effortlessly across borders, the very idea of an American economy is becoming meaningless, as are the notions of an American corporation, American capital, American products, and American technology" (Reich, 1990, p. 3–4, 8–9). If products are no longer "American," what is the point of trying to measure the balance of merchandise trade, or the gap in US–Japan commerce in high-technology goods? While the enthusiasts of globalization want national governments and their agencies to become invisible in the marketplace, many others are made uneasy by such a disappearance. The older ways are more familiar, more comforting – and besides, the people you know and can appeal to (Congress, Parliament, the Treasury) still seem to be in control of economic affairs.
[. . .]

If major corporations have largely broken free from their national roots, this is even more true of the fast-moving, twenty-four-hour-a-day, border-crossing, profit-hunting system of international finance, in which vast sums of capital – described by one investment authority as "the most purely rational thing there is" (Ohmae, 1990, p. 170) – move in and out of a country or a stock according to perceptions of that entity's prospects.

Yet even if money is the most purely rational thing there is, it does not follow that it is immune to instability, panics, and financial flight. Forty years ago, foreign exchange ratios reflected the fundamentals of individual countries' trade balances, and most of the current exchanges that were made related to the flow of goods. Today, the daily volume of foreign exchange trading is *several hundred times* larger than the value of traded goods, and the relationship has altered. Across the world, millions of individual investors, companies, and banks speculate in currencies, many of them automatically following computer-generated indicators that reveal whether (say) the dollar is increasing or decreasing in value relative to other currencies. These players swiftly react to economic data such as the latest trade figures or a rise in interest rates, incidentally making it more difficult for governments and central banks to implement what may be necessary fiscal measures out of fear that international investors may find them unwelcome; a marked reduction in interest rates, judged by a government to be helpful to its country's industries and employment, may be ruled out or at least trimmed because of concern over its effect on the nation's currency. Still more do these investors react to political turbulence such as the threat of a war, or a political assassination. Were the event to be particularly serious – a major earthquake in Tokyo, or the death of the president of the United States – currency markets could be swiftly and seriously destabilized.

The ideological implications of this global system are debated more in Europe than in the laissez-faire United States. The reality nowadays is that any government which offends international finance's demand for unrestricted gain – by increasing personal taxes, for example, or by raising fees on financial transactions – will find its capital has fled and its currency weakened. [. . .] [T]he message is clear: if you do not follow the rules of the market, your economy will suffer. But the market's message ignores important considerations. If, say, a French Socialist government is conscientiously attempting to provide better schools, health care, housing, and public utilities for its citizenry, by what means can it raise the necessary funds without alarming international investors who may be not at all interested in the well-being of those citizens but merely in their own profits? The rational market, by its very nature, is not concerned with social justice and fairness.

Political issues aside, there are practical problems in endowing a single currency – the US dollar – with such an overwhelming responsibility within the international financial system. [. . .]

Orthodox economists offer many reasons why the present financial system will continue. As American deficits grow, foreigners simply hold more dollars. For various structural reasons, it is argued, no other currency can replace the dollar – at least not in the foreseeable future. Therefore, the position of the US dollar remains "unassailable," according to the optimists (Strange, 1990, p. 274). History shows, however, that previous international monetary regimes – such as the one that revolved around the gold standard, the pound sterling, and the City of London prior to 1914 – became ever more difficult to sustain when the hub economy itself began to lose its relative strength and competitiveness. Current economic trends – the diminution of the American share of global assets, the rise of such other currencies as the yen and the ECU, the emergence of new financial centers, the increasing share of American national wealth needed for debt repayment – suggest that the post-1945 international monetary regime may also be drawing to a close, *without* an adequate successor system in view. [. . .]

What have these financial matters to do with preparing for the year 2025, and with the larger problems facing our global society? At first glance, the investment calculations of a multinational company's strategic planners and the daily maneuvers of Tokyo speculators may appear to overlap little with the challenges facing a West African groundnut producer or a Malaysian tin miner. If this is true, it means that the great gap between the rich and poor in today's world is increasing; how, indeed, will a technologically sophisticated, transnational, corporate culture, loyal to no government and beyond the reach of local regulation, coexist with the polyglot, hungry, and dissatisfied masses foreshadowed by a world population of 8 or 10 billion? Moreover, if profound financial instability does occur as a consequence of the fast-flowing but irresponsible system of monetary exchanges, severe shocks to the international trading order are likely to depress developing world commodity prices – coffee, cocoa, ores – most of all. That was a lesson of the 1930s, and of the post-oil-shock 1970s. The continued dependence of developing countries upon such exports suggests that the same would be true today. Events in Central America may have little impact upon Wall Street, but Wall Street's actions could have serious consequences for the developing world.

Even within the industrial democracies themselves, the globalization of production, investment, and services has serious consequences. Until recently, many large companies still retained the characteristics of the typical post-1945 corporation: located in a particular region, the provider of jobs to its skilled blue-collar work force and to layers of managers, the provider also of philanthropic and social goods to the "company town." Although examples still exist of such localist and paternalist firms, many have been compelled by international competition to discard all such loyalties to the town, the region, or the country. "The United States," one prominent American executive observed, "does not have an automatic call on our resources. There is no mind-set that puts the country first" (Reich, 1990, p. 141). In consequence, states, regions, cities, and townships have become "bidders" for the presence of a new factory, or, more often, the retention of an existing plant which a multinational company may be thinking of moving. If the community in question can offer enough inducements – tax concessions, operating subsidies, training grants – as did Danville, Illinois, in 1983 in a bid to win a new forklift assembly plant, it may succeed, at least for a while; if it does not make enough concessions, like Portland, Oregon, in the same bidding war, it will lose. If a union at one plant is willing to agree to the demands of the corporation – as did the General Motors workers in Arlington, Texas, thereby contributing to the closure of the firm's factory in Ypsilanti, Michigan, where the union was less cooperative – it may survive, until the next time. Since communities and unions are bidding for the same jobs, it follows that one region's enhanced (or retained) employment means another region's rising unemployment. Winner or loser, it is clear that there is "uneven bargaining power" between communities and the globalized company (Reich, 1998, p. 295–8).

Within the developed world, globalization also affects the career expectations of individuals and the structure of employment generally. In the United States, which has opened itself to laissez-faire forces more readily than other industrial democracies, lawyers, biotechnology engineers, economics editors, software designers, and strategic planners are in demand because they contribute a high "added value" to whatever they are working upon. The demand for their services is international – the request for the software design, or legal brief, or "op-ed" commentary upon a diplomatic crisis may come from anywhere in the developed world – just as the means of communicating this knowledge (via Express Mail, or fax) are also international. Unlike the fast-food server, or the local policeman or schoolteacher, or the blue-collar worker, these creators and conveyors of high-added-value information are no longer linked to a regional or even a national economy. They have become functioning and prosperous parts of a borderless world – and, like the growing number of their equivalents in Europe, Japan, and Australasia, will remain so just as long as their education, skills, expertise, and inventiveness are in demand from distant consumers.

Much more important, in social and political terms, is the fate of the four-fifths of Americans who are not in such international demand. Skilled blue-collar employees – the core of the traditional high-per-capita-income US work force, and the backbone of the Democratic Party – have lost jobs in the millions as American firms wilted under international competition or relocated industrial production to other countries with lower labor costs. During the 1980s, the United Auto Workers lost 500,000 members even as companies like General Motors were adding to employment abroad. At the same time as high-paying blue-collar jobs were disappearing, millions of new jobs were being created across the United States. Unfortunately, the vast majority of those positions were low-paid casual or unprotected jobs requiring few skills and offering little opportunity, such as work in fast-food stores, gas stations, discount supermarkets, hotels, and cleaning and gardening services. An increasing majority of Americans have found their real standards of living – like the real level of national productivity – stagnating since the mid-1970s. Just as the gap between the upper one-fifth and lower four-fifths of global society has increased, so also, though less drastically, has the upper one-fifth in American society detached itself from the rest.

Although it is too early yet to be certain, these changes in American society – and in societies that go the "American way" – may also affect the debate on North-South relations. A family whose chief wage-earner has lost his job because the factory was moved to Mexico or Thailand is unlikely to be sympathetic to pleas for enhanced development aid to poorer countries. Employees who lack a college education and scramble to retain their low-paying positions as hospital janitors or office cleaners will resent the infiltration of immigrants (whether legal or illegal) willing to work longer hours and for less money. Politicians in constituencies suffering from factory closings by multinationals will be tempted – are already tempted – to push for greater protection of the home market, regardless of what that means for the developing world. Well-heeled professionals, who are college-educated, drive Volvos, contribute to Oxfam, and are sympathetic to environmental concerns, may increasingly recognize the need for unpopular reforms to counter worrying global trends; but that is unlikely to be true for most of their fellow citizens, who are finding it hard to preserve their standards of living.

The implications for the developing world of the financial and communications revolutions and the rise of the multinational corporations are even more sobering. So much of the breathlessly enthusiastic literature about the benefits of globalization focuses upon what is happening in Europe, North America, and Japan, plus certain extensions of that triad (South Korea, Brazil, Australia). But little is said about the rest of the world. From the perspective of laissez-faire theory – from Adam Smith and Cobden to Kenichi Ohmae today – such countries presumably become relevant only when they learn the lessons of the marketplace and possess those features which allow them to compete in the borderless world: a well-educated population, lots of engineers, designers and other professionals, a sophisticated financial structure, good communications, enormous deposits of knowledge (libraries, computers, laboratories), adequate capital and entrepreneurs, and perhaps a fledgling multinational corporation or two. If this has happened in South Korea, why can't it happen in every country of the world?

[. . .] [T]his beguiling theory is too abstract. Not merely would it require the ending of corrupt regimes, excess spending on the military, bureaucratic ineptitude, protection of special interests, lack of legal protection, religious fundamentalism, and all the other obstacles to commerce which exist in many countries in Central America, the Middle East, and sub-Saharan Africa. It would also involve a transformation of the dominant value systems in many developing world societies that are antithetical to the norms of Western rationalism, scientific inquiry, legal theory, and capitalism. Until such a profound change occurs, it is hard to foresee when Ethiopian-based or Philippine-based multinational companies, flush with funds and talented personnel, will begin to move into Japan or New England, making strategic acquisitions as they take *their* historic turn at the center of the global economic stage.

Accepting the logic of the global marketplace will also be difficult because of the structural obstacles that cramp many of today's developing nations. The idealized picture, in which hyperefficient multinational corporations compete to bring their latest products to discriminating consumers across the globe while governments become all but invisible, makes seductive reading; but it ignores the fact that what most poorer nations need is not simply the liberating effects of free-market economics, but also enormous investments in social improvement. In a predominantly agrarian, land-locked African country whose population is doubling every twenty-five years, the most urgent needs would appear to be family planning, environmental protection, health care, education, and basic infrastructure – which free-market, multinational corporations are not likely to be interested in financing. In other words, huge public funds are required – whether in Central Africa or Eastern Europe – before conditions become attractive to investment managers of Japanese and American companies. But how such public funds are to be provided is rarely if ever touched upon by the fans of globalization.

Moreover, if a developing country does manage to reconstitute itself on the East Asian model and enjoys a rise in foreign investment, production, exports, and standards of living, then it could in turn become steadily more susceptible to the relocation of branch plants and jobs as multinationals search for still cheaper regions for manufacture and assembly. According to borderless-world theories, this is not a problem; if the principles of supply and demand really work efficiently, deindustrialization and unemployment ought not to last for long: "In this interlinked economy, there is no such thing as absolute winners and losers, A loser becomes relatively attractive as its currency gets weaker and an unemployed work force emerges that is available at reasonable cost." Just as an American automobile company would be willing to move assembly plants *back* to the United States if its currency and labor costs fell far enough, so would an obliging multinational return to (say) Malaysia or Brazil when it became cheap enough again. Such unimaginative reasoning does not consider whether the working populations and governments of newly industrializing countries are likely to remain complacent when multinational corporations move elsewhere, as happened to a large extent in northern England and the Ohio Valley. An angry native reaction and a backlash against being treated as the economic pawns of First World companies are equally plausible.

[. . .]

NOTE

* This chapter has been adapted from, Kennedy, P., (1993), *Preparing for the Twenty-First Century*, New York, Random House.

REFERENCES

Ohmae, K., (1990), *The Borderless World: Management Lessons in the New Logic of the Global Marketplace*, New York/London.

Reich, R. B., (1990), *The Work of Nations*, pp. 3–4, 8–9.

Strange, S., (1990), 'Finance, Information and Power', *Review of International Studies*, p. 274.

3

WORK IN TRADITIONAL
AND MODERN SOCIETIES*

Craig R. Littler

This chapter explores some of the differences between work in traditional and modern societies. It does so by examining structures of production (economic structures) and the culture of 'work'. It is these frameworks of social organisation and social meaning that shape the nature of work experiences.

Comparing types of economy and types of work organisation is important, especially to overcome the continual tendency to take Western capitalist society as the absolute centre of reference. The purpose in comparing types of economy, however, is not to construct an evolutionary framework or to imply a simple linear evolution. Any evolution can only be indicated by examining *particular* historical developments. Instead, comparison is intended to be a typological process in order to illuminate the particular mechanisms of modern industrial societies and to construct theories which have their roots in more than the quicksand of the present and the contemporary.

STRUCTURES OF PRODUCTION

Production is the totality of operations and processes aimed at procuring for a society its material means of the existence. Stripped to formal essentials, production entails combining resources available from the environment, instruments of labour (tools etc.) and men (labour power), in accordance with certain technical rules, in order to obtain a product that can be used socially. However, this formalism should not suggest that there is a simple logic of tasks or a logic of nature.

[. . .]

In general, [. . .] all exploitation of resources presupposes a certain knowledge of the properties of objects, materials and tools. Productive activity is, thus, an activity governed by technical norms. But where do these technical norms originate? And who controls them? These are some basic questions of work and the experience of work which this chapter will approach in the second section. However, before turning along that path it is important to examine some further aspects of the structure of production.

The combining of factors of production is carried out within the setting of 'production units' – understood in an abstract sense. Such units may be the small family holding, the village community, the tribe as a collection of communities, or an industrial enterprise (Godelier 1978: 62).

The extent to which a 'production unit' is a work group or a work organisation in a modern, Western sense of an explicit economic organisation is highly variable. If we look at one of the simplest hunting and gathering economies – the Copper Eskimos – as an example, then this point becomes clear. The composition of the Eskimo hunting and fishing groups varies throughout the year, according to the kinds of game being hunted and the type of fishing being done. A large number of people are involved in hunting seals during the winter, and at that season the Eskimos live in large communities by the sea. In contrast, during the summer when possibilities for fresh-water fishing and hunting occur, the communities break up into smaller bands and move inland. As the season progresses, the exigencies of deer hunting demand smaller groups still and a further fragmentation occurs. The only organisational continuities are that first, most (though not all) fragmentation occurs along family lines and, second, there is a general division of labour by gender (Udy 1970: 38).

In societies with stable (or relatively stable) cultivation, horticultural and agrarian societies, work organisation is more permanent. In many such societies the production unit was based on the family and such an organisation constituted the sub-structure of most economies. [. . .]. This raises the problem of how does work which is too great a burden for one family get done? Beyond the household, the typical pattern was one of familial reciprocity. Udy (1970) distinguishes between two types: (a) non-routine work (such as building a house) where there is a diffuse quid pro quo obligation, and (b) routine work relating to peak periods (e.g. planting, harvesting) in the farming cycle. The latter form of reciprocity usually entails extensive pooled arrangements, whereby several families work for one another in successive rotation. When the rotation cycle has been completed, all work obligations have been discharged.

The above work arrangements presuppose something: namely an equal distribution of property. In the face of unequal distribution of property, they tend to break down – or be reconstructed. The typical pattern in complex traditional societies was one of family-based work organisation assisted by norms of reciprocity combined with a top-structure of forced labour (or corvée) politically imposed by larger landholders or by the state. In medieval Europe, for example, peasants were obliged to work on their lord's land for anything from one up to seven days per week throughout the year, the average being about three days (Lenski 1966: 268). The lord's claims on peasant-family labour was an essential aspect of work relations (and class relations) of the medieval manor. [. . .]

A form of production nearer to us in time, but reflecting many of the characteristics of the feudal manorial system, is the hacienda system. This was the predominant type of agricultural work organisation in South America in the nineteenth and early twentieth centuries. The hacienda consisted of a very large agricultural estate characterised by (as with the feudal manor) the coexistence on one property of the owner's farm and a number of peasant-economy farms. The landowner let out parcels of land to peasant farmers, who paid the rent by working on his farm. The relative size of the home farm and the peasant holdings varied, but the latter normally accounted for more than half of the cultivated area and the landowner usually retained the grazing lands for himself. In this way there grew up a class of worker bound to the soil and working both on the peasant farms and on the landowner's. The main characteristic of the work relationship was that it was not clearly delimited in scope, since it affected every aspect of the life of the individual. Because the hacienda was in a position to satisfy all the basic needs of the workers and their families, their possibilities of contact with the outside world were reduced to a minimum: the school, the church and the food store were all there on the spot, turning the hacienda, like the manor, into a closed and self-sufficient economic and social system. One result of the relationship of dependency generated by the hacienda system is that the landowner acted as an intermediary between the worker and the world outside and derived profits from his role of middleman between the peasant and the market. Another characteristic of the social system prevailing on the hacienda was a low degree of division of labour, all the peasants having to perform a wide range of tasks. This fitted in with the productive role of the family. A member of the family could replace a (male) worker in his obligations to the hacienda or in his work on the family's own holding. Such work formed part of the ordinary household duties of women and the normal obligations of children, such that the concept of employment in the modern sense had little significance. Since there was neither a clear-cut division of labour nor a rigid separation of roles within the family group, 'employment' and the manifold other daily tasks that had to be performed merged into a single joint activity for all its members (Kay 1974: 69–98).

The hacienda system, then, though it had some peculiar characteristics, typifies the cluster of production relations which existed in many agrarian societies. [. . .]

However one analyses the mutual linkages between the relations and instruments of production, the relations of production represent the immediate framework of work experience. The examples of work within traditional societies, including the hacienda system, point towards a general conclusion, spelt out by Godelier:

> The work is at one and the same time an economic, political and religious act, and is experienced as such. Economic activity then appears as activity with many different meanings and functions, differing each time in accordance with the specific type of relations existing between the different structures of a given society. The economic domain is thus both external and internal to the other structures of social life and this is the origin and basis of the different meanings assumed by exchanges, investments, money, consumption, etc., in different societies, which cannot be reduced to the functions that they assume in a capitalist commodity society and that economic science analyses.
>
> (Godelier 1978: 63)

In other words, the notion of 'work' is one which has evolved out of the modern relations of production. This leads us on to the question: what are the basic elements of these relations?

One basic idea is that of contractual labour – an explicit agreement to perform specified work for a specified time in the future. Such ideas were not unknown in traditional societies: there were ascriptive groups available for hire under limited circumstances in many tribal societies. In addition, mutual associations set up to perform collective works, such as the construction and maintenance of irrigation works, have often appeared (Udy 1970). However, such forms of organisation are not equivalent to the development of wage labour in modern, capitalist economies. The linkage of wage labour to the modern factory system was not inevitable. During the nineteenth century many people did not relish a move into the factory; as Pollard says: 'As long as there was some measure of choice between cottage and factory, the workmen preferred the cottages' (Pollard 1968: 191). Even when they had been recruited many 'peasant-workers' lived on the margins of the factory world with an ambition to leave as soon as possible. Frequently, the entrepreneur's answer to these problems of recruitment was to employ unfree labour. Widespread use was made of paupers and pauper-apprentices, prisoners and ex-prisoners, and lunatics. Some entrepreneurs employed agents to travel the country combing the workhouses and lunatic asylums for people. But this compounded the problem of recruitment, because the early factories became associated with workhouses and prisons in people's minds.

In the event, in every West European society entrepreneurs failed to establish factories on the basis of coerced labour. Instead, labour was deemed to be 'free' of all diffuse and general obligations to employers, hired – not to do specified work, but often to do unspecified work – for a specified time. Wage labour created a world of employers and hired hands. In so doing, these relations of production created 'work' as it is experienced today: 'Those who are employed experience a distinction between their employer's time and their own time. And the employer must *use* the time of his labour, and see it is not wasted: not the task, but the value of time when reduced to money is dominant. Time is now currency: it is not passed but spent' (Thompson 1974: 43). Modern industrial work organisation resulted in a new economy of time, culminating in Henry Ford's moving assembly line in 1914 which chopped the average job down to task duration of 1.19 minutes [. . .]. Time is also reduced to money. Traditional work patterns were often *non*-market oriented. As we have seen, they were based on domestic and familial forms of production, within which people produced for subsistence and were unaccustomed to a money economy. [. . .]

WORK PROCEDURES, IDEOLOGY AND CULTURE

There are enormous conceptual difficulties in talking about ideology and culture, a fact recognised by many authors. [. . .] Bauman has emphasised this point:

> These two requirements of the specifically human condition – ordering and orientation – are as a rule subsumed under two separate headings: social structure and culture. A historical study of circumstances which led to petrification of two inseparable faces of one coin into two, for a long time unconnected, conceptual frameworks – remains to be written. . . . a disproportionately time-consuming effort has been invested by scholars into solving of what under closer scrutiny appears to be a sham and artificial problem. In keeping with the notorious human tendency to hypothesise purely epistemological distinctions, the two analytical concepts coined to describe the two indivisible aspects of the human ordering activity have been taken for two ontologically distinct beings.
>
> (Bauman 1973: 78)

If we adopt this perspective, then thought ceases to be a 'level' which is separate from other levels. Instead, as Godelier argues, 'any social relation necessarily contains an element of thought that is not necessarily either "illusory" or "legitimising", and which forms part of this relation from the moment of its formation' (Godelier 1982: 17 and 19). In relation to work, the material means of existence equally imply a complex set of ideas, rules and understanding. All work activities entail cognitive routines and shared logic which accompany and surround task performances. Such cognitive routines, which may or may not accompany the activity on a conscious level, are both part of the task performance and a constraint in relation to it. It is both constitutive of the activity and stands outside of it. [. . .]

Moreover, cognitive routines have a certain independent momentum, a fact which most people have directly experienced – almost everyone has caught themselves, in moments of absent-mindedness, half-way down the steps of the *wrong* routine. Cognitive routines are based on training, both formal or informal. [. . .]

So far, we have argued that material practices have a subjective element, such as cognitive routines, which are an essential part of their *material* existence. But such routines have to be 'activated' within a framework of specific social relations 'which imposes a determinate form of division of labour by attaching a specific value to a specific task and by linking that task to a specific social category (men/women, elders/young people, master/slave, etc.)' (Godelier 1982: 20). [. . .] [T]he work process itself often involves symbolic elements. As

Godelier points out, 'a labour process often involves symbolic acts through which one acts not upon visible nature, as with implements, but on the invisible forces which control the reproduction of nature and which are thought to be capable of granting or refusing man his wishes: a good harvest, good hunting, etc. This symbolic element in the labour process constitutes a *social* reality that is every bit as real as material actions upon nature' (1982: 32). In the rest of this chapter we will look at some of the relations between material practices (cognitive routines), culture and ideology in particular types of society.

In many simple societies, such as nomadic or horticultural societies, no clear line can be drawn between the cognitive and symbolic aspects of work. [. . .] Work is dyed with the colours of sacredness. There is no English word to express this cultural idea, but there are many words in other cultures. For example, in Maori culture (the Maoris were the original inhabitants of New Zealand) the word for the holy or sacred was 'tapu'. Tapu was applicable to things, to people and to activities. The Maoris were a small dispersed society which practised a simple garden culture, of which by far the largest crop was the kumara, a kind of sweet potato. The planting of the kumara was governed by tapu:

> Before new land was used, the original cover was burnt off, cleared, and broken-up with a hoe (ko) or wooden grubber (timo). This was usually finished in late autumn, before the rains clogged the soil. In spring, before the seed tubers were planted, the ground was dug over. *This was a very tapu operation, following a procedure ritually laid down in every detail.* The whole field was not dug up, but small mounds were formed in a extremely regular pattern, again using the ko. The soil in these mounds was pulverised, after which the seed tubers were distributed at the mounds and planted.
>
> (Schwimmer 1974: 73, emphasis added)

[. . .]

If we look at more complex agrarian societies, [. . .] some broad points can be made. The overwhelming majority of such belief-systems were [. . .] religions oriented to the supernatural rather than humanistically-oriented. As religions, belief in the gods is crucial and service to the gods becomes a (or *the*) central focus of human activity. In addition, the social order was often seen as in some way dependent on the cosmic order: perhaps both orders are thought to enjoy a form of mystical congruence. [. . .]

Given the general characteristics of cosmic ideologies, what has been the relation between them and routine work activities? The answer to this varies with the institutional context of work. As we have seen, the typical pattern in complex traditional societies was one of work organisation based on the family, supplemented by reciprocal assistance amongst the lower classes, combined with a top-structure of forced labour (or corvée) in varying forms and degrees politically imposed by the ruling elite. For example, in ancient Egypt (which was only partly a slave society) the annual corvée involved a mass mobilisation of labour which would normally be used for religious or state purposes. Carlton describes the composition of an expedition under Ramesses IV to collect stone:

> He mobilised 9368 men including the high priest of Amun and other high officials together with the cupboards and some 20 scribes. These were merely the headquarters staff. . . .The main body of the expedition included 91 masters of the horse, baggage train overseers, 50 police and 50 minor administrators, 5000 soldiers, 2000 temple staff, 800 foreign auxiliaries and 900 further officials of the central government. The particular craftsmen who were crucial to the entire undertaking, the draughtsmen, sculptors, stone-dressers and quarrymen, 140 in all, represented a mere fraction of the total force. . . . *A high proportion of the personnel was composed of ritual experts, and the entire operation was dedicated to the gods*, particularly Amun, without whose goodwill it was thought to be

doomed to failure. . . .The whole burden of state economic activity was charged with ritual necessity.

(Carlton 1977: 133–4, emphasis added)

Clearly such forms of work organisation were highly ritualised and the state religion was directly relevant to task performance. However, as has been suggested, the majority of work in agrarian societies was performed in different circumstances by the peasants and a limited segment of artisans. And in relation to such agricultural work and craft work the pre-dominant ideology [. . .] no longer formed the weft and warp of work, but had become a distant clamour of angels and devils. As one writer has pointed out in the English case, 'the hold of orthodox religious views on the mass of the English people was never more than partial' (Budd 1973: 126). [. . .] More generally, the retreat of religion from day-by-day work practices arose from the institutional divorce between state religion and that of the people. Religion became associated with a literate elite, whilst in opposition to this was a 'low intellectual tradition' consisting of magical and semi-magical beliefs and filled with practical matters of peasant technology (Lenski 1966: 208; Thomas 1971: 776–7). [. . .]

In general, then, stratification in complex agrarian societies combined with the typical contempt of the upper classes for manual labour, served to de-ritualise work to some degree, or at least it left the work routines supported by only a semi-sacred and often 'pagan' patina. This is not to say that cosmic ideologies did not attempt (successfully or otherwise) to legitimate tributes, forced labour and other forms of obligation.

So far, we have argued that in simple societies the whole of life tends to be enclosed in a network of magical techniques. In contrast complex traditional societies are characterised by the prevalence of a central worldview, such as a coherent religion, under which 'technique' retreats and becomes secondary: technical activities have little ideological place in these societies. This lack of 'place' permits a certain degree of innovation in work routines but there is no institutionalisation of innovation. In small simple communities innovation is seen as pathological behaviour. For example, in southern Mexico any members of the Oxchuc Indians who invest in new equipment or explore new techniques in order to increase crop yields, or show in any other way their ambition to become wealthy, are distrusted by their neighbours and often accused of practising witchcraft (Siverts 1969). The social environment of complex agrarian societies is not so hostile to innovation; in particular the craft tradition is one in which value is attached to product excellence, which permits the gradual evolution of techniques relatively independently of mythical and religious interpretations of the world. However, as Habermas points out, 'despite considerable differences in their level of development, civilisations, based on an economy dependent on agriculture and craft production, have tolerated technical innovation and organisational improvement only within definite limits' (1971: 94–5).
[. . .]

In modern industrial societies the cultural framework becomes subservient to the development of the forces of production, which in turn are linked to the institutionalisation of scientific and technical development. Modern sciences produce knowledge which is of a form to be technically exploitable and to offer technical control (Habermas 1971: 88 and 99). Innovation as such becomes institutionalised. Indeed the very substantial effects of technical stasis in many industries even for a short period make the rate of innovation the key factor in the rationality of industrial administration. Stinchcombe argues that 'the fundamental characteristic of a rational industrial administration is that it innovates constantly', whether by invention, incremental adaption or by borrowing (1974: 35).

Cognitive routines in modern industrial societies tend to be either technical or legal. Decision-making and behaviour are subsumed under technical rules – this is part of what Weber meant by the notion of 'rationalisation'. Some writers have argued that the end result is not a process of de-ritualisation, but the development of a new ideology of technocracy. For example, Ellul argues that 'technique' has become sacred:

> The individual who lives in the technical milieu knows very well that there is nothing spiritual anywhere. But man cannot live without the sacred. He therefore transfers his sense of the sacred to the very thing which has destroyed its former object: to technique itself [. . .] technique has become the essential mystery.

(1964: 143)

The effects of this process on human choice, according to Ellul, is a state of 'automatism':

> When everything has been measured and calculated mathematically so that the method which has been decided upon is satisfactory from the rational point of view, and when, from the practical point of view, the method is manifestly the most efficient of all those hitherto employed, or those in competition with it, then the technical movement becomes self-directing. I call this process automatism. . . . Technique itself selects among the means to be employed. The human being is no longer in any sense the agent of choice.

(1964: 79–80)

This argument, whereby 'technique' becomes a reality in itself, confuses levels of analysis. It is this very view of technical cognitive routines which represents the ideological aspects and which can be labelled 'technocratic'. Technocracy creates a form of 'thought dependency' by the apotheosis of the expert and the scientific sanctification of the technique. There is no place for choice ('automatism'), because one cannot choose on the basis of ignorance; there is no place for negotiation, because one cannot negotiate about scientific facts.

Technocratic ideology can take many specific historical forms; for example Taylorism [. . .] with its view of the one scientifically determined method of performing work tasks. However, perhaps technocratic ideas were best expressed by the 'New Machine' movement in the 1920s in the United States. This was an association which sought political power and advocated scientific government by 'experts' in all spheres of society: power should pass to the priests of the machine (Maier 1970: 32–4 and 60–1). The New Machine movement failed and this failure underlines that technocratic ideology is a *tendency* in capitalist industrial societies, and not necessarily the predominant ideological framework. But it is the framework within which most work activity takes place and as such it marks a clear distinction from work within traditional societies.

NOTE

* This chapter has been adapted from, Littler, C. (ed.) (1985), *The Experience of Work*, Gower.

REFERENCES

Bauman, Z. (1973), 'The structuralist promise', *British Journal of Sociology*, 24, pp. 67–83.

Budd, S. (1973), *Sociologists and Religion*, Collier-Macmillan.

Carlton, E. (1977), *Ideology and Social Order*, Routledge & Kegan Paul.

Ellul, J. (1964), *The Technological Society*, Vintage Books.

Godelier, M. (1978), 'The object and method of economic anthropology', in D. Seddon (ed.), *Relations of Production*, Frank Cass, pp. 49–126.

Godelier, M. (1982), 'The ideal in the real', in R. Samuel and G. Stedman-Jones (eds), *Culture, Ideology and Politics*, Routledge & Kegan Paul, pp. 12–38.

Kay, C. (1974), 'Comparative development of the European manorial system and the Latin American hacienda system', *Journal of Peasant Studies*, October, pp. 69–98.

Lenski, G. (1966), *Power and Privilege*, McGraw-Hill.

Maier, C. S. (1970), 'Between Taylorism and technocracy: European ideologies and the vision of industrial productivity in the 1920s', *The Journal of Contemporary History*, 5, 2.

Pollard, S. (1968), *The Genesis of Modern Management*, Penguin.

Schwimmer, E. (1974), *The World of the Maori*, A. H. & A.W. Reed.

Siverts, H. (1969), 'Ethnic stability and boundary dynamics in Southern Mexico', in F. Barth (ed.), *Ethnic Groups and Boundaries*, Little, Brown.

Stinchcombe, A. L. (1974), *Creating Efficient Industrial Administration*, Academic Press.

Thomas, K. (1971), *Religion and the Decline of Magic*, Penguin.

Thompson, E. P. (1974), 'Time, work-discipline and industrial capitalism' in M. W. Flinn and T. C. Smout (eds), *Essays in Social History*, Clarendon Press, pp. 39–77.

Udy, S. H. (1970), *Work in Traditional and Modern Society*, Prentice-Hall.

4

WORK*

C. Wright Mills

Work may be a mere source of livelihood, or the most significant part of one's inner life; it may be experienced as expiation, or as exuberant expression of self; as bounden duty, or as the development of man's universal nature. Neither love nor hatred of work is inherent in man, or inherent in any given line of work. For work has no intrinsic meaning.

No adequate history of the meanings of work has been written. One can, however, trace the influences of various philosophies of work, which have filtered down to modern workers and which deeply modify their work as well as their leisure.

While the modern white-collar worker has no articulate philosophy of work, his feelings about it and his experiences of it influence his satisfactions and frustrations, the whole tone of his life. Whatever the effects of his work, known to him or not, they are the net result of the work as an activity, plus the meanings he brings to it, plus the views that others hold of it.

MEANINGS OF WORK

To the ancient Greeks, in whose society mechanical labor was done by slaves, work brutalized the mind, made man unfit for the practice of virtue.† It was a necessary material evil, which the elite, in their search for changeless vision, should avoid. The Hebrews also looked upon work as 'painful drudgery,' to which, they added, man is condemned by sin. In so far as work atoned for sin, however, it was worth while, yet Ecclesiastes, for example, asserts that 'The labor of man does not satisfy the soul.' [. . .]

In primitive Christianity, work was seen as punishment for sin but also as serving the ulterior ends of charity, health of body and soul, warding off the evil thoughts of idleness. But work being of this world, was of no worth in itself. [. . .]

With Luther, work was first established in the modern mind as 'the base and key to life.' While continuing to say that work is natural to fallen man, Luther, echoing Paul, added that all who can work should do so. Idleness is an unnatural and evil evasion. To maintain oneself by work is a way of serving God. With this, the great split between religious piety and worldly activity is resolved; profession becomes 'calling,' and work is valued as a religious path to salvation.

Calvin's idea of predestination, far from leading in practice to idle apathy, prodded man further into the rhythm of modern work. It was necessary to act in the world rationally and methodically and continuously and hard, as if one were certain of being among those elected. It is God's will that everyone must work, but it is not God's will that one should lust after the fruits even of one's own labor; they must be reinvested to allow and to spur still more labor. Not contemplation, but strong-willed, austere, untiring work, based on religious conviction, will ease guilt and lead to the good and pious life.

The 'this-worldly asceticism' of early Protestantism placed a premium upon and justified the styles of conduct and feeling required in its agents by modern capitalism. The Protestant sects encouraged and justified the social development of a type of man capable of ceaseless, methodical labor. [. . .]

Locke's notion that labor was the origin of individual ownership and the source of all economic value, as elaborated by Adam Smith, became a keystone of the liberal economic system: work was now a controlling factor in the wealth of nations, but it was a soulless business, a harsh justification for the toiling grind of nineteenth-century populations, and for the economic man, who was motivated in work by the money he earned.

But there was another concept of work which evolved in the Renaissance; some men of that exuberant time saw work as a spur rather than a drag on man's development as man. By his own activity, man could accomplish anything; through work, man became creator. How better could he fill his hours? [. . .]

During the nineteenth century there began to be reactions against the Utilitarian meaning assigned to work by classical economics, reactions that drew upon this Renaissance exuberance. Men, such as Tolstoy, Carlyle, Ruskin, and William Morris, turned backward; others, such as Marx and Engels, looked forward. But both groups drew upon the Renaissance view of man as tool user. [. . .]

In Marx we encounter a full-scale analysis of the meaning of work in human development as well as of the distortions of this development in capitalist society. Here the essence of the human being rests upon his work. [. . .] Capitalist production, thought Marx, who accepted the humanist ideal of classic German idealism of the all-round personality, has twisted men into alien and specialized animal-like and depersonalized creatures.

Historically, most views of work have ascribed to it an extrinsic meaning. [. . .] Ruskin's famous outburst, ' "there is no wealth but life," the argument of the Socialist who urges that production should be organized for service, not for profit, are but different attempts to emphasize the instrumental character of economic activities by reference to an ideal which is held to express the true nature of man.' But there are also those who ascribe to work an intrinsic worth. All philosophies of work may be divided into these two views, although in a curious way Carlyle managed to combine the two.

1. The various forms of Protestantism, which (along with classical economics) have been the most influential doctrines in modern times, see work activity as ulterior to religious sanctions; gratifications from work are not intrinsic to the activity and experience, but are religious rewards. By work one gains a religious status and assures oneself of being among the elect. If work is compulsive it is due to the painful guilt that arises when one does not work.

2 The Renaissance view of work, which sees it as intrinsically meaningful, is centered in the technical craftsmanship – the manual and mental operations – of the work process itself; it sees the reasons for work in the work itself and not in any ulterior realm or

consequence. Not income, not way of salvation, not status, not power over other people, but the technical processes themselves are gratifying.

Neither of these views, however – the secularized gospel of work as compulsion, nor the humanist view of work as craftsmanship – now has great influence among modern populations. For most employees, work has a generally unpleasant quality. [. . .] For the white-collar masses, as for wage earners generally, work seems to serve neither God nor whatever they may experience as divine in themselves. In them there is no taut will-to-work, and few positive gratifications from their daily round.

The gospel of work has been central to the historic tradition of America, to its image of itself, and to the images the rest of the world has of America. The crisis and decline of that gospel are of wide and deep meaning. [. . .] 'When work becomes just work, activity undertaken only for reason of subsistence, the spirit which fired our nation to its present greatness has died to a spark. An ominous apathy cloaks the smoldering discontent and restlessness of the management men of tomorrow.'

To understand the significance of this gospel and its decline, we must understand the very spirit of twentieth-century America. That the historical work ethic of the old middle-class entrepreneurs has not deeply gripped the people of the new society is one of the most crucial psychological implications of the structural decline of the old middle classes. The new middle class, despite the old middle-class origin of many of its members, has never been deeply involved in the older work ethic, and on this point has been from the beginning non-bourgeois in mentality.

At the same time, the second historically important model of meaningful work and gratification – craftsmanship – has never belonged to the new middle classes, either by tradition or by the nature of their work. Nevertheless, the model of craftsmanship lies, however vaguely, [at the] back of most serious studies of worker dissatisfaction today, of most positive statements of worker gratification, [. . .]. Therefore, it is worth considering in some detail, in order that we may then gauge in just what respects its realization is impossible for the modern white-collar worker.

THE IDEAL OF CRAFTSMANSHIP

Craftsmanship as a fully idealized model of work gratification involves six major features: There is no ulterior motive in work other than the product being made and the processes of its creation. The details of daily work are meaningful because they are not detached in the worker's mind from the product of the work. The worker is free to control his own working action. The craftsman is thus able to learn from his work; and to use and develop his capacities and skills in its prosecution. There is no split of work and play, or work and culture. The craftsman's way of livelihood determines and infuses his entire mode of living.

I.   The hope in good work, William Morris remarked, is hope of product and hope of pleasure in the work itself; the supreme concern, the whole attention, is with the quality of the product and the skill of its making. There is an inner relation between the craftsman and the thing he makes, from the image he first forms of it through its completion, which goes beyond the mere legal relations of property and makes the craftsman's will-to-work spontaneous and even exuberant.

II. [. . .] What is actually necessary for work-as-craftsmanship, [. . .] is that the tie between the product and the producer be psychologically possible; if the producer does not legally own the product he must own it psychologically in the sense that he knows what goes into it by way of skill, sweat, and material and that his own skill and sweat are visible to him. [. . .]

The craftsman has an image of the completed product, and even though he does not make it all, he sees the place of his part in the whole, and thus understands the meaning of his exertion in terms of that whole. The satisfaction he has in the result infuses the means of achieving it, and in this way his work is not only meaningful to him but also partakes of the consummatory satisfaction he has in the product. If work, in some of its phases, has the taint of travail and vexation and mechanical drudgery, still the craftsman is carried over these junctures by keen anticipation. He may even gain positive satisfaction from encountering a resistance and conquering it, feeling his work and will as powerfully victorious over the recalcitrance of materials and the malice of things. Indeed, without this resistance he would gain less satisfaction in being finally victorious over that which at first obstinately resists his will. [. . .]

III. The workman is free to begin his work according to his own plan and, during the activity by which it is shaped, he is free to modify its form and the manner of its creation. [. . .] This continual joining of plan and activity brings even more firmly together the consummation of work and its instrumental activities, infusing the latter with the joy of the former. It also means that his sphere of independent action is large and rational to him. He is responsible for its outcome and free to assume that responsibility. His problems and difficulties must be solved by him, in terms of the shape he wants the final outcome to assume.

IV. The craftsman's work is thus a means of developing his skill, as well as a means of developing himself as a man. It is not that self-development is an ulterior goal, but that such development is the cumulative result obtained by devotion to and practice of his skills. As he gives it the quality of his own mind and skill, he is also further developing his own nature; in this simple sense, he lives in and through his work, which confesses and reveals him to the world.

V. In the craftsman pattern there is no split of work and play, of work and culture. If play is supposed to be an activity, exercised for its own sake, having no aim other than gratifying the actor, then work is supposed to be an activity performed to economic value or for some other ulterior result. Play is something you do to be happily occupied, but if work occupies you happily, it is also play, although it is also serious, just as play is to the child. [. . .] The craftsman or artist expresses himself at the same time and in the same act as he creates value. His work is a poem in action. He is at work and at play in the same act.

'Work' and 'culture' are not, as Gentile has held, separate spheres, the first dealing with means, the second with ends in themselves; as Tilgher, Sorel, and others have indicated, either work or culture may be an end in itself, a means, or may contain segments of both ends and means. In the craft model of activity, 'consumption' and 'production' are blended in the same act; active craftsmanship, which is both play and work, is the medium of culture; and for the craftsman there is no split between the worlds of culture and work.

VI. The craftsman's work is the mainspring of the only life he knows; he does not flee from work into a separate sphere of leisure; he brings to his non-working hours the values and qualities developed and employed in his working time. His idle conversation is shop talk; his friends follow the same lines of work as he, and share a kinship of feeling and thought. The leisure William Morris called for was 'leisure to think about our work, that faithful daily companion . . .'

In order to give his work the freshness of creativity, the craftsman must at times open himself up to those influences that only affect us when our attentions are relaxed. Thus for the craftsman, apart from mere animal rest, leisure may occur in such intermittent

periods as are necessary for individuality in his work. As he brings to his leisure the capacity and problems of his work, so he brings back into work those sensitivities he would not gain in periods of high, sustained tension necessary for solid work.
[. . .]

In constructing this model of craftsmanship, we do not mean to imply that there ever was a community in which work carried all these meanings. Whether the medieval artisan approximated the model as closely as some writers seem to assume, we do not know; but we entertain serious doubts that this is so; we lack enough psychological knowledge of medieval populations properly to judge. At any rate, for our purposes it is enough to know that at different times and in different occupations, the work men do has carried one or more features of craftsmanship.

With such a model in mind, a glance at the occupational world of the modern worker is enough to make clear that practically none of these aspects are now relevant to modern work experience. The model of craftsmanship has become an anachronism. We use the model as an explicit ideal in terms of which we can summarize the working conditions and the personal meaning work has in modern work-worlds, and especially to white-collar people.

THE CONDITIONS OF MODERN WORK

As practice, craftsmanship has largely been trivialized into 'hobbies,' part of leisure not of work; or if work – a marketable activity – it is the work of scattered mechanics in handicraft trades, and of professionals who manage to remain free. As ethic, craftsmanship is confined to minuscule groups of privileged professionals and intellectuals.

The entire shift from the rural world of the small entrepreneur to the urban society of the dependent employee has instituted the property conditions of alienation from product and processes of work. Of course, dependent occupations vary in the extent of initiative they allow and invite, and many self-employed enterprisers are neither as independent nor as enterprising as commonly supposed. Nevertheless, in almost any job, the employee sells a degree of his independence; his working life is within the domain of others; the level of his skills that are used and the areas in which he may exercise independent decisions are subject to management by others. Probably at least ten or twelve million people worked during the 'thirties at tasks below the skill level of which they were easily capable; and, as school attendance increases and more jobs are routinized, the number of people who must work below their capacities will increase.

There is considerable truth in the statement that those who find free expression of self in their work are those who securely own the property with which they work, or those whose work-freedom does not entail the ownership of property. [. . .]

The objective alienation of man from the product and the process of work is entailed by the legal framework of modern capitalism and the modern division of labor. The worker does not own the product or the tools of his production. In the labor contract he sells his time, energy, and skill into the power of others. To understand self-alienation we need not accept the metaphysical view that man's self is most crucially expressed in work-activity. In all work involving the personality market, as we have seen, one's personality and personal traits become part of the means of production. In this sense a person instrumentalizes and externalizes intimate features of his person and disposition. In certain white-collar areas, the rise of personality markets has carried self and social alienation to explicit extremes.
[. . .]

The detailed division of labor means, of course, that the individual does not carry through the whole process of work to its final product; but it also means that under many modern conditions the process itself is invisible to him. The product as the goal of his work is legally and psychologically detached from him, and this detachment cuts the nerve of meaning which work might otherwise gain from its technical processes. Even on the professional levels of white-collar work, not to speak of wage-work and the lower white-collar tasks, the chance to develop and use individual rationality is often destroyed by the centralization of decision and the formal rationality that bureaucracy entails. The expropriation which modern work organization has carried through thus goes far beyond the expropriation of ownership; rationality itself has been expropriated from work and any total view and understanding of its process. No longer free to plan his work, much less to modify the plan to which he is subordinated, the individual is to a great extent managed and manipulated in his work.

The world market, of which Marx spoke as the alien power over men, has in many areas been replaced by the bureaucratized enterprise. Not in the market as such but centralized administrative decisions determine when men work and how fast. Yet the more and the harder men work, the more they build up that which dominates their work as an alien force, the commodity; so also, the more and the harder the white-collar man works, the more he builds up the enterprise outside himself, which is, as we have seen, duly made a fetish and thus indirectly justified. The enterprise is not the institutional shadow of great men, as perhaps it seemed under the old captain of industry; nor is it the instrument through which men realize themselves in work, as in small-scale production. The enterprise is an impersonal and alien Name, and the more that is placed in it, the less is placed in man.

As tool becomes machine, man is estranged from the intellectual potentialities and aspects of work; and each individual is routinized in the name of increased and cheaper per unit productivity. The whole unit and meaning of time is modified; man's 'life-time,' wrote Marx, is transformed into 'working-time.' In tying down individuals to particular tasks and jobs, the division of labor 'lays the foundation of that all-engrossing system of specializing and sorting men, that development in a man of one single faculty at the expense of all other faculties, which caused A. Ferguson, the master of Adam Smith, to exclaim: "We make a nation of Helots, and have no free citizens." '

The introduction of office machinery and sales devices has been mechanizing the office and the salesroom, the two big locales of white-collar work. Since the 'twenties it has increased the division of white-collar labor, recomposed personnel, and lowered skill levels. Routine operations in minutely subdivided organizations have replaced the bustling interest of work in well-known groups. Even on managerial and professional levels, the growth of rational bureaucracies has made work more like factory production. The managerial demiurge is constantly furthering all these trends: mechanization, more minute division of labor, the use of less skilled and less expensive workers.

In its early stages, a new division of labor may specialize men in such a way as to increase their levels of skill; but later, especially when whole operations are split and mechanized, such division develops certain facilities at the expense of others and narrows all of them. And as it comes more fully under mechanization and centralized management, it levels men off again as automatons; both integrated by the authority which makes them interdependent and keeps each in his own routine. Thus, in the division of labor, the open development and free exercise of skills are managed and closed.

The alienating conditions of modern work now include the salaried employees as well as the wage-workers. There are few, if any, features of wage-work (except heavy toil – which is decreasingly a factor in wage-work) that do not also characterize at least some white-collar work. For here, too, the human traits of the individual, from his physique to his psychic disposition, become units in the functionally rational calculation of managers. None of the features of work as craftsmanship is prevalent in office and salesroom, and, in addition, some features of white-collar work, such as the personality market, go well beyond the alienating conditions of wage-work.

Yet, as Henri De Man has pointed out, we cannot assume that the employee makes comparisons between the ideal of work as craftsmanship and his own working experience. We cannot compare the idealized portrait of the craftsman with that of the auto worker and on that basis impute any psychological state to the auto worker. We cannot fruitfully compare the psychological condition of the old merchant's assistant with the modern saleslady, or the old-fashioned bookkeeper with the IBM machine attendant. For the historical destruction of craftsmanship and of the old office does not enter the consciousness of the modern wage-worker or white-collar employee; much less is their absence felt by him as a crisis, as it might have been if, in the course of the last generation, his father or mother had been in the craft condition – but, statistically speaking, they have not been. It is slow historical fact, long gone by in any dramatic consequence and not of psychological relevance to the present generation. Only the psychological imagination of the historian makes it possible to write of such comparisons as if they were of psychological import. The craft life would be immediately available as a fact of their consciousness only if in the lifetime of the modern employees they had experienced a shift from the one condition to the other, which they have not; or if they had grasped it as an ideal meaning of work, which they have not.

But if the work white-collar people do is not connected with its resultant product, and if there is no intrinsic connection between work and the rest of their life then they must accept their work as meaningless in itself, perform it with more or less disgruntlement, and seek meanings elsewhere. [. . .]

If white-collar people are not free to control their working actions they, in time, habitually submit to the orders of others and, in so far as they try to act freely, do so in other spheres. If they do not learn from their work or develop themselves in doing it, in time, they cease trying to do so, often having no interest in self-development even in other areas. If there is a split between their work and play, and their work and culture, they admit that split as a common-sense fact of existence. If their way of earning a living does not infuse their mode of living, they try to build their real life outside their work. Work becomes a sacrifice of time, necessary to building a life outside of it.

NOTES

* This chapter has been adapted from, Mills, C. Wright (1956) *White Collar: The American Middle Class*, New York, Oxford University Press.
† In this historical sketch of philosophies of work I have drawn upon Adriano Tilgher's *Work: What It Has Meant to Men through the Ages* (New York: Harcourt, Brace, 1930).

SECTION 2: UNDERSTANDING ORGANISATIONS

INTRODUCTION

The first section was concerned with the nature of the modern organisation and its impact; and the different ways in which work has been, is, and can be organised in different times and places and circumstances.

It was about the implications of the modern form of organisation for employees. The modern organisation – that strange phenomenon – matters greatly to us, as employees, citizens and consumers. It relies on us holding certain values and attitudes; but it also affects our attitudes and values – towards ourselves and our society.

But what is this 'modern organisation' and how did it develop? Where did it come from and how did it develop its characteristic features? These are the concerns of this second section.

Section 2 has two objectives. First to identify the main features of the new modern form of work organisation as it emerged during the nineteenth century, and the processes that produced it. What were its advantages and origins and prerequisites? Second, how was this new phenomenon – the new work organisation – defined and analysed and explained by contemporary theorists and how have these early theories influenced current thinking? This issue is important not out of an interest in the history of ideas but for the simple reason – explained more fully in chapters 6 and 7 – that early attempts to theorise these new organisations were and remain extremely influential on more recent approaches to their understanding. This section offers an overview of two contrasted ways in which modern organisations – the banks and building societies and universities and retailers and fast food organisations and all the other myriad organisations which surround us and cater for our needs and employ us – actually work. It will offer two contrasted forms of explanation for their structures, their activities, their decision-making – for how they work. These two approaches are based in theory – in fact you will not be surprised to learn they are based in precisely the theories we discuss in this section – but they go far beyond these origins and offer powerful explanations for the organisational structures and actions we see around us. In fact I would be very surprised if you have not already used both types of explanation before you even started to read this book.

Chapter 5: The emergence of new work forms – Graeme Salaman

This chapter offers a broad overview of the historical development of the modern organisation. It contains a lot of material and uses a number of historical sources. This chapter is about how and why the phenomenon that we know as the modern organisation developed, and what it developed from and how it developed. As noted earlier there is a risk that the modern organisation is so familiar to us, so taken-for-granted – that we fail to see it as just one way of organising work, and fail to recognise how it developed sometimes painfully, uncertainly and hesitantly – from earlier alternative forms.

The chapter addresses three issues:

the forms of work from which the new organisation developed, the nature of the process of development, the key features of the new organisation as it emerged throughout the nineteenth century.

An obvious question arising from this chapter – and it is one to which we will return in the final section – is how far modern organisations still reflect or have managed to move radically away from, the core features of the new type of organisation that are described here.

Chapter 6: Classic theories of bureaucracy – Graeme Salaman

The modern work organisation represented a radical and dramatic break with earlier ways of organising work. What changed was not just the way people worked – important as that was – but, as the readings from Littler and Mills in the first section suggest, the way people related to their work, related to those for and with whom they worked. It even affected their basic ways of life, values and ways of seeing and understanding themselves and their place in the world. The new work organisation was an incredibly potent and dramatic social change. As such it attracted a great deal of analysis and speculation. In chapter 6 three highly important eighteenth century theorists' views of the nature and implications of the new type of organisation are presented and considered.

These three theories are offered here not out of any academic respect for theory for its own sake but quite simply because these three theories have fundamentally defined the key ways in which we still think about modern organisations: how they work and their consequences for employees and society.

And this last point is important. All of the theories described in this chapter are far more than mere theories of modern organisations; they are also theories of the impact of these organisations on the surrounding society. Each of the theorists whose work is described here was interested not simply or solely in the modern organisation *per se* but in the ways in which these startling new phenomena heralded fundamental changes in society and specifically occasioned changes in social values and social stability and division.

Chapter 7: Work organizations, managerial strategies and control – David Dunkerley

Chapter 6 was about nineteenth century theorists whose work still dominates our thinking on organisations. Now it is time to bring us more up to date. Durkheim, Weber and Marx left a legacy that still influences current organisational theory in many ways. These influences – on theories of organisation – are discussed in the next section. But Weber in particular left more than a way of thinking about organisations; he left us with a model of organisation – bureaucracy. And it is this model that is discussed in this section.

Weber clearly states the benefits of bureaucracy – which is defined in this chapter by Dunkerley

> The decisive reason for the advance of bureaucratic organisation has always been its purely technical superiority over any other form of organisation. The fully developed bureaucratic mechanism compares with other organisations exactly as does the machine with the non-mechanical forms of production . . . Today it is primarily the capitalist market economy which demands the official business of the administration be discharged precisely, unambiguously, continuously and with as much speed as possible. Bureau-cratisation offers above all the optimum possibility for carrying through the principle of specialising administrative functions according to purely objective considerations. Individual performances are allocated to functionaries who have specialised training and who by practice learn more and more. The 'objective' discharge of business primarily means a discharge of business according to calculable rules and without regard for persons.
>
> (Weber, 1948, p. 214–5)

These are strong claims: that bureaucracy is the most efficient form of organisation, that it creates speedy, predictable, fair, rule-based, skilful business management. They are claims that may seem surprising today when we are exposed on every side to critiques of bureaucracy and to organisational attempts apparently to move away from bureaucratic principles.

However this chapter has two closely connected themes. The first is about bureaucracy and some of the limitations of this form of organisation in practice. The second theme builds on the assessment of bureaucracy as a model of organisation. If bureaucracy is not always appropriate, if other forms of organisations may be more suitable for certain sorts of organisations, or certain sizes of organisations, then is it possible for organisational structures to vary with key organisational circumstances? If so, how? And how far is it possible for organisational structure to be chosen?

Chapter 8: Studying organisations: an introduction – Paul Thompson and David McHugh

The objectives of this chapter are very clear: the chapter sets out admirably clearly, two important and distinctly different ways of thinking about and seeing and studying organisations. It is about theories of organisations, specifically what it calls mainstream and critical approaches. These theories derive ultimately from the classic theories discussed earlier in chapter 6. But these are of much more than merely historic interest. These theories not only determine how researchers study and describe organisations: they also influence how managers try to run and to change organisations. Ultimately, then, these are very practical indeed.

The importance of these two opposed approaches to organisational analysis is not limited simply to their respective merits and limitations. The existence of these two approaches emphasises that any and all understandings of organisations are ultimately theoretical, and ultimately, contested. No-one has access to undisputed truth about organisations. Be wary of anyone who claims such access.

Chapter 9: Struggle and resistance – Graeme Salaman

The approach described – and critiqued – in chapter 8 sets out a clear and powerful view of what organisations are like – why they take the form they do, how they work. This mainstream approach is very important because undoubtedly it catches a critical element of organisations. Clearly organisations are extraordinarily efficient. However, as indicated by Thompson and McHugh, and earlier by Needle, although the mainstream approach is extremely powerful; although very obviously organisations do – indeed must – display these features they can also display other less efficient qualities: they are characterised by sectionalism, politics and limited rationality. Chapter 9 discusses these. The previous chapter presented a view of organisations where the purposes of the organisation are clear, agreed, shared; where decisions are taken on clear and rational grounds; where all staff know and agree what they are doing and work cooperatively together for the shared larger organisation purpose; where the structure and processes of the organisation are carefully designed to ensure efficiency and where management strives to ensure coordination and control for the achievement of the organisation's goals. The same approach was discussed and presented in chapter 1. This may describe some organisations, or an aspect of organisations, but to me it seems an attractive but rather an idealised picture – in much the same way that Max Weber's picture of bureaucracy was not necessarily an empirical description of actual, bureaucracy but an idealised version of what a pure bureaucracy should look like if it were to realise to the fullest degree the rationality and calculability on which it was based.

This chapter discusses in some detail one way in which this idealised picture of the rational consensual harmonious organisation may need to be corrected. The focus of the chapter is on conflict within the organisation. Conflict is something that is largely missing from the mainstream approach. Within that view organisations are consensual phenomena: people agree about what they are trying to achieve; they are all committed to the same goals; their behaviour is informed by these shared goals and values; organisational processes and decisions are determined only by the rational analysis of the best means of achieving shared goals. But chapter 9 tells a different story. Here the 'dark side' of organisations is explored.

5

THE EMERGENCE OF NEW
WORK FORMS*

Graeme Salaman

Despite the uneven rate of development of organizations within the industrial period, and the fact that some early enterprises anticipated the innovations of the period, it is legitimate and useful to speak of the tendencies which can be seen as characteristic of the early industrial organization. There was, as Pollard notes, a 'common thread running through that process of economic transformation' (Pollard, 1965: 103). First and foremost under industrial capitalism work became organized around profit. Labour power was bought and sold like any commodity, organized around the pursuit of profit by capital. [. . .] As guild handicraft gave way to the domestic system of production, work became increasingly subject to the control of capital, and the worker lost his independence. Even before those changes and innovations in technique and work organization which are associated with the industrial period and which permitted the flowering of the capitalist system, work had begun to display the prime feature of work in capitalism: that it involved the sale and purchase of labour power in pursuit of profit, with all its attendant implications for the emergence of class relations between buyer and seller, the owner of capital and the seller of labour. In the industrial period the subordination of production to capital and the pursuit of profit not only became more wide spread and obvious; it became the principle which ultimately guided the design of work organizations, employment relations and work technology as well as the principle determining relations between employed and employers – although, as we see, this principle of employment was not automatically and entirely realized in actual relations, and prior forms of work and employment persisted for many years. It took some time for both parties to learn 'the rules of the game', as Hobsbawm called them. But whether the participants sought to define the employment relationship entirely in terms of the new principle or not (and as the nineteenth century proceeded they became increasingly concerned to define it in pure market terms), the essential nature of the employment relationship was established. [. . .]

The next most obvious feature of the organization of the industrial period was the concentration of the work force – with all the implications for its standard of living – and the organization of work and control. The significance of the concentration of workers did not lie in the subsequent size of the enterprise. [. . .] The key significance lay in the possibilities of dividing work, and in the implications of this for control and discipline.

Divided work must also be coordinated and re-integrated work. The flow of work and the integration of divided processes required management and a disciplined work force. Herein lay the major feature of the factory system, which gave rise to the need for new work habits and a new conception of time – 'by the division of labour; the supervision of labour; fines; bells and clocks; money incentives; preachings and schoolings, the suppression of fairs and sports – new labour habits were formed, and a new time-discipline was imposed' (Thompson, 1967: 90). [. . .]

Marx, for example, discusses two ways in which factory manufacture arises. In one, the capitalist brings together a variety of discrete trades each of which, before, separately contributed to the construction of one item. He gives the example of the manufacture of carriages which required contributions from a number of independent crafts. The other way occurs when the capitalist employs a number of people who do the same work. Each worker previously constructed (possibly with some assistance) the complete product. Soon, when the workers are together, the work is divided and redistributed; just as in the first case, the independent craftsmen soon lost their control over the whole area of their craft and became 'confined in one groove'. In both cases, the work becomes divided so that it becomes the product of a 'union of artificers' who perform just one of the required operations (Marx, 1954: 318–19).

The advantages to be gained by gathering the workers together and dividing labour were striking and, to the entrepreneur, attractive. For one thing, as Pollard notes, the putting-out system's great advantage over handicraft was the opportunities it offered the organizing merchant/entrepreneur to initiate some division of labour. By the same token, the factory offered the opportunity to take this division of work even further. Production in a single factory also had the advantage that it enabled 'a much closer supervision of the work in process than was possible with the domestic system' (Dobb, 1963: 145). And once production was organized and dominated by capital – whether in the form of merchant capital, or by some of the producers themselves – the capitalist merchant-manufacturer had an increasingly close interest in promoting improvements in the instruments and methods of production. 'The very division of labour . . . prepared the ground from which mechanical invention could eventually spring' (Dobb, 1963: 145).

Landes supports this view of the development of the factory system – that it offered an opportunity to the entrepreneur to take advantage of new forms of technology and at the same time to cope with some of the more severe inadequacies and internal contradictions of the older forms of production, the most serious of which was the problem of control. With the putting-out system, the entrepreneur found it difficult to control the behaviour and, most importantly, the level of output of his dispersed, home-based workers.

He had no way of compelling his workers to do a given number of hours of labour; the domestic weaver or craftsman was master of his time, starting and stopping when he desired. And while the employer could raise the piece rates with a view to encouraging diligence, he usually found that this actually reduced output. The worker . . . preferred leisure to income after a certain point.

(Landes, 1969: 59)

So, just when the entrepreneur wanted an increase in production he found himself frustrated by the 'irrational' traditionalism of the workers. Wage cuts were equally ineffective. These resulted either in the workers leaving, or in their embezzling even more of the merchant's raw materials. It was this inherent inadequacy of the putting-out system in the face of increased demand that led in turn to the entrepreneurs' demand for new work technologies and new opportunities for control and work organization and integration offered by the factory system.

But, as Landes remarks, the factory was not simply a larger work unit; it was a

> system of production, resting on a characteristic definition of the functions and
> responsibilities of the different participants in the productive process . . . the specialization
> of productive functions was pushed further in the factory than it had been in shops and
> cottages; at the same time, the difficulties of manipulating men and materials within a
> limited area gave rise to improvements in layout and organization.
>
> (Landes, 1969: 2)

And these improvements in turn were closely related to the employment of machines.
Machines not only replaced – or reorganized [. . .] – manual labour; they made the
concentration of workers in factories necessary and profitable. By demanding more energy
than domestic supply could provide and by being more productive than hand labour these
machines caused not only the concentration of labour, but also its employment as 'hands',
as machine operators rather than craftsmen.
[. . .]
   Clearly the relationship between factory concentration and the design and installation of
machines was two-way: each encouraged the other, and the same is true of the relationship
between the development of machine-based factories and the organization of work; the
factories made possible, and took advantage of, the increasing specialization of labour. As
Dobb remarks:

> revolution in technique acquired a cumulative impetus of its own, since each advance of
> the machine tended to have as its consequence a greater specialization of the units of its
> attendant human team; and division of labour, by simplifying individual work-
> movements, facilitated yet further inventions whereby these simplified movements were
> imitated by a machine.
>
> (Dobb, 1963: 268)

Allied to these mutually supporting developments were two others which also fuelled the
cycle of specialization and mechanization: the growing productivity of labour, and therefore
of capital for further investment, and the increasing concentration of production and
ownership.
   The mechanization and specialization of work in the early factories undoubtedly resulted
in increased labour productivity. But from the employees' point of view they resulted in the
large-scale reduction of work skills – the deskilling of factory work, and the transformation
of the worker's relationship to his product, his tools, his materials, his work itself. If, on the
one hand, there was 'the employer, who not only hired the labour and marketed the finished
product, but supplied the capital equipment and oversaw its use', there was, on the other
'the worker, no longer capable of owning and furnishing the means of production and
reduced to the status of a hand' (Landes, 1969: 2).
   With the introduction of fragmented, specialized work and mechanization on a large
scale, the entrepreneur found himself with a new major problem. Solutions to this problem
constitute one of the most important influences on factory organization. They have an
impact on every aspect of work design, management structure and employment practices.
The problem was that of control, coordination and discipline.
   In the early days of the industrial period, the problem of control had a number of aspects:
recruitment; training and work control work discipline in general (or of the new work ethic,
as it is sometimes known).
   Recruitment was a problem not only because of shortage of labour, but because of
potential employees' unwillingness to enter the new factories. Numerous commentators

of the period noted the 'aversion of workers to entering the new large enterprises with their unaccustomed rules and disciplines' (Pollard, 1965: 160). So great was the resistance, even among the landless and dispossessed, that coercion was often used: convict labour was impressed, for example, in Welsh lead mines; and the establishment of workhouse-manufactories and the forcible use of pauper labour, particularly pauper apprentices, was necessary for 'the pauper children represented the only type of labour which in many areas could be driven into them, and even then it was usually by force and in ignorance of conditions.' (Pollard, 1965: 165)

[. . .]

Certainly the problems of control and discipline loomed very large indeed for the early entrepreneur/employer, as did the associated problem of legitimacy. We can distinguish two inter-related aspects: discipline and work control.

The first priority with the new, factory work force was to encourage the employees to develop 'appropriate' and 'responsible' attitudes towards work regulation and discipline, and towards the new form of employment relationship based on the cash nexus. The widespread concern with sexual morals, drinking habits, religious attitudes, bad language and thrift was an attempt on the one hand to destroy pre-industrial habits and moralities, and on the other to inculcate attitudes of obedience towards factory regulations, punctuality, responsibility with materials and so on. It was considered necessary to change – or improve – the worker's character before he would become amenable to factory regulations and factory inducements: 'A man who has no care for the morrow, and who lives for the passing moment, cannot bring his mind to indulge the severe discipline, and to make the patient and toilsome exertions which are required to form a good mechanic' (Quoted in Pollard, 1965: 196). What was required by the new factories was a 'new breed of worker', broken to the inexorable demands of the clock (Thompson, 1967), and willing to react obediently and appropriately to the employers' manipulation of controls and sanctions. Traditional attitudes and priorities had to be replaced by modern rationality.

The preoccupation with the workers' character, morality, sexual habits, religious devotions, etc. might, as Pollard notes, 'seem to today's observer to be both impertinent and irrelevant to the worker's performance, but in fact it was critical, for unless the workmen *wished* to become "respectable" in the current sense, none of the other incentives would bite.' (Pollard, 1965: 269).

It was appreciated that if 'Idleness, Extravagance, Waste and Immorality' were to be reduced it was necessary to achieve an entirely new morality. The employees' work and out-of-work lives had to be improved. Hence the frequency of efforts both inside and outside the factory to improve the levels of 'morality' and respectability among the new working class. As Pollard writes:

> The worker who left the background of his domestic workshop or peasant holding for the factory, entered a new culture as well as a new sense of direction. It was not only that 'the new economic order needed . . . part humans: soulless, de-personalized, disembodied, who could become members, or little wheels, rather, of a complex mechanism.' It was also that men who were non-accumulative, non-acquisitive, accustomed to work for subsistence, not for maximization of income, had to be made obedient to the cash stimulus, and obedient in such a way as to react precisely to the stimuli provided.
>
> (Pollard, 1965: 254)

Such efforts were accompanied by intra-factory attempts to regulate and direct the work of the hands. Factory work required regularity and integration. If jobs were now subdivided, each hand was now interdependent to an entirely new extent. Previously, if a craftsman wished to regulate his own speed and amount of work he affected no one but himself. But with divided and mechanized labour, regularity of effort and of intensity of effort became crucial. Prefactory work involved a variety of tasks, and an irregularity of levels of effort and of performance. It entailed periods of intense labour followed by periods of licence. And even when such work took the form of employment, it would not place a predominant value on maximizing levels of rewards. All this was incompatible with the factory system. It is worth quoting at length the assessment of a contemporary commentator, Andrew Ure:

> The main difficulty did not to my apprehension, lie so much in the invention of a proper self-acting mechanism for drawing out and twisting cotton into a continuous thread, as in the distribution of the different members of the apparatus into one cooperative body, in impelling each organ with its appropriate delicacy and speed, and above all, in training human beings to renounce their desultory habits of work, and to identify themselves with the unvarying regularity of the complex automaton.
>
> (Ure, quoted in Bendix, 1963: 59)

Factory work involves specialization, sub-division and fragmentation. Decisions about the general rules and procedures and detailed work specifications are vested in experts, managers or machinery. The speed and quality of work cannot remain with the individual workers. Levels and standards of effort and intensity must be carefully controlled, coordinated and monitored. These features required a new 'rational' work ethic on the part of the hands. Much of the structure and history of the early factories must be regarded as various managerial efforts to resolve the problem of control, a problem which was exacerbated by the resistance and obduracy of the employees as they struggled to resist attempts to regulate them, strove to develop 'strategies of independence', or to push back the 'frontier of control'. All forms of employment contain the potential for conflict. But the type of employment relationships characteristic of the factory system created a greater potential than any previous system had created. The need, within the new order, for discipline and orderliness; the need to destroy traditional work habits and speeds; the attack on traditional work relationships and skills; the emergence of the cash-nexus as a basis of employment; the sheer fact of exploitation and degradation, all encouraged the development of a new form of conflict – *class* conflict (see Thompson, 1968; Foster, 1974; Morris, 1979). For at the same time that conditions deteriorated and deprivations increased, skills were demolished and the employment relationship came to be defined by both parties as one characterized by the market criterion: the cash nexus.

Such were the major innovations of the factory system in its early stages: concentration of workers, specialization and division of work, the use of machinery, and a related concern both inside and outside the factory with inculcating the 'proper' attitudes of compliance to factory discipline and installing control systems to achieve the regularity and predictability of wage labour. In themselves these were tremendous changes in the nature of work; and, as such, as shall be seen, they attracted the attention of the early theorists. Towards the end of the nineteenth century other characteristic features emerged – features which may be regarded as typical of the mature factory system: the development of management and bureaucracy, and the increasing emergence of rationalized, direct control systems. These two features are closely connected.

With the increasing size of the enterprise the entrepreneur was faced with a serious problem – how to manage the factory. In previous periods, and during the years prior to the industrial period, shortage of managers and of management procedures was a major blockage to expansion. Where entrepreneurs relied on managers or agents they more often than not found themselves faced by embezzlement, incompetence, theft and various dishonest practices. When managers were left in control, the question was how they in turn might be controlled.

Yet by the time the increased division of labour, technological innovations and the use of inanimate power sources made concentration attractive, it was obvious that the function of management had to grow to take over decisions previously left to individual craftsmen, to carry out their specialist management functions, and to achieve control and coordination.

The work of this new specialism of management contained two elements: the management and organization of the work of shop-floor employees, and specialist management services. To some degree these two functions supported each other; as for example, the imposition of increasingly direct control of employees, and of efforts to measure and regard increases in work effort assisted, among other factors, the development of more ambitious accountancy and planning departments, as well as facilitating the expansion of management *per se*.

Gradually the problem of control of the managers themselves was resolved by the adoption of what are now known as bureaucratic systems. Whereas in the early stages the agent was likely to see his position as a resource to be exploited for what he could get out of it, gradually a manager's job became distinguished from his personal property and his rewards were defined in terms of regular salaries. Again, while at the end of the eighteenth century managers were frequently chosen from within the entrepreneur's family (in an effort to gain trustworthiness), by the middle of the nineteenth century, 'the trustworthiness of managers and their professional standing had risen sufficiently to make their appointment less agonizing. Indeed, the replacement of nepotism by merit became one of the more significant aspects of the growing rationalization of industry' (Pollard, 1965: 146). This tendency, which Pollard exaggerates (see Nichols, 1969), was assisted by the development of increasingly relevant technical training. Although training in management itself did not emerge during the period, specialist and technical training improved considerably.

During the course of industrialization, as factories grew in size and the management function grew, we can find evidence of another innovation on a considerable scale: the formalization of rules and procedures. Some entrepreneurs went to surprisingly detailed extremes in their attempts to anticipate, and legislate for, work events and exigencies, as they systematized impersonal rules and procedures to replace more *ad hoc* regulations.

As Pollard remarks, 'Work rules, formalized, impersonal and occasionally printed, were symbolic of the new industrial relations. Many rules dealt with disciplinary matters only, but quite a few laid down the organization of the firm itself' (Pollard, 1963: 258).

Furthermore, as the division of manual work increased, and grew more differentiated and specialized, as work became increasingly divided, or fragmented, management was required to develop new, coordinating and integrating functions. Litterer (1961) suggests that in North America managerial responses to this problem were to instigate procedures to achieve vertical and horizontal integration, such as production-control systems, cost accountancy, information systems and the installation of policies and procedures which were used to guide and constrain the decisions of subordinate managers. He also makes the point that these various procedures are identical to the conditions that Weber [. . .] cited as major elements of the process of bureaucratization of the enterprise: clear definition of functions and relationships, clear lines of communication, centralized information etc. Bureaucracy was a method of control, or as Goldman and Van Houten put it: 'Specifically bureaucratic mechanisms, notably the detailed division of labour, formalized hierarchy, and the isolation of technical knowledge from workers, proved the most successful means of effecting both social control and efficiency' (Goldman and Van Houten, 1980: 113).

Alongside the development of management and of bureaucracy went another key development – the move from *indirect* to *direct* control and employment, which was allied to the increasing intensification of the employment contract. This tendency in particular must not be exaggerated. Certainly the shift towards direct control and employment was critical to the development of the factory system. It is a key tendency, articulating as it does the priorities and problems of profits and accumulation. But the change did not happen overnight. Littler (1980) argues convincingly for the sporadic and uneven and lengthy emergence of direct control – of the way in which, in the early work organizations, the priorities of capitalism were 'funnelled through, and limited by, the social continuities from the pre-industrial period' (Littler, 1980: 160). Furthermore, [. . .] the transition from pre-industrial to the characteristic features of capitalist work organization was resisted by those who found themselves consequently de-skilled and disadvantaged.

Although the work organizations of the early industrial period demonstrate many of the features of present-day organizations, in one significant respect they retained pre-industrial aspects. This is particularly true of the nature of employment relations in the early factories. Initially much employment in the factories was sub-contracted to foremen who arranged the employment, control and payment of his workers. This system of sub-contract continued for many years. From the employers' point of view, in the early stages of industrialization it offered the great attraction that it helped to resolve the problems of management by avoiding them. They were the responsibility of the subcontractor. And since he very often was able to maintain a more or less traditional relationship with his employees, he too was able to avoid problems of man-management. As Bendix (1963) notes, there is an inverse relationship between the diminishing strength of these traditional relationships between sub-contractor and employees and the increasing division of labour in, and bureau-cratization of, the technical and administrative organization of industrial enterprises.

But in the early days the traditional attitudes of labour that so infuriated the entrepreneur eager to take advantage of increased demand actually assisted the management of labour through sub-contract, because traditional ties and relationships between employers and employees persisted. As Bendix expresses it: the 'sub-contractors, whose middle-man role often depended upon their technical skills, could manage the work force of the early enterprise more or less on the basis of the existing and cumulative traditions of the master–apprentice relationship.' (Bendix, 1963: 55) Employment relations in the early factory were, largely because of sub-contract, characterized by traditional ties, and, as far as the entrepreneur was concerned; coloured by traditional conceptions of the responsibility of the master for his hands. They were permeated by what Mill called the 'theory of dependence' whereby the poor are seen as children unable to think for themselves, who require the protection of their superiors so long as they demonstrate deference and virtue. But this is not to say that these relations were not exploitative, arbitrary and harsh. Personal relations can encourage personal arbitrariness and exploitation (Littler, 1980). Indeed, many contemporaries had occasion in the early stages of industrialization to note and condemn the manner in which middlemen and contractors exploited their workers.
[. . .]

Gradually, as industrialization got under way, and early entrepreneurs were replaced by their sons, or agents, a new conception of the employment relationship began to emerge, replacing the traditionalism of the theory of dependence with the rationality of capitalist accountancy. Under this new philosophy, management control could not be exercised via the channels of traditional master–apprentice relations. It required something new: both sides had to define the relationship in terms of naked self-interest, in market terms. The new generation of industrialists did not believe that their workers' work performance could be controlled on a personal basis: 'rather they tended to regard the workers as factors of production, *whose cost could be calculated*' (Bendix, 1963: 57; emphasis in the original).

From the entrepreneurs' point of view traditionalism was an obstacle to the efficient and rational organization of the enterprise. [. . .] [E]ntrepreneurs, faced with a declining rate of profit, were anxious to use their labour more efficiently and systematically. The extensive use of labour, through long hours of work, was gradually replaced by the intensive use of labour, as hours of work shortened, but the amount, and the sort of effort required, was increasingly controlled. The new factory system involved the substitution of formal, centralized controls for the emergent, traditional, decentralized, sub-contracted controls of the early factory. As Nelson has demonstrated, this process had three elements:

> a technological dynamic, as technical innovation produced, often inadvertently, fundamental changes in the factory environment and in the human relationships that derived from it; a managerial dynamic, as administrators attempted to impose order and system on the manufacturing organization; and a personnel dynamic, as managers began deliberate efforts to organize and control the factory labour force.
>
> (Nelson, 1975: ix)

[. . .]

Sub-contract employment was gradually replaced by direct employment. Within the enterprise the number of salaried, white-collar and managerial employees grew as managerial, administrative and technical functions developed, and subdivided. A new scale, and type of business enterprise was born. Most important of all was the new philosophy of management and employment. Partly as a result of the new scale of business, partly because of falling rates of profit, increasing attention was given to rationalizing work and employment in the drive for a higher pace of work. This search was based upon the application of market principles to employment, bureaucratic and direct control principles and mechanisms to supervision and management, and engineering principles to work design. Systematic management – soon to be institutionalized in the work and teaching of F. W. Taylor with his Scientific Management – was the engineer's response to the problems posed by inefficiency and the increasing scale of employing organizations. It found its reflection in the developing 'instrumentality' of the employees.

As Babbage noticed, the early days of traditional attitudes had their advantages for employers, not least of which was the consequent cheapness of labour (Hobsbawm, 1968; Babbage, 1835) but a major disadvantage was the difficulties such attitudes posed for the installation of more intensive and efficient work forms. By the middle of the nineteenth century both managers and men were developing more market-oriented attitudes towards the employment contract. Both parties learnt to adjust their behaviour to the 'rules of the game', the worker's attitude towards the employment relationship and the wage/effort bargain becoming characterized by market rather than by traditional criteria. Not surprisingly this had repercussions for the development and manifestation of industrial conflict: more heavily bureaucratized and rationalized companies became interested in defining the employment relationship in terms of a wage/effort bargain. This resulted in increasing conflict around the question of job control and productivity.

These, then, in very general terms, are the major features and developments of the new work organizations of the nineteenth century. How were these conceptualized and theorized about by the early social theorists?

NOTE

* This chapter has been adapted from, Salaman, G., (1981), *Work Organisations, and Class Structure*, M.E. Sharpe, New York.

REFERENCES

Babbage, C., (1835), *On the Economy of Machinery and Manufactures*, Charles Knight, London.

Bendix, R., (1963), *Work and Authority in Industry*, Harper and Row, New York.

Dobb, M., (1963), *Studies in the Development of Capitalism*, Routledge and Kegan Paul, London.

Dunkerley, D., and Salaman, G., (eds) (1980), *The International Yearbook of Organizational Studies*, Vol. 1, Routledge and Kegan Paul, London.

Foster, J., (1974), *Class Struggle and the Industrial Revolution*, Methuen, London.

Goldman, P. and Van Houten, D., (1980), 'Managerial Strategy in Turn-of-the-century American Industry', in Dunkerley, D. and Salaman, G., (eds), op. cit., pp. 108–41.

Hobsbawm, E. J., (1968), *Labouring Men*, Weidenfeld and Nicolson, London.

Landes, D. S., (1969), *The Unbound Prometheus*, Cambridge University Press, Cambridge.

Litterer, J., (1961), 'Systematic Management: the Search for Order and Integration', *Business History Review*, 35, pp. 461–76.

Littler, C., (1980), 'Internal Contract and the Transition to Modern Work Systems', in Dunkerley, D. and Salaman, G., (eds.), op. cit., pp. 157–85.

Marx, K., (1954), *Capital*, Vol. I, Progress Publishers, Moscow.

Morris, R. J., (1979), *Class and Class Consciousness in the Industrial Revolution, 1780–1850*, Macmillan, London.

Nelson, D., (1975), *Managers and Workers*, University of Wisconsin Press.

Nichols, T., (1969), *Ownership Control and Ideology*, Allen and Unwin, London.

Pollard, S., (1965), *The Genesis of Modern Management*, Edward Arnold, London.

Thompson, E. P., (1967), 'Time, Work Discipline and Industrial Capitalism', *Past and Present*, 38, pp. 55–97.

Thompson, E. P., (1968), *The Making of the English Working Class*, Penguin Books, Harmondsworth.

Weber, M., (1964) *The Theory of Social and Economic Organization*, Free Press, New York.

6

CLASSIC THEORIES OF BUREAUCRACY*

Graeme Salaman

We shall restrict our attention to the relevant works of Durkheim, Weber and Marx. [. . .] [E]ach theorist developed an analysis of the major principles of the new organizations which connects directly with his conceptualization of the society within which they emerge. Each theorist also assesses the social and personal implications of the new forms of organization, and advances a theory of organizational structure.

DURKHEIM AND THE DIVISION OF LABOUR

For Durkheim the important point about the increasing differentiation and specialization of the division of labour was not the principles underlying the new work forms, but the implications of the new differentiation for social solidarity. The difference between Durkheim and the other theorists is one of degree. Both the other theorists were concerned with the possibility of societal instability followed by the development of conflict relations between privileged (or exploiting) and negatively privileged (or exploited) classes. Nevertheless, Durkheim's preoccupation with the significance of the division of labour for societal stability and order distinguishes him from the other theorists as surely as do the conclusions he draws.

Durkheim's prime concern was with how it is that societies hold together. He distinguishes two different kinds of solidarity, one based on the high degree of resemblance of the individuals, wherein the individual is absorbed into the society to such a degree that individuality itself is barely developed. Members are very similar to each other. This is mechanical solidarity. In the other type, organic solidarity, the parts of the society and individuals are differentiated and individualized. Here solidarity comes from functional interdependence and exchange-relationships.

Organic solidarity – in which society is held together by the interdependence of differentiated units, operating separately but always on the basis of some shared precontractual morality – is a consequence of the development of the division of labour. Durkheim insists that there is no necessary threat to stability in the growth of individualism or of specialization or of market relations. These simply change the basis of social solidarity, they do not destroy it.

The conception of the 'isolated individual', entering into exchange relationships in order to maximize his personal returns, is itself, according to Durkheim, a product of social development and presupposes a moral order . . . the spread of the ideals of individualism is not a symptom of a pathological condition of society, but on the contrary is the 'normal' and healthy expression of the social transformations that are engendering a new form of social solidarity.

(Giddens, 1978: 10–11)

[. . .] The important point is that Durkheim argued that the function of generating social solidarity was, in primitive societies, performed by certain factors and institutions which had, in modern society, been replaced by the division of labour, which far from signalling the end of solidarity and morality, merely represented a new method of creating social solidarity. [. . .] [T]he increasing development and differentiation of the division of labour was a source not of instability and conflict but of stability and social solidarity. Such a view is in marked contrast to Marx's and, to a lesser degree, Weber's assessment of the consequences of new work relationships and forms. It would also seem to be in conflict with observable events and tendencies. Since Durkheim was not unaware of the empirical facts of industrialization and the implications of new work organizations and relationships, he found it necessary, in order to save his thesis, to devote some analysis to what he called 'abnormal forms' of the division of labour. These occur when the process of development of the division of labour as it should naturally develop is obstructed and distorted by various factors. The thesis is saved in face of strongly contrary evidence – that the division of labour frequently produces conflict, instability and division, not solidarity – by defining the conditions under which these 'abnormal' consequences emerge as in some way atypical or unhealthy, i.e. as deviations from the expected which require explanation by reference to special, pathological factors rather than to the fact of the division of labour itself.
[. . .]
These 'abnormal' forms are the result, argues Durkheim, of three conditions. First, the division of labour is often not 'spontaneous' [. . .].

Durkheim is aware, then, that despite the formal freedom of workers in industrial societies, numerous circumstances operate to limit freedom of choice and equality of opportunity. He notes the importance of class and inherited privilege in distorting the spontaneity of the division of labour. If the division of labour is to be characterized by spontaneity, then individuals' aptitudes and preferences need to be matched by the demands of their work. [. . .] Furthermore, exchange relations must also be free from constraint: no one party should be able (because of his resources or position) to exploit or dominate the other party. [. . .]

Secondly, the division of labour can produce abnormal effects because it is 'anomic'. The anomic division of labour is regarded as a result of the uneven development of economic conditions and social solidarity, of the rapidity of industrialization which has moved ahead of the necessary developments in social regulation. As a result, the economy is unregulated and liable to crises, work is increasingly specialized and mechanized, with serious consequences for the workers. [. . .] The problems of industrial organization are attributed not to the system *per se*, with its inherent priorities and relationships, but to the fact that the organization of work in its entirety has developed so fast that it is largely unregulated and not governed by bodies of moral rules and procedures. From this 'anomic' (i.e. lacking regulation and moral control) condition the 'pathologies' of industrialization stem.

Finally, the third factor responsible for 'abnormal' development of the division of labour concerns the fact of organization itself. Durkheim ascribes some of the problems of industrialization to the inefficiency and inadequacies of management and organization. When functional specialization and interdependence within the enterprise are so poorly designed and coordinated as to allow 'incoherence and disorder', then such conditions will not give rise to smooth integration at the societal level. This is a problem of work design, of management, or, indeed, of coordination. Durkheim was confident that with time, increased functional differentiation would bring about increased solidarity at work. [. . .]

For Durkheim, most of the personal pathologies of the new industrial order were attributed to the prevalence, within that order, of anomie. [. . .] As a result of the rapidity of industrialization, relationships within the enterprise and the individual employee's aspirations lost their moral character, i.e. were no longer bound by acceptable rules. They became unregulated, meaningless, anomic. [. . .]

[I]n some ways Durkheim's development and use of the concept anomie can be compared to Marx's use of the concept alienation, though the two concepts differ drastically [. . .]. For Durkheim, anomie resulted from the lack of social control; alienation, on the other hand, *results* from certain sorts of social control. Horton describes anomie as follows: 'Cultural constraints are ineffective; values are conflicting or absent, goals are not adjusted to opportunity structures or vice versa, or individuals are not adequately socialized to cultural directives' (Horton, 1964: 285).

Durkheim saw modern economic life as characterized by constant and pervasive anomie. Anomie, remarks Horton, has become institutionalized as self-interest and the unchecked search for self-interest dominates economic life. Traditional restraints have been overwhelmed. The result is a characteristic pathological mental condition of the citizen, or employee, whose aspirations are unlimited, and whose lot is meaningless egotism.

WEBER

Weber regarded the organizational developments described earlier as constituting the development of *bureaucracy*, a type of organization which articulated a wholly new principle of organization and which represented a radical departure from traditional organizational forms in a number of respects, namely, the basis of authority within the organization, the methods and principles of control, and the basis of decision-making and planning.

All systems of coordinated social action require some mechanism of control and coordination, and some element of 'voluntary submission'. Such submission of the subordinate and controlled to the dominant controller rests upon the attitudes of the subordinate and his perception of the nature of the relationship and the characteristic of his superior. Such attitudes, Weber argues, are of three broad sorts: rational, traditional, and charismatic.

The notion that obedience is due to the superior, or the rules he had promulgated, because such control represents, and derives from, the 'legally established impersonal order' clearly constitutes a major departure from more traditional or personal bases of control and obedience. It rests, Weber argues, on the acceptance of a series of ideas concerning the nature and origin of the underlying legal norms. [. . .] In the main these consist of organization on the basis of impersonal rules, the elimination of personal, subjective factors from decision-making or selection, the clear and formal specifications of responsibilities, and the organization of the offices hierarchically. Incumbents of bureaucratic positions are controlled by 'strict and systematic' discipline, are subject to elaborate systems of rules and procedures, are rewarded by regular salaries, and are involved in bureaucratic careers, i.e. they are expected to rise (according to merit and performance) through the hierarchically arranged offices.

Weber sees bureaucracy as characteristic of many aspects of social life – 'the Church and state, of armies, political parties . . .'. He also sees it as characteristic of economic enterprises. The development of capitalism has been marked, he writes, by the progressive expropriation of workers from the means of production, by the increase in size of the enterprise, by increased specialization and mechanization, and the increase in the functions and size of management. With the introduction of capital accounting, which makes possible a rational assessment of profits and losses in money terms, the extensive, essentially traditional utilization of labour gives way to more systematic, rational and intensive use of labour: 'All the non-human means of production become fixed or working capital; all the workers become "hands" . . . even the management itself becomes expropriated and assumes the formal status of an official' (Weber, 1964: 259).

Furthermore, not only are capitalist enterprises increasingly bureaucratic, but '. . . the capitalistic system has undeniably played a major role in the development of bureaucracy.' And, Weber continues, that development,

> largely under capitalistic auspices has created an urgent need for stable, strict, intensive, and calculable administration . . . capitalism in its modern stages of development strongly tends to foster the development of bureaucracy, though both capitalism and bureaucracy have arisen from many different historical sources. Conversely, capitalism is the most rational economic basis for bureaucratic administration and enables it to develop in its most rational form . . .
>
> (Weber, 1964: 338)

According to Weber, capitalism and bureaucracy both depend on the same basic principle or attitude: that of rationality. In order to understand what is meant by this it is necessary briefly to outline Weber's analysis of the nature and origins of capitalism (Weber, 1930).

Capitalism, Weber insists, is not the same as the drive for profit. Capitalism as an economic system or attitude is distinctive for its 'pursuit of profit, and forever *renewed* profit, by means of continuous rational capitalistic enterprise' (Weber, 1930: 17). Capitalism must be distinguished from traditional, pre-rational attitudes and economic systems.

> . . . it is one of the fundamental characteristics of an individualistic capitalistic economy that it is rationalized on the basis of rigorous calculation, directed with foresight and caution towards the economic success which is sought in sharp contrast to the hand-to-mouth existence of the peasant, and to the privileged traditionalism of the guild craftsman and of the adventurers' capitalism, oriented to the exploitation of political opportunities and irrational speculation.
>
> (Weber, 1930: 76)

Weber locates the origins of this capitalist rationality in the personal psychological consequences and anxieties of Calvinism. Briefly he argues that the empirical relationship between Protestantism and early capitalist activity is not the result of the formal doctrine of Protestantism but of the impact of Protestant beliefs and practices upon the believer. Thus he emphasizes the distinctive features of rational capitalism – the vigorous and systematic pursuit of wealth coupled with a reluctance to consume the profit thus generated in conspicuous consumption or personal pleasures – and relates these to Protestantism's emphasis on asceticism and on the individual's whole-hearted commitment to his calling. Supplying the motive power for these involvements is the individual's anxiety about his personal salvation, exacerbated by his relative lack of institutional supports within the formal Church.

These are the origins of the 'spirit of capitalism' – an attitude which was necessary to the development of capitalism as a distinctive form of economy based on the pursuit of profit through the use of formally free labour.

Also necessary was the emergence of institutions which could further the capitalist pursuit of profit through rational means, i.e. capital accounting and bureaucracy. These institutions are based on the same rational principles. Both are essential to the development of capitalism as an economic system. It was in conjunction with the emergence of the spirit of capitalism that the rational institutions of the industrial societies achieved their full potential. The rationality of capitalism had to be echoed by the rationality of bureaucracy and the anti-traditionalism of capital accountancy. What, then, was this rationality that it characterized all these separate developments?

When Weber described an institution – say capital accounting, or bureaucracy, or the English legal system – as rational, he was making a number of precise points: (a) he was distinguishing the institution or behaviour pattern sharply from traditionalism, in ways specified below; (b) he was describing the institution, not evaluating it. Rationality for Weber, whatever its current implications in normal usage, was not synonymous with 'sensible', efficient or modern, although it could be related closely to these other conditions; (c) rationality itself was of two forms – 'formal' and 'substantive'. Whereas the first refers to the installation (or possibility) of accurate calculations of the nature – costs; quantities, profits, results etc. – of decisions, or to the organization of conduct around certain explicit, formalized rules and principles, the second refers to the relationship between results and overall, general guiding principles.

In these terms bureaucracy, capital accounting and modern capitalism as institutionalized economic activity are rational in the formal sense, because of their employment of explicit rules and principles which make possible exact quantitative assessment of the impact and costs of decisions. The combination of formally rational institutions and the spirit of modern capitalism has created the modern capitalist economy: 'Exact calculation – the basis of everything else – is only possible on the basis of free labour.' (Weber, 1930: 22).

Once two types of rationality are distinguished, conflict between them becomes possible. Weber himself notes, for example, that the achievement of high standards of formal rationality within an economy is dependent on a number of factors, of which one is the expropriation of the individual worker from the means of production, and his exposure to 'a stringent discipline . . . controlling both the speed of work and standardization and quality of products' (Weber, 1964: 246–7). Thus formal rationality depends on the management's extensive control over shop-floor personnel and functions. Such control must, if it is to maximize formal rationality, be unhampered by restrictions or 'irrational obstacles', such as 'the existence of [workers'] rights to participate in management'. But such formally rational procedures contravene other, generally held values about desirable ways of treating workers, of democracy etc. It may be that '. . . the maximum of formal rationality in capital accounting is possible only where the workers are subjected to the authority of business management.' But, continues Weber, 'This is a further specific element of substantive irrationality in the modern economic order.' (Weber, 1964: 248).

The same conflict between formal and substantive rationality is apparent within bureaucracies. Weber recognizes the achievements of modern bureaucracies. 'Experience tends universally to show,' he writes, 'that the purely bureaucratic type of administrative organization . . . is, from a purely technical point of view, capable of attaining the highest degree of efficiency and is in this sense formally the most rational known means of carrying out imperative control over human beings' (Weber, 1964: 337). But he recognizes that bureaucratic rationality and efficiency may conflict. The expression 'efficiency' must be seen against some commitment to certain values and goals. These may be held by some members of the organization, but not by others. An obvious possibility is for formally rational procedures to conflict with the interests of subordinate members of the organization. Or formally rational procedures may obstruct the achievement of substantive rationality. Clearly, Weber's notion of substantive rationality cannot usefully be used without some analysis of the values underlying such assessments, and the social location of such values. According to *which* group's interests and values, for example, can the formal rationality of the division of labour within modern capitalism, as analysed by Weber, or the hierarchic and detailed structure of work and control within modern bureaucracies, be regarded as substantively rational?

To summarize: Weber's analysis of the nature of the new organizational forms of the nineteenth century focused attention on:

(a) the development of organizations with radically new forms and mechanisms of control, which he called bureaucracies. These were distinctive for their use of direct, detailed and specific control, represented in elaborate and strict rules and procedures. Incumbents of positions within these bureaucracies were selected and treated on the basis of their merit, performance and knowledge, not on the basis of personal attributes. They were rewarded by fixed salaries and the promise of careers within the bureaucracy;

(b) these new organizations involved a totally new basis of authority. Orders, and superiors, were obeyed because they were seen by subordinates to reflect acceptable rational-legal norms. Personal and traditional ties between leader and led are irrelevant to the bureaucracy;

(c) these new organizations are described as rational, and this rationality which is also found in other institutions of modern society, is closely related to, and supportive of the developing spirit of capitalism. This rationality constitutes a decisive break with traditional attitudes and values. In its formal manifestation it consists of systems of calculable, quantifiable and explicit procedures and rules. These formally rational procedures are responsible for the achievements bureaucracy supplies for capitalism. But Weber acknowledges the likelihood of conflict between the procedures designed to achieve formal rationality and other societal values. [. . .]

In general, Weber's interest is in the changes in values and priorities which accompanied the process of industrialization, particularly the gradual transcendence of traditionalism. Weber's analysis also focuses on the emerging structure of organizational control and the establishment, at both management and shop-floor levels, of systems of direct control over personnel and performance. As management developed, so the managers found themselves involved in structures of bureaucratic control.

Weber's work is not applicable only to white-collar and managerial levels. He is aware that the new industrial organizations require – if they are to be formally rational – the expropriation of workers from traditional areas of discretion and autonomy, their subjection to strict and stringent discipline, the fragmentation and specialization of their jobs.

The social and personal consequences of the new organizations are revealed in three ways: through classes, and their inter-relationships, which, being based on an individual's ability to sell goods or services within an economic order, develop; in Capitalism, from the position or function of employees of the new work organizations; through the process of rationalization of all aspects and institutions of modern society of which the development of bureaucracy is a major part, and which Weber sees as an emerging feature of Western society; and through the progressive expropriation of employees, workers, managers and officials – from their work, their product, their personal preferences and judgements. [. . .]

As Giddens and others have noted, the emergence of new forms of 'rational' organization is an integral part of the overall process of rationalization which Weber saw as increasingly dominating all aspects of Western society and culture. Typically, this rationalization of the world was, in the first place, anti-traditional. It disenchanted the world by sweeping aside magic and superstition and replacing them with clear, consistent, explicit and, finally, scientific and calculable principles. The progress is apparent in many aspects of institutional and cultural life. It is most clearly revealed in the emergence of new forms and principles of organization.

[. . .]

Rationalization has devastating consequences for the lives and attitudes of individuals, for it means 'that there are no mysterious incalculable forces that come into play, but rather that one can, in principle, master all things by calculation' (Gerth and Mills, 1948: 139). The result is the disenchantment of the world: 'Reality has become dreary, flat and utilitarian, leaving a great void in the souls of men which they seek to fill by furious activity and through various devices and substitutes' (Freund, 1968: 24). Of great importance in the spread of this rationalization has been the emergence and dominance of bureaucratic organizations.

These organizations also affect the lives of individuals directly, by controlling and dominating them through their employment. We have already noted that for Weber, employment within capitalist organization meant the increasing control of the employees as employers attempted to achieve organizational rational systems and procedures in the pursuit of profit. [. . .] Weber argued that within capitalism production is carried out within large organizations, and these can only operate rationally with 'formally free' labour which has no ownership of, or rights over, the means of production. The workers must be expropriated. Control must pass to the owners, or their agents. Large-scale organization is only possible with centralized control; this cannot be achieved if the workers are not fully expropriated. This expropriation is the result of the rationality of capitalistic industry and organization, which requires the free use of large numbers of workers and the centralization of control – 'unified control', 'continuous supervision', coordination and 'stringent discipline'.

The expropriation of workers, being a result of the depersonalization of labour within capitalism, and its use purely for economic production is also required by the needs for centralized control, which results in the emergence of management, for this group takes over the control, monitoring and decision-making of the workers. This group assumes responsibility for the calculation and planning. The alienation of the employee is further increased by mechanization of work. [. . .]

The process of expropriation of employees from control over their work, products and labour is not restricted only to shop-floor employees [. . .]. The process applies also to 'white-collar' workers and to management itself. Weber points to the split between owners and their managers, and notes that this implies the expropriation of such managers, who, like bureaucrats, are selected for their technical ability, rewarded by salaries, and do not own or have any rights over their jobs.

The development of capitalism itself also furthers the application and diffusion of rationality. Capitalism – like bureaucracy – requires the elimination of all non-rational elements. Calculation, impersonality, predictability are the necessary qualities of social relations. The rationality of capitalism is echoed in the rationality of bureaucracy. Both require the expropriation of the employee, the depersonalization of relationships, the supremacy of impersonal calculations. [. . .]

Finally, Weber clearly felt that the very essence of capitalism itself – 'rational conduct on the basis of the idea of the calling' – had given rise to institutionalized capitalism, to a dominating and oppressive way of life, which, in its relentless materialism, destroys traditional values and replaces them with the empty goal of meaningless consumerism. Capitalism as a form of economic order represents the triumph of rationality, with all its consequences:

> The Puritan wanted to work in a calling; we are forced to do so. For when asceticism was carried out of monastic cells into everyday life, and began to dominate worldly morality,

it did its part in building the tremendous cosmos of the modern economic order. This order is now bound to the technical and economic conditions of machine production which today determine the lives of all the individuals who are born into this mechanism, not only those directly concerned with economic acquisition, with irresistible force. Perhaps it will so determine them until the last ton of fossilized coal is burnt. In Baxter's view the care for external goods should only lie on the shoulders of the 'saint like a light cloak, which can be thrown aside at any moment.' But fate decreed that cloak should become an iron cage. Since asceticism undertook to remodel the world and to work out its ideals in the world, material goods have gained an increasing and finally inexorable power over the lives of men as at no previous period in history. Today the spirit of religious asceticism – whither finally, who knows? – has escaped from the cage. But victorious capitalism, since it rests on mechanical foundation, needs its supports no longer.

(Weber, 1930: 181–2)

MARX

Marx maintains that the nature and organization of work in modern large-scale work organizations reflect the essential nature of the employment relationship, which in turn determines all other aspects of society since it establishes the basic groupings (classes) and their relationships and is therefore regarded as the key feature of capitalism. Capitalism as a form of economy and society is revealed through the organization of work and the nature of work relationships. Under capitalism work relationships are characterized by the sale and purchase of labour power. Those with capital buy labour power to achieve profit, which they use to add to their capital and thus to strengthen their position as capitalists and employers. This relationship gives two classes which are in conflict with each other, at least potentially, if not always in practice.

At work this conflict relationship between expropriating employer/capitalist and expropriated employee gives rise to a number of necessary features of work under capitalism: the need for management to direct and organize the labour *power* that is purchased, and to control and discipline potentially recalcitrant employees whose commitment is always unreliable and who may at any moment demonstrate their hostility to their work, their product and their employer.

Since the search for profit from the use of purchased and exploited labour power creates conflict between employer and employee, greater efficiency at achieving profit is inevitably and irrevocably interconnected with greater control and discipline. Measures designed to achieve greater efficiency or productivity or profitability also entail (sometimes directly and explicitly) tighter control over employees, or reduction in the costs (to the employer) of employee recalcitrance or hostility. How could it be otherwise, Marx writes, when:

The directing motive, the end and aim of capitalist production, is to extract the greatest possible amount of surplus-value, and consequently to exploit labour-power to the fullest possible extent. As the number of cooperating labourers increases, so too does their resistance to the domination of capital, and with it the necessity for capital to overcome this resistance by counter-pressure. The control exercised by the capitalist is not only a special function, due to the nature of the social labour-process, and peculiar to that process, but it is, at the same time, a function of the exploitation of a social labour-process, and is consequently rooted in the unavoidable antagonism between the exploiter and the living and labouring raw material he exploits.

(Marx, 1954: 313)

This basic overlapping of the search for profit with the need for greater control results in the politicization of all aspects of work organization. In the first place the design of work, the distribution of work rewards, the level of wages, the state of work conditions etc. reveal the primacy of profit over all other considerations, and demonstrate class-based assumptions about the value and moral worth of the 'hands'. Secondly, the design of work, the use of technology, mechanization, bureaucratization, the development of supervision and management, the emergence of specialist groups within the enterprise are all part and parcel of capital's efforts to increase profitability, cheapen labour, reduce the impact of employees' antipathies and resistance, and increase discipline and control. The division of labour at work is a way to achieve greater control and profitability. Marx writes: 'Division of labour within the workshop implies the undisputed authority of the capitalist over men, that are but parts of a mechanism that belongs to him' (Marx, 1954: 336).

Technology is used to cheapen labour, and to de-skill it, and thus make it easier to obtain and transfer workers. By converting the worker into 'a crippled monstrosity, by forcing his detail dexterity at the expense of a world of productive capabilities and instincts' (Marx, 1954: 340), the employer is able to concentrate skill in the hands of reliable agents – managers. 'Intelligence in production expands in one direction, because it vanishes in many others. What is lost by the detail labourers, is concentrated in the capital that employs them' (Marx, 1954: 341).

The same analysis applies to management itself. While Marx admits that all large-scale enterprises require some coordination, management in the capitalist enterprise is necessitated by the attempt to achieve profit from the employment of alienated labour-power. Capitalism, he writes, requires managers as an army requires officers, to command in the name of the capitalist. The functions of management and the hierarchic structure of capitalist enterprises with their bureaucratic features reflect the attempt to increase labour's profitability, and acquiescence.

These features of work in capitalism have two major consequences: conflict relations between employer and employee, or capitalist and proletariat and the alienation of the worker.

Work relationships between employer and employee are, to Marx, unavoidably exploitative and, therefore, contentious. All aspects of the design of work, and work arrangements in general, plus the fact and design of organization, reflect this basic antipathy. But this potential conflict is not necessarily explicit, or realized. The organization of work under capitalism establishes the basic class groupings. But these classes are by no means necessarily self-conscious groups. Rather they are often either collections of disparate groups, or mere aggregates of people who occupy the same social and economic position but who are – as yet – unaware of their similarities and of their shared conflict of interest with their employers.

Certain essential aspects of capitalism assist the development of *class consciousness* among the proletariat. The nature of work itself – mechanization, degrading activities, de-skilling; the low wages allocated to labour, and the tendency for these to decrease; the increasing pressure of work – the exhaustion of long hours, or of intensively organized work regimes, add to the deprivations of the employees, and encourage the development of hostility.

Certain aspects of the organization of work assist the development of class consciousness among the proletariat by revealing the real nature of the relationship between capitalist and proletariat, and by facilitating the growth of solidarity. Marx stresses the importance of work deprivations, both in the nature of work itself and in the conditions and rewards of work. He stresses the significance of mechanization, by which the worker becomes 'an appendage of the machine', and of the tendency to degraded and de-skilled work which means that '. . . it is only the simplest, most monotonous and most easily acquired knack that is required of him' (Marx and Engels, 1970: 41). He argues that the decreasing skill of manual work is directly allied to the tendency for wages to decrease: 'as the repulsiveness of the work increases, the wages decrease' (Marx and Engels, 1970: 41).

The concentration of workers into factories assists their awareness of their common circumstances, Marx argues, as does their shared exposure to often brutal and demanding work discipline. As a result, and slowly, the proletariat begins to resist the capitalist. Initially as individuals, then as groups and then as the work people of a factory or a locality, the workers struggle against their employers. Initially such struggles mistake the nature of their oppressor, and turn on machinery, or the factory itself. But gradually, as mechanization and market pressures force the growing homogeneity of the proletariat, struggles between the two classes become more common, and more explicitly *class* conflicts. The proletariat becomes organized, through the formation of unions and, overcoming internal divisions, increasingly engages the bourgeoisie in struggles which culminate in the victory of the proletariat. In a striking passage Marx and Engels write: 'What the bourgeoisie, therefore, produces above all, is its own gravediggers. Its fall and the victory of the proletariat are equally inevitable' (Marx and Engels, 1970: 46).

Work under capitalism, then, not only reveals the very essence of this form of society; it exposes those who sell their labour power to such deprivation and indignity that collectively they realize their shared predicament and begin to oppose the system, in order to change it. This is the social consequence of such work circumstance. On the individual level, Marx argues that, under capitalism, the worker is *alienated*. [. . .] The main idea behind the assertion that capitalist society is alienating is that within such a society individuals become separated from various of their attributes, activities, aptitudes and relationships, in the sense that they lose control over, lose any involvement in, become estranged from, their own activities and products, even, indeed, their own potential creativity, and sensuousness. [. . .]

What constitutes the alienation of labour? First, that the work is *external* to the worker, that it is not part of his nature; and that, consequently, he does not fulfill himself in his work but denies himself, has a feeling of misery rather than well-being, does not develop freely his mental and physical energies but is physically exhausted and mentally debased. The worker, therefore, feels himself at home only during his leisure time, whereas at work he feels homeless. His work is not voluntary, but imposed, *forced labour*. It is not satisfaction of a need, but only a means for satisfying other needs. Its alien character is clearly shown by the fact that as soon as there is no physical or other compulsion it is avoided like the plague . . .

We arrive at the result that man (the worker) feels himself to be freely active only in his animal function – eating, drinking and procreating, or at most also in his dwelling and in personal adornment – while in his human functions he is reduced to an animal.

(Marx, 1954: 124–5)

By selling his labour power to the capitalist, by, consequently, being dominated and directed by design of work, technology, supervision, organization in the production of a product he will not own, and which will be sold in order to achieve more expropriated profit, the worker, according to Marx, not only becomes separated from his activities, his creativity, his products. He also supports his own domination and exploitation by creating profit which will be used to finance more employment of the same sort, or more machinery, which itself exacerbates alienation. The workers' products become their master (Avineri, 1968: 121), since past labour is used to finance new machinery, whereby the workers' faculties will be increasingly suppressed. It is in this sense that Marx says capital dominates labour, and the past dominates the present.
[. . .]

[. . .] These are the elements of alienation: that the worker not only loses control, and becomes dominated, loses possibility for expression, as his activity becomes directed and designed in the pursuit of profit, but also that these products, and the profit they generate, increase the power of the capitalist and finance more oppressive work arrangements. In this sense worker and work products are not only separated from the worker, they are *hostile* to him.

SUMMARY

[. . .]

This chapter explored the ideas of three key theorists on the new organisations. Certain similarities and differences emerged. If, in general terms, the theorists agreed in what was occurring, they differed sharply on the origins and implications of the changes. There was agreement, for example, on the personal deprivations and indignities suffered by workers in the new work organizations. There was agreement that these were occasioned by technology, work organization, the division of labour, de-skilling etc. There was agreement that these developments could – or, in the case of Marx, would – result in societal instability through the emergence of classes and class conflict. There was agreement that the new work organizations represented entirely new principles of organization – rationality, the market, individualism and anti-traditionalism, and new forms of organization which articulated these principles. There was agreement that the new organizational forms not only constituted a major threat to societal stability; they also represented a major risk to personal freedom and autonomy. Modern work forms are seen by all three theorists to result in the domination of the individual, so that he has lost control over aspects of his work, his activity, his nature.

There is also basic disagreement, however; most importantly, about the *origins* of these 'pathologies', classes and organizations. Crudely, it is possible to see a major distinction between Marx and Durkheim, with Weber occupying a centre position. For Marx, these various developments in the organization of work, with their attendant consequences for society and the individual, are nothing less than the direct expression of a new, emergent form of economy – capitalism. These are no incidental problems, no results of the process of *industrialization*. They are, quite unequivocally, the direct statement of capitalist priorities and values. For Durkheim, however, the key development is that of industrialization. The personal costs, the pathologies of work and work conflicts, are deviations, unhealthy consequences of a too rapid process of industrialization. While their consequences for personal freedom and well-being, and for social integration, are noted (and regretted), Durkheim is quite clear that they are curable, abnormal forms of institutions and activities which should, normally, be assisting the integration and stability of society. Their elimination requires reform, argues Durkheim, not revolution. 'Anomie' and class conflict follow the lack of regulation of industrial relations, and the unsynchronized developments of the division of labour. These circumstances could be altered by the development of the regulatory role of the state and the setting up of occupational associations operating as intermediate centres of regulation and solidarity. They are the result of the unconditional development of the division of labour, not of *capitalism*.

This position does not however stop Durkheim from mounting a vigorous critique of the personal costs of industrialization, costs which follow the breakdown of control and moral regulation. [. . .]

Weber occupies an intermediate position. The key [. . .] variable is the spread of rationality in bureaucracy and capitalism. Although he is aware of the distinguishing features of capitalism, and notes the close connections between capitalism – and capitalist rationality – and the development of bureaucracy, he also, crucially, notes that bureaucracy, with the modes of appropriation or 'alienation' that accompany it, together with the development of rational institutions (accountancy etc.) would be a necessary feature of a socialist society. He argues, as we have noted:

> . . . the capitalist system has undeniably played a major role in the development of bureaucracy . . . Its development, largely under capitalistic auspices, has created an urgent need for stable, strict, intensive, and calculable administration . . .[and] capitalism in its modern stages of development strongly tends to foster the development of bureaucracy . . . Conversely, capitalism is the most rational economic basis for bureaucratic administration and enables it to develop in the most rational form.
>
> (Weber, 1964: 338)

But, at the same time, capitalism is by no means alone in this close relationship with bureaucracy and rationality. Indeed, the only alternative to bureaucracy is 'reversion in every field to small-scale organization or administrative dilettantism, for "socialism" would . . . require a still higher degree of formal bureaucratization than capitalism' (Weber, 1964: 339).

Inevitably associated with bureaucracy is the widespread expropriation of the employee – of all grades and sorts – and their exposure to the values and criteria of rationality. All grades of worker or employee are expropriated from ownership of the means of production under rational bureaucracy, not just shop-floor workers, as in Marx. For Weber, the most significant features of modern work organizations – and their personal consequences – are not restricted to capitalist societies, although he argues for a close link between the development of capitalism and bureaucracy. Thus the increase in the degree and form of the division of labour derives not simply from capitalism *per se*, but from the emergence of rationality in modern Western societies; a development which relates closely to the development of capitalism, but is not synonymous with it.

There is a complicated relationship between the approaches and preoccupations of the theorists discussed above and more recent organizational theory. Some of the early themes have continued to excite interest and concern; but often in a rather muted form. Others have almost disappeared. At the same time conventional organization theory has developed its own interests. Often these relate closely to managerial problems of morale and organizational design. All in all, there has been a shift from interest in the societal level – the relationship between organizations and the societies within which they exist; the societal implications of organizational structures etc. – to the organizational level. [. . .]

Nevertheless, it is plain that the three theoretical traditions outlined by Durkheim, Weber and Marx still exercise an enormous influence over more recent organization theory, most of which can be seen to articulate some version of the concepts, assumptions and problematics developed in the early theorists' reactions to the startling organizational developments of the early industrial period. This is not to say, however, that all modern organization theory can be regarded in this way; for much of it takes its problematics from what are seen as more practical considerations. Nor is it to claim that the ancestry of all modern organization theory in classic concerns is always clear, or that modern organization theory always does justice to the theory from which it springs. But it is being asserted that both the perspectives of analysis clearly delineated in the works of the early theorists, and the characteristic foci of those traditions (the pathologies of organizational work; a theory of organizational structure; and a theory of class or stratification within organizations) continue to dominate the sociology of organizations.

NOTE

* This chapter has been adapted from, Salaman, G., (1981), *Work Organisations, and Class Structure*, M. E. Sharpe, New York.

REFERENCES

Avineri, S., (1968), *The Social and Political Thought of Karl Marx*, Cambridge University Press, Cambridge.

Freund, J., (1968), *The Sociology of Max Weber*, Allen Lane, London.

Gerth, H. H. and Mills, C. Wright, (1948), *From Max Weber: Essays in Sociology*, Routledge and Kegan Paul, London.

Giddens, A., (1978), *Durkheim*, Fontana Paperbooks, London.

Horton, J., (1964), 'The Dehumanisation of Anomie and Alienation: a Problem in the Ideology of Sociology', *British Journal of Sociology*, Vol. XV, no. 4, pp. 283–300.

Marx, K., (1954), *Capital*, Vol. 1, Progress Publishers, Moscow.

Marx, K. and Engels, F., (1970) 'Manifesto of the Communist Party', in *Selected Works*, Lawrence and Wishart, London.

Weber, M., (1930), *The Protestant Ethic and the Spirit of Capitalism*, Allen Unwin, London.

Weber, M., (1964), *The Theory Social and Economic Organization*, Free Press, New York.

7

WORK ORGANIZATIONS, MANAGERIAL STRATEGIES AND CONTROL*

David Dunkerley

INTRODUCTION

[. . .]

THE DEFINITION OF ORGANIZATION AND BUREAUCRACY

In everyday speech the verb 'to organize' implies that order is being created from a potentially chaotic situation. Similarly when the noun 'organization' is used, both in common parlance and in a strictly sociological sense, the notion of order springs to mind. Order being created so that a set of predefined objectives may be achieved; order so that members of an organization are aware of and carry out their prescribed functions; order so that the whole functions as such. Subsumed within this concept of order is a host of functions that can be seen to operate within organizations and a fundamental aim of this unit is to examine those functions that collectively give rise to certain patterns of work activity directly resulting from organization and the fact of people being organized.

A useful way of looking at what organization comprises is, in fact, to see what it does not comprise. In this sense we can make a distinction between those associations that can reasonably be labelled organizations and those that cannot. As an example, contrast the association or social grouping we label 'the family' and compare this to another social grouping labelled 'the modern factory'. Immediately there are obvious points of difference. Perhaps size is the variable that springs most readily to mind. The contemporary family, consisting typically of two adults with two or perhaps three children, clearly operates on a different scale from, say, IBM, which encompasses many thousands of people throughout the world.

Accompanying this factor of size is the issue of complexity. The functions of the family, whilst in some dispute amongst sociologists of the family, are small compared with the functions of the modern corporation although perhaps quite enough for such a small unit to cope with at any one time. Social relations within the family are of a personal informal kind with sentiment playing a key role in these relations. In comparison, the sheer size and complexity of large organizations tend towards relations being formal and impersonal. Furthermore, the large organization has a clearly defined set of goals and a clearly defined set of means of achieving these goals. In the case of the family unit, objectives tend to be far more loosely understood and often they are not achieved by strictly rational means.

[. . .]

Some well-known definitions of organization perhaps clarify the matter. J. Thompson (1967, p. 397) has suggested that from the outset organization has always been 'an instrument, a deliberate and rational means for attaining known goals'. Parsons (1956, p. 63) defines organizations thus, 'As a formal analytical point of reference, primacy of orientation to the attainment of a specific goal is used as the defining characteristic of an organization which distinguishes it from other types of social system.'

[. . .]

One way forward is still to accept that *goals* are important both in distinguishing organizations from non-organizations and in terms of providing some clues as to what actually happens in organizations in practice. But in order to arrive at this position it has to be recognized that the goals of an organization are themselves abstractions and that for the ordinary member of the organization they may have little immediate relevance in the course of carrying out day-to-day organizational functions.

Perrow (1961, p. 855) distinguishes between the official goals of an organization – 'the general purposes of the organization are put forth in the charter, annual reports, public statements by key executives and other authoritative pronouncements', – and the operative goals which 'designate the ends sought through the actual operating policies of the organization; they tell us what the organization actually is trying to do, regardless of what the official goals say are the aims'. It will be shown below how the reality of organizational functioning is partly shaped by this distinction. At this stage it is sufficient to be aware that what senior members of an organization claim it is doing may, in practice, be different from what it actually does. [. . .]

The most systematic analysis of organizations as rational structures has been that presented by Max Weber who was specifically concerned with bureaucracy rather than all forms of organization. For Weber, organization takes many forms, including the modern state, the political party, the church and the industrial firm. Each type of organization, by definition, has a leader and a specific administrative function. Both leader(s) and administrators are organized or ordered into specific types of social relationships according to the type of rule to which action in the organization is oriented. It was what Weber referred to as 'legal-rational' rule, authority and belief that forms the basis of bureaucracy. Thus, orders are obeyed because of a belief that the order-giver is acting legitimately, according to an agreed-upon set of legal rules and regulations.

A set of characteristics define bureaucracy, that most rational of organizational forms typified by specific conceptions of legitimacy and principles of authority. These characteristics, which apply to all members of a bureaucracy, can be listed as:

1 The staff members are personally free, observing only the impersonal duties of their office.
2 There is a clear hierarchy of offices.
3 The functions of the offices are clearly specified.
4 Officials are appointed in the basis of a contract.
5 They are selected on the basis of a professional qualification, ideally substantiated by a diploma gained through examination.
6 They have a money salary and usually pension rights. The salary is graded according to position in the hierarchy. The official can always leave the post, and, under certain circumstances, it may also be terminated.

7 The official's post is his sole or major occupation.
8 There is a career structure and promotion is possible either by seniority or merit and according to the judgement of superiors.
9 The official may appropriate neither the post nor the resources which go with it.
10 He is subject to a unified control and disciplinary system.

(Albrow, 1970, pp. 44–5)

The modern bureaucratic organization, then, characterises a particular form of rationality. Indeed, Weber goes further in suggesting that 'The peculiarity of modern culture, and specifically of its technical and economic basis, demands this very "calculability" of results' (Weber, 1948, p. 215).

[. . .] It is, though, interesting to note that Weber commented on the rationalization of work being at its most extreme in the case of the scientific management movement in the United States which he said, 'enjoys the greatest triumphs in the rational conditioning and training of work performances' (Weber, 1948, p. 261). The triumphs he referred to basically consisted of the massive dehumanization and impersonal nature of work. [. . .]

There is a danger here of equating rationality with efficiency without appreciating that we must ask efficient for whom, and for what? An underlying reason for the growth of scientific management was the pursuit of efficiency (as well as [. . .] the aim of achieving greater managerial control). [. . .] Weber's bureaucracy is an 'ideal type' – an exaggeration of key tendencies, the manifestation of rationality. But its explanatory utility and its empirical efficiency must, as Albrow (1970) shows, be investigated, not assumed.

[. . .]

Weber, essentially, was arguing that a major determinant of an increasingly important type of organization – the bureaucracy – was the requirement to implement a dominant modern method of problem identification and problem-solving: rationality with all its consequences for explicit, formal, calculability. But do organizations reflect this rationality? Is rationality always synonymous with efficiency? Do other factors also influence organizational structure?

[. . .]

BUREAUCRACY – FUNCTIONAL OR DYSFUNCTIONAL AND FOR WHOM?

Weber established much of the agenda with which sociologists discuss the determinants of organizational structure by identifying the issues considered here: are organizations (bureaucracies) rational, for whom are they rational? Or, even more broadly, how are they structured, and why?

[. . .]

In an important article written as long ago as 1940 entitled 'Bureaucratic Structure and Personality', Robert Merton initially set out to describe the ways in which certain features of the structure of organizations may be affected by the personalities of members of the organization. The argument is this: those people in powerful positions in organizations, the decision-makers, demand control in the organization and essentially this control arises from ensuring that the behaviour of subordinates is reliable. Reliable behaviour, in turn, stresses the need for predictability and accountability within the organization. These features for establishing control arise from an attempt to introduce standardization of techniques (for example, through the introduction of techniques associated with scientific management).

When a situation arises whereby members of an organization are constantly pressured into reliability, certain effects follow. In the first place, there is a reduction in personalized relationships. Thus, a more bureaucratic style of management is adopted since formal relationships, in Weber's analysis, leads to people in organizations being treated not as people but merely as office-holders. Second, an over-internalization of the rules of the organization may occur, suggesting that the function of the rules is changed whereby rule-following becomes an end in itself rather than as a means of achieving the goals of the organization. Third, an emphasis on control can lead to the position where categorization is so restricted that the search for alternatives that is essential to decision-making becomes self-restricted.

These three effects do, in fact, have the function that was originally aimed for – making behaviour of people in organizations highly predictable. Yet behaviour becomes so predictable that it is also highly rigid. The sense of common purpose and development of a strong *esprit de corps* leads to defence of behaviour and structure by members when confronted by external pressure. In this way the original demand for control from the top occasioned by the demand for reliability is certainly satisfied but equally the defensibility of individual action is increased and the amount of difficulty with clients increases.

Clearly, we have here a situation often referred to as 'red tape', a situation when we can use the word bureaucracy in a pejorative sense. By taking the same characteristics as Weber we can see that instead of these characteristics having positive functional effects, they may in certain circumstances have negative and dysfunctional effects as far as the management of the organization is concerned. [. . .]

In pursuing our argument that organization structure itself may be used as a powerful source of control within organizations the early work of Alvin Gouldner is most significant. [. . .]

We have seen that in his analysis of bureaucracy, Weber placed great emphasis upon the function of impersonal and abstract rules that exist in all organizations. What Weber did not do sufficiently thoroughly, in Gouldner's view, was to address the issue of who makes the rules and how they are made. These questions are not only important ones from the point of view of how organizations function, they are important in that they can inform us about how power is distributed in organizations and how control is exercised. A related issue that is taken up by Gouldner and largely neglected by Weber concerns the ends that are served by the particular rules.

With these issues in mind, let us now turn to the case study undertaken by Gouldner and published as *Patterns of Industrial Bureaucracy* (1954) and *Wildcat Strike* (1965). The study centred on a gypsum mine situated in a rural and relatively closed community. The traditional values and structure of this local community appeared influential in determining the values and structure of the gypsum mine and were certainly more influential than a pattern of rational formal organization. What rules there were appeared to be implicit rather than rules defined by formal bureaucratic exigency. This 'structure' of informal implicit rules was described by Gouldner as an 'indulgency pattern' insofar as an informal pattern of management–worker relations existed and a pattern of harmony and peace characterised the operation of the organization.

This indulgency pattern was not a causally related phenomenon in terms of technology or environment. Indeed, a later section will show that such deterministic views should be rejected. It is true that a fit existed between the values and orientation of the local community and the way in which the organization actually functioned. This fit had evolved over many years and was largely founded upon a common definition of the situation that had never been challenged or had apparently needed to be challenged. Gouldner's account shows what happened when such a challenge was made.

[. . .] As might be predicted the goals of the company as a whole were oriented towards profit and maximum output. Company objectives accorded with the kinds of rational and formal imperatives described by Weber and were in sharp contrast with the docile indulgency of the local plant. Furthermore, the company's head office was aware that output and achievement at local level were far lower than could have been possible.

The death of the local manager provided the company with an opportunity to replace him by an outside manager whose orientation would be more in accord with the company as a whole rather than the ways of the local community. The new manager saw the existing indulgency pattern as non-rational and set about dismantling it through the imposition of a set of formal rules and through the introduction of more sophisticated technology. [. . .]

It is perhaps not surprising to learn that this disruption from outside of a system that seemed, to organization members at least, stable and functional, with established values, meaning and definitions, should lead to immense dissatisfaction. A new situation of uncertainty prevailed in which established assumptions were being under-mined. It is interesting to note the reaction of the workforce. The men were realistic enough to recognize that they could not express their grievances in terms of a demand for a return to the *status quo*. The main grievance that was both rational and legitimate (in their view) was a demand for higher wages. In fact, management conceded this demand but minor crises still arose.
[. . .]

From this brief description a number of relevant issues arise. The original position at the gypsum mine was one where power was not needed or exerted since consent rather than control and coercion influenced activities. The situation moved to one where power needed to be explicitly exerted since the traditional structure had been so disrupted. This exertion of power arose through the mechanism of imposing certain features of 'organization' in a rational and purposive manner. Interestingly, Gouldner goes on to describe the occurrence of a wildcat strike through which the workers' demands were articulated. The consequence was an even more rigid application of the rules by the manager and a further tightening of supervision. What we see happening here is the operation of a vicious circle. Management were virtually forced into a position of using more and more formal and explicit rules and authority. The workforce responded with more resistance, leading to a management reaction of even greater control. Eventually the wildcat strike was settled by an even greater imposition by management of formal rules, the total collapse of the former indulgency pattern and a reinforcement of impersonal attitudes.
[. . .]

Gouldner's case study and the theoretical issues arising from it clearly move our analysis further. [. . .] Rather than accepting the perhaps simplistic notion that an organization is either bureaucratic or not, his empirical analysis suggests different types or patterns of bureaucracy (hence the title of the 1954 book, *Patterns of Industrial Bureaucracy*). These patterns he calls mock, representative and punishment-centred bureaucracies. For our purpose mock bureaucracy – displaying a situation where bureaucracy does not really exist except as a form of gloss for outside agencies – can be ignored.

The two patterns of representative and punishment-centred bureaucracy display very different characteristics. The former typifies a situation where the rules are both enforced by management and obeyed by workers; where few tensions are generated with little overt conflict; and where there is joint support for the rules buttressed by informal senti-ments, mutual participation, initiation and the education of workers and management. Punishment-centred bureaucracy, on the other hand, represents a situation where the rules are either enforced by workers or management and evaded by the other; where tension and open conflict are rife; and where the system is enforced by punishment and supported by the informal sentiments of *either* workers *or* management.

[. . .][A]n organization possessing bureaucratic characteristics may in turn possess functional and dysfunctional features. A central feature, that of a demand for control from above, has been shown to have a variety of effects, many of which are unintended and unanticipated by management. Part of this picture also suggests that complex organizations in their operation possess contradictory tendencies. These contradictions, as we have seen from Gouldner's study, may produce a vicious circle of increasing control that produces more and more dysfunctioning of the organization.

Peter Blau, writing in the 1950s again, took the Weberian model of bureaucracy as his starting point and set about observing the actual operation of organizations with this model in mind. Rather than starting with the issue of control and the demand for it from management, Blau's central concern was with the issue of rationality which, you will recall, was central to Weber's analysis and indeed represented a much wider concern to Weber than that of bureaucracy itself in that the latter is an example of a large-scale process of rationalization in modern society.

[. . .]

Blau argues in his book *The Dynamics of Bureaucracy* (1955) that in Weber's writings on bureaucracy there is a basic premise – that people will only behave in a rational way if their job or work task is highly structured.

Thus for rationality to prevail throughout the organization it becomes necessary for there to be low discretion roles where individual organization members are denied the opportunity of using their own judgement, where each role in the organization is as prescribed as possible by management.

[. . .]

In the light of these implications that Blau derives from Weber's work, he (Blau) studied two government agencies in the United States – a federal law enforcement agency and a state employment agency. Blau was concerned to examine how the formally and officially defined rules and regulations of these two organizations were carried out in practice.

The studies themselves can be examined quite briefly from the point of view of their major findings. In the state employment agency the rules and procedures for finding jobs were laid down centrally, in accord with what Weber suggests. At the local agency level it was found that certain adjustments were made with the aim of allocating the unemployed to jobs more expeditiously. Each agency official was regularly assessed for performance, the main criterion of assessment being the number of job placements as recorded by the agency. One interpretation of the assessment procedure was that it engendered a spirit of competition amongst agency officials which in turn was thought to have positive effects on efficiency and productivity. What Blau in fact found was that there was rather more cooperation than competition amongst officials to the extent that the formal rules and procedures were adjusted such that the statistical recordings of placements aided those who on the face of it were less productive.

In the case of the federal law enforcement agency Blau discovered that the official rules could in fact be dysfunctional for the organization. The corollary of this was that when infringement occurred, as it appeared to on a regular basis, the organization was more effective from the point of view of achieving its stated goals. As one example, Blau describes how one central rule of the agency was to report any attempted bribery of the agency workers. By ignoring the rule, the latter were then in a strong position at a later date should they wish to gain cooperation from those who had attempted to bribe them. From an organizational point of view, the flagrant ignoring of the official rule was, in fact, highly functional and the goals were much more likely to be achieved under these circumstances.

Interpreting these empirical findings we see that the original formal model of bureaucracy could benefit from some modification. The rules laid down by the organization were, as Weber suggests, impersonal and abstract; the actual operation of these rules was shown to be dysfunctional, both in terms of the extent to which the goals of the organization were being achieved and in terms of the negative effects upon employees as could be manifested in lower individual productivity and higher job dissatisfaction. The suggestion then is that some type of organizational structure other than formal bureaucracy could be more functional. Blau himself argues for greater decentralization in organizations, a more participative role for employees and the opportunity for people to use their discretion in employees and the opportunity for people to use their discretion in interpreting rules and procedures. In addition to such a strategy directly affecting the work roles of people and 'enlarging' or 'enriching' their jobs, it also means a significantly different type of organization structure might be appropriate. It is Blau's contention that such changes would be functional for management and worker alike.

We shall see in the next section that Blau's argument has been influential amongst later writers who argue that a very real choice can exist in the design of organization structure and that structure itself is not some God-given pre-determined phenomenon but one that is capable of adaptation to particular circumstances. From the point of view of the present argument we can see that bureaucracy in its 'pure form' is not necessarily as functional as might be assumed from a reading of Weber's account. [. . .]

The last of our empirical examples in this section is a study carried out by the French sociologist Michel Crozier and published as *The Bureaucratic Phenomenon* (1964), a study of the strategies of involvement in two French state bureaucracies – a clerical agency and tobacco factories. The results of the study have much in common with our other examples especially with regard to a kind of vicious circle of greater inefficiency and ineffectiveness in organizations arising from an increased emphasis on bureaucratic imposition.

Bureaucracy, Crozier suggests, can be beneficial to both organization and individual in certain circumstances. For example, detailed specifications of jobs have obvious advantages for management and the organization in general as we have already discussed; for the employee, subject to these specifications, there are also advantages in that there need only be the smallest amount of involvement in the organization and its work. Equally, employers, it is argued, may wish to reduce the amount of discretion available to their supervisors and this can be achieved by the existence of low discretion roles for employees where the task is well defined and structured.

When a process of bureaucratization is undergone, then, one consequence might be the emergence in the one organization of two rather distinct sub-cultures with rather different ends being pursued and using different tactics to safeguard their own respective interests. Each group with its own sub-culture has in mind strategies that will ensure relative independence from the other group and will have as a central aim that of maintaining or increasing its discretion. One way of achieving these tactics is to make behaviour unpredictable. [. . .]

An interesting example from Crozier's work is from one of the tobacco factories (a state monopoly) where the production workers were dependent on the maintenance workers. The latter thus perceived themselves (rightly) in a position of power *vis-à-vis* the former in that only they could carry out the necessary repairs, only they could stop the production workers losing money when vital machinery was out of action. From this and other examples, Crozier comments that:

> Each group fights to preserve and enlarge the area upon which it has discretion, attempts to limit its dependence upon other groups and to accept such dependence only insofar as it is a safeguard against another and more feared one, and finally prefers retreatism if there is no choice but submission. The group's freedom of action and the power structure appear to be clearly at the core of all these strategies.
>
> (Crozier, 1964, p. 156)

Erratic rule-following and behaving 'bureaucratically' may therefore be viewed as a mechanism of self-protection. Crozier's explanation is in terms of making behaviour less predictable in the sense of others not knowing when or how rules will be followed. Whether or not rules are followed therefore creates an air of uncertainty in the organization and generally a way of reducing uncertainty and enhancing predictability is through the acquisition of information.

Crozier's clerical agency study shows this very well in that the agency gave every sign of being highly bureaucratized – very impersonal and with a rigid hierarchy. [. . .] The divisional head, in this instance, was dependent on information flowing upwards from the section chiefs. But the section chiefs were competing with one another for resources and so tended to slant the information being sent upwards in order to secure a greater share of the resources. The divisional head then received either inaccurate information or contrived misinformation upon which he had to make decisions and solve problems.

The outcome is a particularly rigid organization structure, minimal commitment and the articulation of various defence mechanisms to maintain the status quo. The situation, however, deteriorates through the by now familiar vicious circle. Management, when they become aware of the fact that they are losing or have lost control of the situation, resort to the rules and procedures in an attempt to regain a grip. We see, though, from Crozier's analysis that emphasizing centralization and lowering the discretion of tasks is likely to reduce the effectiveness of the actual operation and in this sense bureaucracy and the process of imposition have negative rather than positive consequences.

[. . .]

Bureaucratic structures – some implications

Some of the implications of the above studies can now be examined. Each of us is at times astonished at the way operations are carried out in complex organizations. Each of us could probably think of more efficient ways of performing tasks in organizations and yet these ways are often not adopted by the management of such enterprises. Bureaucratic intransigence and red tape often appear as unnecessary problems and yet they frequently occur and are rarely overcome. The reasons for such phenomena are many as the above examples have suggested but certain common elements emerge that are worth highlighting.

In the first place, bureaucratic dysfunctioning often appears to arise from the attempts by management to increase control in the organization. Such attempts at control may derive from the need for greater efficiency or may be seen as management asserting its power – the two, of course, are not mutually exclusive.

In Weber's original statement on bureaucratic structures the issue of control is central. The formal structure of an organization may be so designed as to maximize the exercise of control by those possessing legitimate power in the organization. Weber regarded the modern organization as a highly rational form of administration in which each of the characteristics is designed to enhance the rationality of the whole.

Yet the examples discussed above suggest that, in reality, the position is likely to differ from that perceived and analysed by Weber. The empirical studies have demonstrated that the very characteristics that in the ideal-type construct lead to a highly functional arrangement, may in other circumstances combine to produce a highly dysfunctional organization. Furthermore, the examples are all directly or indirectly concerned with issues of control and with how management may exert or regain control over their subordinates. Whether this is control for its own sake or control to increase efficiency is an issue that we turn to below.

A major problem with Weber's analysis that subsequent research has highlighted is the fact that bureaucracy is not necessarily to be seen as a unitary concept. [. . .] The point is that management appears to be able to choose different types of organization according to the circumstance; in turn this suggests that there are alternative control structures.

Gouldner's study shows clearly that the control strategies arising from organization structure can vary quite considerably from very tight formalized arrangements (punishment-centred) through to very loose informal settings as in mock bureaucracy. It would appear that the use of these different strategies depends upon the perception of management as to the appropriateness of structure to wider conditions.

[. . .]

The extended discussion above on Gouldner's work highlights this distinction. Representative bureaucracy has been shown to be based upon agreement of the rules by all in the organization and where the rules are justified from a technical point of view. Punishment-centred bureaucracy is characterized by the rules being imposed from above. As we have seen from Gouldner's work, it is not merely this distinction which is of interest, but also the raising of the question as to where the rules in an organization originate and for what purpose. In turn, the suggestion is that control in organizations may be obtained by either direct or indirect means.

Direct control may be achieved by a high centralization of decision-making in the organization. [. . .]

Indirect control may be achieved through invoking the bureaucratic rules. The imposition of the system of rules in the organization ensures a standardization in functioning. In turn, this standardization may be yet another way of ensuring the low level of discretion in the work roles of the majority of organization members.

[. . .]

ORGANIZATION STRUCTURE AND THE ROLE OF CHOICE

[. . .]

Our attention here is focused upon an examination of what may be referred to as the formal characteristics of complex organizations as seen in a series of studies that temporally largely succeed the case studies looked at above.

In essence what is being sought is an answer to the question of whether and how much choice can exist in the type of organization structure adopted. Hidden within such a general question are a number of issues e.g. Whose choice are we talking about? Is there a certain inexorability about organization form? What are the consequences of adopting one type of structure rather than another? It is not, then, simply a matter of looking at the extent of choice but also the kinds of rationale lying behind the making of such decisions.

[. . .]

The change in direction to which we are referring eventually came to be known as 'contingency theory'. This theory, which will be outlined below, argued that the formal structure of organizations might vary according to the circumstances of the organization. Whereas early management and administrative theorists had focused upon seeking the best (and by implication, the only) structure for an organization and providing prescriptions for the best span of control, the best type of decision-making and so forth, a perspective began to emerge suggesting that management design the structure of their organizations in the light of certain 'contingencies' within which the organization operated. So by the early 1960s it was becoming clear that certain structural aspects of work organizations such as those indicated above (span of control, communication structure, etc.) were more appropriate and indeed successful in achieving the goals of the organization in certain definable types of environment. This was a major move forward in getting away from looking at the best or optimal ingredients applicable to all organizations covering all circumstances.

[. . .]

Joan Woodward's study of industrial firms in South East Essex (Woodward, 1965) is regarded as something of a classic in the industrial sociology literature. Although she was initially interested in examining the relationships between organizational structure and business performance, her enquiries developed by taking 'technology' as a key variable, finding that technology, not size, seemed to be a way of explaining variations that were found in structural characteristics. On the basis of technology the organizations in the sample were classified into a variety of type ranging from small-batch and unit production through to process production. Clearly, the degree of technical complexity was the key issue. Woodward found that firms within the same band of production system had similar forms of structure. Thus the degree of technical complexity appeared to be related to characteristics such as the span of control of first-line supervisors, the number of levels in the hierarchy and the ratio of managers and staff to total personnel. Interestingly, both unit production and process production firms seemed to display relatively non-bureaucratic structures (certainly when compared to the highly formalized bureaucratic structure that was characteristic of mass production firms). Woodward explains this phenomenon in terms of the central problem of the types of technology. The central problem for unit production firms, she argues, is product development, for process firms it is marketing. In both instances the stress is upon innovation where a formal bureaucratic structure would be inappropriate. Mass production firms, on the other hand, encourage bureaucratic structure because the central concern is control both of administration and production. Findings such as these obviously represented a major breakthrough. After all, it became clear that looking for the best type of structure on a universal basis was inappropriate. [. . .] We can see from Woodward's work that technology was found to be the contingent factor. Although Woodward perhaps over-emphasized the one variable of technology and possibly her findings are most applicable to small firms, the importance of her work should not be under-estimated. [. . .]

The other study [. . .] was undertaken by Burns and Stalker (1961). On the basis of empirical investigation of a sample of firms connected with the Scottish electronics industry two distinct systems of management practice and control resulting in distinct organization types could be observed. These Burns and Stalker termed 'mechanistic' and 'organic' types. These two types of organizational control were, in turn, found to be appropriate to particular types of environment. The hall-marks of an organic structure are adaptability, flexibility and low structure whereas the mechanistic structure approaches the bureaucratic forms described earlier. In practice what we can observe is that an organic structure is more appropriate to those organizations where there is a need to be innovative. The pressure of innovation suggests a structure that can respond to environmental variations rapidly so it is necessarily loosely defined and flexible. Equally, the organization tends not to be formalized nor are roles too closely structured. On the other hand, when the environment is stable a mechanistic structure is more relevant. As with Woodward's work, Burns and Stalker's findings have provided a stimulus for further work and have contributed to the now well-established contingency approach outlined below.

[. . .]

Amongst these early contingency approaches it is to some extent also possible to include Gouldner's work that has already been discussed at some length. You will recall that two significant types of bureaucracy were distinguished – representative and punishment-centred – largely on the basis of type of authority. [. . .]

We can see then a pattern developing in which elements of bureaucratic structure tend to correlate with each other and different organizational patterns of structure suggest different types of organizational control. We can also see that key contingent factors have been stressed including technology and environment. It is also worth noting that these researchers were broadly committed to a 'systems' model of organization and in so doing have considered an analogy with a living organism. In Burns and Stalker's work, for example, there is constant reference to the 'survival' of the system, the adaptation it needs to make to its environment and generally seeking ways of improving the overall performance of the system. Although later contingency writers have moved away from a systems perspective, the latter has promoted an orientation that has been developed by the former – an orientation upon formal characteristics with little or no regard for the actual individuals who inhabit the organization's offices and perform organizational roles and activities.

The empirical study of ten organizations upon which Lawrence and Lorsch's book *Organization and Environment* (1967) is based was concerned to answer the question of the form of organization that was required in order to deal with various and varying market and economic conditions. Through the use of an organic analogy the organization is seen to comprise an inter-related system, the elements of which are influenced by the environment. The central proposition arising from this systems perspective is that organizations are internally differentiated and must achieve a certain level of integration that allows for adaptation to the environment. They argue, for example, that

> . . . in a more diverse and dynamic field, such as the plastics industry, effective organizations have to be highly differentiated and highly integrated. In a more stable and less diverse environment, like the container industry, effective organizations have to be less differentiated, but they must still achieve a high degree of integration.
>
> (Lawrence and Lorsch, 1967, p. 10)

[. . .]

By now you should be gaining a clear impression that during the 1960s the various contemporary empirical studies were suggesting, if not demanding, a re-assessment of the way organizations were analysed and that the time had come to formulate a theoretical scheme that could incorporate the many new findings that were rapidly rendering 'traditional' theory redundant and inappropriate. Lawrence and Lorsch's work is important in that they attempted such a re-orientation by looking at the effects on management of the contingency approach. [. . .]

In examining the contingency 'model' in more detail it is useful to draw upon the integrative work of Burrell and Morgan (1979, pp. 167–81) in providing a clear statement of the basic principles derived from the empirical studies.

(a) Contingency theory argues that the analogy of a biological organism is appropriate for the study of complex organizations.

(b) The theory employs an 'open systems' perspective, i.e. one which emphasizes the importance of the environment within which an organization operates.

(c) There is an interdependence between an organization and its environment.

(d) Those using contingency theory tend to focus upon the organization per se and seek to separate it from the environment.

(e) It is the actual nature of relations between organization and environment that constitutes the primary focus of contingency theorists.

(f) The 'survival need' for the organization is perceived as the central relationship between organization and environment.

(g) Each organization, in addition to being a sub-system of the environment, consists of a number of interdependent sub-systems each of which is a 'functional imperative' in relation to the total process, i.e. there are a number of essential processes which must be achieved within each organization.

(h) The sub-system or key processes comprise the strategic control, the operational, the human and the managerial. These four interact and engage in a process of mutual influence with themselves and their environments.

(i) There is considerable variation in each of the sub-systems stressing strategic, technological and organizational choices.

(j) Environments may be distinguished by the degree of uncertainty they experience, bearing in mind that the notion of a stable, predictable environment is perhaps only theoretically possible.

From these principles a number of issues arise that have subsequently been investigated empirically and to which the rest of this section is directed. In the first place, the use of a systems perspective, as hinted above, has tended to lead to investigations focusing far more upon organization structure than upon what people actually do in organizations. Second, the model suggests that an element of choice exists in the design of organizations that has not, at least in the literature reviewed so far, been adequately dealt with. And third, [. . .] choice of structure raises the spectre of 'whose choice?' and thence on to questions concerning power and its implementation in organizations. Although [. . .] power has not been a major concern of systems theory, the development of contingency theory has placed it very firmly on the agenda.

With regard to the first of these issues – the emphasis on formal structure – one of the most extreme positions has been that adopted by Blau and Schoenherr in their book *The Structure of Organizations* (1971) where they argue that in looking at organizations, the researcher has to choose between concentrating on social structures or social relations. [. . .] They write in their preface that,

> . . . a choice must be made between examining sociopsychological processes within an organization, taking its basic structure as given, and investigating the interdependence in the structure of organizations, while ignoring the details of daily relations and of human relations.
>
> (Blau and Schoenherr, 1971)

The point, as Blau and Schoenherr see it, is that organizational structures can have a major constraining influence on human activities and as such are a valid target for analysis. The extreme position they adopt on this issue can be seen when they state that their approach involves,

> reducing living human beings to boxes on organizational charts and then further reducing these charts to quantitative variables . . . it is legitimate in as much as concern is with the formal structure in its own right rather than with the people in it.
>
> (Blau and Schoenherr, 1971, p. 18)

[. . .] Such an approach is heavily influenced by a positivistic sociology and whilst it may have some legitimacy within its own pre-determined parameters, it does present a picture of reality that is grossly biased. In particular, a sterile view of organizations is presented in which the struggles of individuals and groups, the political processes that are the everyday stuff of organizations, are ignored. [. . .] [T]hese processes are absolutely central to all organizations and no understanding is complete without taking cognizance of them.

Nevertheless in the early 1970s the approach advocated and adopted by Blau and Schoenherr had a considerable following. It was really the series of studies undertaken at the University of Aston led by David Hickson and Derek Pugh that typified, in the UK at least, a change of focus in organizational analysis, one that had a significant effect on the direction of organization studies for at least a decade. Initially, the central concern of the Aston researchers was with this question of organization structure – how could it be conceptualized, measured and interpreted? Having defined structure and scientifically measured it, the aim was to arrive at dimensions of structure that would enable organizations to be compared and contrasted. [. . .]

The conceptual scheme arrived at shows the complexity of the programme. Put at its most basic level the variables can be arranged as in the figure below.

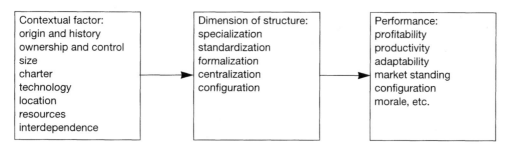

Contextual factor:	Dimension of structure:	Performance:
origin and history	specialization	profitability
ownership and control	standardization	productivity
size	formalization	adaptability
charter	centralization	market standing
technology	configuration	configuration
location		morale, etc.
resources		
interdependence		

Figure 7.1

[. . .] Such data are, of course, open to criticism but for the present let us continue with the examination of the research programme. The data were collected from 52 work organizations in the West Midlands, sampled from all organizations employing more than 250 employees.

In brief, it was noted that when the data were collated according to the conceptual scheme a number of the dimensions proved to be highly correlated. Sophisticated statistical work showed that four principal factors accounted for the variance in the data: the *structuring of activities* (standardization, specialization and formalization), *concentration of authority* (autonomy, centralization, percentage of workflow superordinates and standardization in selection and advancement); *line control of workflow* (percentage of superordinates, degree of formalization of role performance recording and standardization in selection and advancement); and *relative size of supportive component* (the amount of auxiliary, nonworkflow activities such as clerical, transport or catering functions).

By profiling organizations in terms of these four structural factors the Aston researchers claimed to have made a significant discovery by generating an empirically grounded theory of organization. As Pugh and Hickson put it,

> In so far as the original primary dimensions . . . were drawn from a literature saturated with the Weberian view of bureaucracy, this multi-factor result has immediate implications for what might be called the Weberian stereotype. *It is demonstrated here that bureaucracy is not unitary, but that organizations may be bureaucratic in any of a number of ways . . . The concept of the bureaucratic type is no longer useful.*
>
> (Pugh and Hickson, 1976, p. 61, my emphasis)

This non-unitary conception of bureaucracy is illustrated below in terms of seven types of organization structure arranged in a developmental sequence from full bureaucracy to an implicitly structured organization.

Further analysis was undertaken in an attempt to find out why organization structures vary. This analysis suggests that size is related to an increase in the structuring of organizational activities and to a decreased concentration of authority. Technology, they found, was a less influential predictor of structure than size (although a re-analysis of the data by Aldrich (1972) disputes this conclusion).

[. . .]

Both the original work done by the Aston researchers and some of their later cross-national studies have suggested a certain inexorable advance of organization structures akin

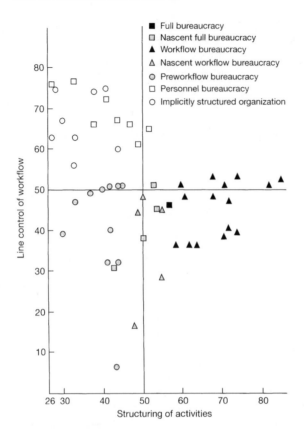

Figure 7.2 Structuring of activities and line control of workflow
Source: Pugh and Hickson, 1976, p. 117 (As reproduced with permission by Gowar Publishing Ltd.)

to a logic of industrialism (Kerr *et al.*, 1973). Thus, although cultural and political differences exist between nations these, it has been argued, are less important than the fact of the existence and growth of large-scale organization. One interpretation of the Aston studies is that a 'logic of organization' prevails in all industrial societies producing, in its turn, a convergence of these societies regardless of political and cultural differences. A useful collection of papers that, *inter alia*, explores such issues is to be found in Lammers and Hickson (1979).

In a paper written before the Aston studies were undertaken, Gouldner (1955) suggested that it was not so much a convergence of logic, but one of sentiment that was occurring. He talks of the despair inherent in arriving at deterministic theories of the kind that would make, say, organization structure determined by size or technology or location. These factors are not necessarily determinant of anything insofar as designers of organizations have choice and can bring their own values to bear on the construction of organizations.

What is the relevance of Gouldner's argument to the present discussion? One interpretation of the Aston studies is that bureaucracy in one form or another is inevitable, that size of organization appears to facilitate the development of bureaucracy, that even if the operation is too small for 'size' to be conducive then technology could well be a determinant.

John Child (1972) has introduced a critique of organization theory that parallels Gouldner's argument. [. . .] He starts from the observation that the way that the research was conducted meant that 'process' could not be examined, 'research designed to establish statistically the presence of associations between organizational characteristics usually leave underlying processes to be inferred . . . adequate explanation derives from an understanding of process, and in this regard the "fact" of a statistically established relationship does not "speak for itself"(Child, 1972, pp. 1–2).

[. . .] One way of remedying this shortcoming is, according to Child, to place an emphasis on the role of 'strategic choice'.

> Incorporation of the process whereby strategic decisions are made directs attention onto the degree of choice which can be exercised in respect of organizational design, whereas many available models direct attention exclusively onto the constraints involved. *They imply in this way that organizational behaviour can be understood by reference to functional imperatives rather than to political action.*
>
> (Child, 1972, p. 2, my emphasis)

Child, then, is arguing that the focus should not be upon constraints but upon choice in design. Almost by definition, therefore, Child rejects both a technological and an environmental determinism that characterized much of the work on organizations operating within a systems framework. [. . .]

Child is sceptical as to whether the notion of technology *per se* has much value as a theoretical strategy. He writes, 'Rather than concentrating upon the technological adjuncts of executing tasks, and on the technical logic whereby such tasks are linked, *there would seem to be a good case for focusing upon the work itself*' (Child, 1972, p. 5, my emphasis). [. . .]

Child is critical of determinist positions involving causal relations between size and structure. Specialization may, then, have little to do with the size of organizations but rather more to do with being part of an elaborate system of management control.

This overall view of organization structure now has a wide currency. What we can see is that it is now accepted that a far greater degree of choice is open to controllers of organizations as to the actual structure adopted. The current position, then, has come a long way from those who originally believed in a universalistic approach to organization structure and design. The principles of scientific management provide such an example of a universalistic approach in which an optimal or best way of organizing was elaborated. We have seen that the contingency approach eschews such sweeping statements by arguing that organization structure may depend upon a range of contingencies including technology, goals and environment.

[. . .]

CONCLUSIONS

A deliberately wide-ranging approach has been taken [. . .] in order to examine the nature of organization structures themselves and to survey some of the more important and significant empirical and theoretical studies that have incrementally shed light on the topic since Weber's original statement about the nature of bureaucratic organizations.

This review should have made it clear that the study of organization structure in its own right has undergone some dramatic shifts of emphasis but that underlying most of the work in the area has been the emphasis of the bureaucratic tradition. Such an emphasis has been both a help and a hindrance to the development of our knowledge. It should be clear, though, why Weber's model of bureaucracy and the rationale for the model were initially examined. What is interesting is not only the debate that later researchers have had over this model but also the way in which so many features relating to the nature of work derive from it.

It is important to regard the issues in the unit as more than a chronological catalogue of the way in which academic thinking has developed. Each of the studies has contributed something to the debate and has incrementally increased our knowledge of work organizations. Whilst the early studies might today have an air of obviousness about them their contemporary significance should not be under-played.

This incremental knowledge leaves us today where we know that management has at its disposal a variety of strategies of control. [. . .]

One area, in particular, has been shown [. . .] to have been especially important – that of managerial choice over strategy in the light of a variety of contingent factors that are both internal and external to the organization. Some of these factors (for example, the prevailing economic conditions) appear to shift the balance of power in organizations such that management itself needs to interfere very little for it to regain lost positions of power and control. By the same token, labour in conditions of recession is placed in a remarkably weak position *vis-à-vis* the employer. [. . .]

Such a recognition is important and stands as a corrective to Braverman's position of scientific management being the main control strategy available to management. We have seen [. . .] that a range of control strategies is available to management and that their differential employment is dependent upon the kinds of internal and external contingencies discussed above. The position has been reached, then, whereby not only do work organizations themselves clearly possess a variety of control devices that can be operated through their structures but also that employers may employ different strategies at different times, in different organizations and over different types of labour. Thus a picture of considerable complexity is painted. The elements of this complex picture have been discussed in this unit in order to demonstrate how knowledge of the structuring of organizations and the deployment of managerial strategies through these structures can more adequately enable us to understand how the work of individuals is designed and controlled in both direct and subtle ways.

NOTE

* This chapter has been adapted from, The Open University (1985) DE325 *Work and Society*, Block 3 *Processes and Control*, Unit 10 'Work organizations, managerial strategies and control', Milton Keynes, The Open University.

REFERENCES

Albrow, M. (1970) *Bureaucracy*, Pall Mall.

Aldrich, H. (1972) 'Technology and Organizational Structure: a Re-examination of the Findings of the Aston Group', *Administrative Science Quarterly*, 17, pp. 26–42.

Blau, P. (1955) *The Dynamics of Bureaucracy*, University of Chicago Press.

Blau, P. and Schoenherr, R. (1971) *The Structure of Organizations*, Basic Books.

Burns, T. and Stalker, G. (1961) *The Management of Innovation*, Tavistock.

Burrell, G. and Morgan, G. (1979) *Sociological Paradigms and Organizational Analysis*, Heinemann Educational Books.

Child, J. (1972) 'Organization Structure, Environment and Performance: the Role of Strategic Choice', *Sociology*, 6, pp. 1–22.

Child, J. and Mansfield, R. (1972) 'Technology, Size and Organization Structure', *Sociology*, 6, pp. 369–93.

Crozier, M. (1964) *The Bureaucratic Phenomenon*, Tavistock.

Gouldner, A. (1954) *Patterns of Industrial Bureaucracy*, The Free Press.

Gouldner, A. (1955) 'Metaphysical Pathos and the Theory of Bureaucracy', *American Political Science Review*, 49, pp. 496–507.

Gouldner, A. (1965) *Wildcat Strike*, The Free Press.

Kerr, C., Dunlop, J., Harbison, F. and Myers, C. (1973) *Industrialism and Industrial Man*, Penguin.

Lammers, C. J. and Hickson, D. (1979) *Organizations Alike and Unlike*, Routledge and Kegan Paul.

Lawrence, P. and Lorsch, J. (1967) *Organization and Environment: Managing Differentiation and Integration*, Harvard University Press.

Merton, R. (1940) 'Bureaucratic Structure and Personality', *Social Forces*, 18, pp. 560–8.

Parsons, T. (1956) 'Suggestions for a Sociological Approach to the Theory of Organizations', *Administrative Science Quarterly*, 1, pp. 63–85 and 225–39.

Perrow, C. (1961) 'The Analysis of Goals in Organizations', *American Sociological Review*, 26, pp. 854–66.

Pugh, D. and Hickson, D. (1976) *Organizational Structure in its Context: the Aston Programme I*, Saxon House.

Thompson, J. (1967) *Organizations in Action*, McGraw-Hill.

Weber, M. (1948) *From Max Weber: Essays in Sociology*, translated, edited and with an Introduction by H. Gerth and C. W. Mills, Routledge and Kegan Paul.

Woodward, J. (1965) *Industrial Organization: Theory and Practice*, Oxford University Press.

8

STUDYING ORGANISATIONS: AN INTRODUCTION*

Paul Thompson and David McHugh

[. . .]

DOMAIN ASSUMPTIONS OF MAINSTREAM APPROACHES

This section seeks to spell out the underlying or 'domain' assumptions in mainstream organisation theory. Though there are varieties and differences, a number of dominant ways of thinking can be identified.

Organisations as goal-seekers

If organisations are consciously created instruments, then their purpose can be defined in terms of goal-seeking. This is unexceptional and, in fact, provides a means of distinguishing organisations from social institutions (for example, families) or movements (for example, feminism), which do not manifest systematic structures and processes for controlling relations between means and ends. But further definition is more controversial. Goals are seen as preferred states which organisations and their members attempt to achieve through collective and co-ordinated action [. . .] In this 'goal model', action and values are seen in terms of consensual collectivities. Goals are formulated, policies and objectives flow from them, and inputs in the form of activities are created, which, in turn produce outputs that allow for realisation of goals and organisational success.

Though there may be vague reference to 'environmental influences', the starting point tends to be located within, rather than outside the organisation: 'there is an assumption that the organisation has some capacity to resist environmental constraints and set its own pattern' (Benson, 1977: 5). It is true to say that obstacles and variations in these processes *are* acknowledged. Members of organisations may have goals which are contradictory to senior management; creating gaps between formal and informal, official and operative, goals and actual policies (Perrow, 1979). For example, scientific and technical workers tend to be much more committed to their job than to their company, and tensions arise between employees' desire to pursue research projects for their intrinsic value and pressure on employers to monitor and even close down those projects (Randle and Rainnie, 1994).

Furthermore, sub-units of the organisation develop a life of their own, partial devolution of responsibility resulting in goal displacement (Selznick, 1949). It is management's job to ensure the best possible fit between the goals of different 'stakeholders'. Emphasis on goals does not enable distinctions between different forms of organisational activity. Various classification schemas exist based on types of goal-seeking which are beyond the scope of our argument. [. . .]

In search of the rational-efficient organisation

The emphasis on collective goal-seeking can only be sustained by a vision of organisations as *rational* instruments or tools; indeed this was a prime theme of Classical Management Theory, which formed the basis of modern organisational analysis. When we talk of rationality, we normally refer to the logical nature of beliefs or actions. This is an aspect of mainstream perspectives, but the basic feature concerns the development of suitable means to reach specific ends. It therefore becomes inseparable from a notion of *efficiency*. The emphasis is on rationally designed structures and practices resting on processes of calculated planning which will maximise organisational effectiveness. Some traditional theorists have described this in terms of the 'one best way' to run organisations. A more acceptable version of the rational model recognises the contingent nature of the process: 'Organisational arrangements are viewed as the outcomes of means–end decisions to bring situational circumstances and structures into alignment in order to enhance efficiency' (Bryman, 1984: 392).

Most mainstream texts continue to deny that there is one formula to fit every situation, but any serious examination of popular management writing and the associated business fads shows that the search for blueprints and formulas has not been forgotten (Pascale, 1990; Huczynski 1993). This can be seen by the rash of books imitating the American bestseller *In Search of Excellence* (Peters and Waterman, 1982). All examine the activities of companies to find the winning formula. At the level of the individual, the equivalent is the endless exhortation to become the 'successful manager', the 'one-minute manager' and so on. Interestingly Peters and Waterman attack the 'rational model' embodied in the classical theorists such as Weber and F.W. Taylor. But their objection is actually to a particular type of rational action that is based on following rules, techniques and structural devices. They quote Selznick approvingly: 'It [the organisation] refers to an expendable tool, a rational instrument engineered to do a job . . . the transformation of an engineered, technical arrangement of building blocks into a social organism' (1982: 98). For them the key role is played by the distinctive values or culture of an organisation, for this has the effect of binding the various participants together. This is what has apparently made Eastman Kodak, McDonald's, Texas Instruments and other companies successful. . . . The magic formula may differ, but the framework of rational action = efficiency remains the same.

Order and hierarchy

Mainstream theory is strongly influenced by ideas of organisations as cooperative social systems; self-regulating bodies, tending towards a state of equilibrium and order. This, in turn, rests partly on a notion that organisations are or should be *unitary* bodies combining the activities, values and interests of all their participants. Each part of the system plays a positive, functional role in this process, for example by generating binding social values. Thus the organisation is a system of interrelated parts or sub-units, for example departments, groups and individuals; each functioning to mobilise resources towards meeting wider goals. These parts are at the same time differentiated and interdependent, aiding processes of integration and co-ordination.

The managerial requirement to integrate potentially diverse goals and activities, could, of course, take place in a number of ways. But mainstream theory has tended to emphasise the advantages of a particular pattern of roles and responsibilities. [. . .]

Such an interpretation of the division of labour has always played a leading role in ideas of how to sustain the social solidarity necessary for the survival of the 'organism' of society or enterprise. Current managerial rhetoric is awash with terms such as 'empowering' the workforce and self-managed teams, which suggest a different way of doing things. [. . .]

Managerialism

Part of management's social engineering role is to maintain the maximum degree of harmony and generate feelings of belonging in the workforce, reflecting literally the definition of organisation as 'form into an orderly whole'. Common to all versions of rational efficiency is that the logical basis of action is held to reside with the manager. In contrast, employees who restrict or oppose such action are frequently held to be acting irrationally, governed by a 'logic of sentiment', rather than one of efficiency. The more overtly managerial writers are understandably full of references to what management *should* do, and in this sense are clearly *prescriptive* in nature. For some, the role of organisational analysis is to 'help managers in organisations understand how far their behaviour can positively influence their subordinate's productivity' (W. Clay Hamner, quoted in Karmel, 1980).

Effectiveness becomes synonymous with management effectiveness, and options in debates are situated within that framework. Donaldson (1985: 86) disputes this by arguing that though both are concerned with systems effectiveness, their viewpoints are distinguishable. After all, if they were the same, there would be no point in supplying prescriptions. This is true, but the parameters are strictly circumscribed, as in the example supplied – that an organisational analyst might advise greater or less socialisation into company beliefs, with no question of the legitimacy of the beliefs themselves.

Not all mainstream writing is openly managerialist. But the underlying assumptions seldom stray too far. In the preface to a recent popular textbook (Buchanan and Huczynski, 1985), Lupton remarks that social scientists should not attach themselves to any one organisational group or its problems. But he then gives two examples of key 'puzzles'. Why and in what conditions do workgroups restrict output? What are the origins and costs of impeding technical innovation? Similarly Karmel (1980) identifies key questions. Why do people sabotage equipment? Why does the introduction of a computer make many people unhappy? Why do subordinates not obey? Alternative 'puzzles', such as why are alienating technologies designed in the first place, are conspicuous by their absence. In addition the way such problems are defined, and the recurrent use of the term *practitioners* can only refer to management practices.

A science of organisations

In terms of methodology, many mainstream writers take what Benson (1977) refers to as a 'simple positivist view'. That is, they tend towards the use of methods and a view of reality borrowed from the natural sciences. There are two particularly important features involved. First, there is great emphasis on *measurement* of organisational phenomena for example, types of structures, technologies, leadership styles, and even the fit between them. Secondly, there is an attempt to discover clear cause and effect relationships, Donaldson (1985: 84) stating the need to 'reaffirm the commitment to valid general causal laws as the goal'. He asserts the superiority of science over lay accounts, which is hardly the point. It is a question of the nature of the scientific approach, particularly the mistaken emphasis on laws. The fact that no one can actually identify any does not seem to worry Donaldson, as this is no proof that they may not yet be discovered in the future! Inevitably under the mantle of science – whether administrative, organisational or behavioural – these generalisations are intended to apply to *all* organisations. On this basis, analysis and intervention can be used to predict and control events, and make prescriptive recommendations. Stress on technique rather than values matches the idea of organisations as technical instruments. When combined, these attitudes towards scientific intervention into the organisation itself tend to be taken for granted rather than treated as problematic. Some criticisms have been raised alongside the exposition but the next section opens this out more comprehensively.

An evaluation of mainstream perspectives

Mainstream perspectives are not homogeneous and there are tensions [. . .] between concepts derived from Weber, Durkheim and other key figures. There is also much of value in the body of ideas, both in terms of the issues raised and empirical work generated. Nevertheless, we can identify the outline of a number of interrelated criticisms, many of which are followed up in other chapters. *Rationality* and *efficiency* have been important themes, and no one should deny that they are legitimate aspects of organisational analysis. But in mainstream theory they are presented largely in neutral terms, as if rationality was a simple determinant of organisational structures, processes and goals. Processes are reduced to a matter of technique; devising the appropriate kind of structure, or best fit with a particular environment. A cosy picture is developed of a functional relationship between rational organisations and a rational society. This perspective removes issues of politics, power and control from organisational choices, and critical questions concerning means and ends. Donaldson (1985: 101) tries to get round this by separating the latter; 'The concern with rational means rather than values is part of what makes such studies apolitical'. But there are as many contestable choices to be made about how to design jobs or authority structures as there are about the ends to which they are put.

A rational *model* emphasising features such as calculability is further confused with rationality or reasonableness *as such*. As Fischer and Sirriani put it: 'For the critical theorist, mainstream writers have confused the rational model of efficient administrative behaviour with organisational rationality itself . . . organisations must be conceptualised as tools for the pursuit of personal, group or class interests' (1984: 10–11). Furthermore, traditional notions underestimate the role of rationality and efficiency as ideological constructs which help to legitimise the positions, rewards and activities of dominant groups (Salaman, 1979: 177–82). For example, when changes such as mergers or closures take place, they are often described in terms of *rationalisation*, as the decision of managers or boards of directors are inevitable and the only way of doing things. It is important to acknowledge the contested nature of rationality, underpinned by the struggle for scarce organisational and social resources; and indeed, this is the direction taken by an increased range of organisational theorists (Bryman, 1984).

This is insufficiently recognised in mainstream perspectives because they are underlaid by an assumption of harmony of interests. This is reproduced in another crucial sphere, that of the division of labour. The way that tasks, functions and jobs are divided, with the consequent specialisation and hierarchies, is all too often regarded as an unproblematic, technical or functional necessity. The origins and workings of the division of labour is neglected as an issue, influenced by analyses which emphasise differentiation and interdependence. As a consequence, many deep-rooted features of organisational life – inequality, conflict, domination and subordination, manipulation – are written out of the script in favour of behavioural questions associated with efficiency or motivation. Some of these features may be seen as pathological or temporary phenomena arising from breakdowns in organisational systems, rather than a fundamental product of the structuring of the division of labour.

Notions of social harmony have also distorted an understanding of *goals*. As we saw earlier, mainstream writings have made some progress towards acknowledging goal diversity and uncertainty. This is welcome, but there are still weaknesses. Oppositional goals cannot be confined to the 'personal'. As Clegg and Dunkerley observe: 'There is no notion of rational structural sources of opposition being generated in the normal processes of organisation' (1980: 317). A sense of reification is still present, in which the organisation is treated as a thing, and the only legitimate goal-seeking collectivity. Problems cannot be avoided by the use of the 'stakeholder' model (Donaldson, 1985: 24), which postulates a spurious pluralism in which goals are held to be the result of a relatively equal trade-off between the preferences of competing, but co-operative groups (employees, managers, owners, customers). Nor is it enough for Donaldson to assert that the higher levels of management simply 'edit and select' from competing claims.

The notion that formal organisations, made up of different members, are constituted to co-ordinate wider goals as if they are a form of social contract (Albrow, 1973: 408), underestimates the extent to which dominant power groupings have set those goals and shaped the appropriate structures. In practice, co-ordination or co-operation may reflect pressure, constraint or acquiescence to power as much as shared goals. [. . .]

So, there *is* a sense in which we can refer to 'organisations' having policies or goals, but they have to be clearly recognised as frequently the property of particular individuals or groups. [. . .] As we saw earlier, to define or classify organisations in terms of goal-seeking distorts the differences between them. We need to differentiate between different types of goals and the wider economic and political influences upon them; and to consider how they are constructed and in whose benefit they operate. The example used earlier of direct selling companies is illustrative of alternative *organising logics* that can operate between and even within organisations. Different logics lead to the choice of particular managerial mechanisms.

The failure to analyse these processes adequately underlines the extent to which organisational analysis remains consciously or implicitly management-orientated. Texts remain a curious and confusing mixture of analysis and prescription. Emphasis on a stream of advice and solutions to managers consistently undermines the generation of valid and realistic knowledge of organisational processes. Two qualifying points to this criticism need to be made: first, there *is* a need to study management as an activity; second, an openly 'management science' servicing the needs of such groups inevitably reflects existing socio-economic relations. But such an orientation is particularly dangerous to a broader organisational analysis. As Watson (Watson, 1980) points out, management requirements are likely to focus on short-term pragmatic relevance related to task achievement, or towards the ideological expedience of unitary and consensual views of organisational life. Theorists can become, in Baritz's (1960) words, 'servants of power', enmeshed in restrictive client relationships within the business firm. The problem is less that of the corruption arising from lucrative contracts (though it is worrying when yesterday's advocates of participation become today's advisers on union-busting) than that of knowledge and problem-solving on management terms. Thus Organisational Theory is helping to constitute a particular reality without critically analysing it, and runs the risk of reducing theory and practice to a technology of social control.

Not only does this limit the ability of analysis to be a resource for a wider range of participants, it has the negative consequence of ignoring lower-level employees except as objects or in their defined 'roles' (Salaman, 1979: 47). Limitations arise from the service role itself. Reed observes, 'organisation theory has presented management with a stock of "moral fictions" (such as "managerial effectiveness") that disguise the social reality of contemporary management practice' (1985: 95). Despite or perhaps because of that role, there are frequent complaints that official theory propagated to business students and managers is out of touch with the 'real world'.

In conclusion, we would argue that mainstream perspectives have often functioned as theories of regulation and are bound up in the purposes and practices of organisational control. This has prevented the development of 'any coherent or consensual theoretical object of the organisation' (Clegg and Dunkerley, 1980: 213). Instead organisational and societal reality has tended to be taken for granted, with emphasis on that which is prescriptive and short term. Viewing organisations as natural systems and as largely autonomous bodies has produced a limited capacity to explain historical changes and the political and economic contexts in which organisations operate. The overall objections of critical theory are summed up by Fischer and Sirriani: 'Common to all of the approaches is a concern over the conservative/elitist bias of organisational theory, a general absence of social class analysis, a failure to connect the organisation to the political economy of the larger social and historical context, a general neglect of political and bureaucratic power, and the ideological uses of scientific organisational analysis' (1984: 5).

DOMAIN ASSUMPTIONS OF A CRITICAL APPROACH

Like their mainstream counterpart, critical perspectives are based on a variety of ideas and theoretical sources. The starting point is obviously critique itself: the identification of the weaknesses, limitations and ideological functions of orthodoxy. The two traditions are not always different on every point, and there are some partly overlapping objectives for some of the strands of thought, including humanisation of work processes and non-bureaucratic forms of organisation. Nevertheless through the critique an outline of a different agenda begins to emerge, with a concern for issues of power, control, domination, conflict, exploitation and legitimation. What of the more positive alternative? What do we mean by critical? Any alternative perspectives necessarily start from different guidelines and assumptions about organisations and society. Though the issues overlap, we have followed the convention of the equivalent mainstream section and divide it into parts.

Reflexivity

Critical perspectives must first of all be *reflexive*. That is they must have the capacity to reflect upon themselves, so that values, practices and knowledge are not taken for granted. Nor can we take our own experiences for granted. [. . .]

In fact, our inability to experience large organisations directly in the same way – as individuals or small groups, subordinates or power holders – creates special problems for studying organisation, problems which are often resolved through the use of unsatisfactory substitutes such as metaphors – organisations are 'like' machines, garbage cans or prisons (Sandelands and Srivatsan, 1993).

We have referred previously to unproblematic conceptions of phenomena such as goals and productivity. But a key example of a problematic conception would be that of gender. Existing analyses have largely treated gender divisions as irrelevant, or in practice invisible, despite: 'the persistent fact that women's position in any organisation differs from men in the same organisations' (Woolf, 1977: 7). In this sense, orthodoxy has been as much 'male-stream' as mainstream (Mills and Tancred, 1992).

Instead of reflecting the concerns of established power-groups, organisational theory should reflect critically on and challenge existing attitudes and practices. It can draw on the distinction between practical and technical rationality identified by Habermas (1971) and subsequently espoused by many other radical writers. Technical rationality is based on the instrumental pursuit of taken-for-granted goals such as 'efficiency'. In contrast, practical rationality emphasises conscious and enlightened reflection which would clarify alternative goals and actions based on the widest communication and political dialogue. These concepts are, in themselves, rooted in Weber's differentiation between a formal rationality concerned with calculable techniques and procedures, and substantive rationality which emphasises the values and the desired ends of action.

The embeddedness of organisations

A further guiding principle is the necessity to be *historical* and *contextual*. Organisational theory and practice can only be understood as something in process, otherwise the search for general propositions and instant prescriptions becomes disconnected from reality, as it has done in conventional ahistorical approaches (Littler, 1980: 157). It is also necessary to counter the tendency to see organisations as free-floating and autonomous; and the concentration on the micro-level of analysis, or single enterprise. This means locating organisational processes within their structural setting, examining the interaction with economic forces, political cultures and communities. To return to the gender example, it is impossible to understand the emergence and development of the sexual division of labour in organisations only from within. We have to go outside, to the family and patriarchal structures in society as a whole in order to reflect back.

This approach means more than diffuse references to the environment. In theoretical terms, organisational issues cannot be comprehended outside of the totality constituted by capitalist society in general and the mode of production in particular (Burrell, 1980). Donaldson objects to this on the grounds that locating explanations within the wider social system denies that organisational phenomena are topics of enquiry in their own right. But no convincing argument is put forward to justify the desirability or possibility of such analytical autonomy, to say nothing of seemingly denying the validity of the work of Weber, Marx and Durkheim. Donaldson raises a more pertinent point when he argues that, 'the notion of totality is a reference to everything – nothing is left out' (1985: 124). It is indeed important to avoid reducing totality to a meaningless level of generality: we do not always learn very much from general references to the effects of capitalism and patriarchy. There may not be a smooth fit between organisations and each part of the 'totality', but it is possible and necessary to show the concrete ways in which organisations are embedded in specific social, political and economic structures.

[. . .]

Dialectics and contradiction

Many critical theorists (for example, Benson, 1977; Storey, 1983) utilise the notion of dialectical perspectives as a crucial means of explaining the dynamic of organisational change. In abstract terms a dialectical process refers to a movement from thesis to antithesis and synthesis and derives from Hegel and Marx. More frequently it is used to denote a reciprocal interaction, between structure and human agency or between conflicting groups. [. . .]

The most direct application of dialectical perspectives to work organisations is expressed in the idea of a reciprocal relation between managerial control and worker resistance. Management control strategies are fundamentally a means of dealing with contradictions, uncertainties and crises in their socioeconomic environment. New methods of control inevitably provoke and shape forms of employee resistance and sometimes counter-'strategies'. Over a period of time, management responses are likely to develop into alternative control methods, blending with and going beyond the old. For example, piecework was introduced as a means for management to set targets and control through monetary incentives. But the shop floor frequently devised ways of asserting their own controls over output and earnings. In the 1970s employers in the motor industry responded by establishing new payment systems based on 'measured day rates', but still using control techniques based on work study and measurement. Over a period of time workers developed their own methods of adaptation and resistance, so the cycle continues.

This kind of perspective puts more substance into the traditional idea of an interaction between formal and informal dimensions of organisational life. However it is formulated, we can view organisations as continually having to respond to and counter *disorganisation*: a process which is underpinned by the divergent goals and interests discussed earlier in this chapter. Those who command organisations are required to mobilise a variety of resources to counter disorganisation. Although the actors themselves may not see it in these terms, we can pull together a variety of practices under the conceptual umbrellas of power, control and persuasion or consent. The factors underlying such choices and the different forms managerial and employee action take will be key and recurrent themes of this book.

Social transformation

The fact that we have argued against prescription does not mean a lack of interest in the 'practical' or the applied. We have tried to approach this in a number of ways. First, by giving an account and evaluation of up-to-date empirical research into work organisations, rather than the make-believe simulations that accompany many conventional texts. This involves critically examining as an issue in its own right the interventions made by social scientists as researchers or consultants. Second, by always analysing theories and practices together and as part of specific economic and political contexts. Showing how theories are used by managerial and other groups may sound unexceptional. But the dominant tradition has been to treat the major theories of organisation and management primarily as ideas systems and historically sequenced. The result is that most students do not get a realistic and informed view of the practicality of theory. In addition the impression is often given that theories developed in the past are outdated and 'wrong' compared to the latest favoured perspective. When these are inevitably replaced, cynicism about theory and organisational analysis is the likely result.

But alternative 'practicalities' have to go further than this and provide resources for social transformation. In this context, Benson adds a further aspect of a dialectical perspective, that of *praxis*, drawing on the previously discussed notion of practical rationality. Praxis involves developing analytical resources which go beyond reflexivity and can help members of organisations constrained by existing relations of ownership and power to reflect critically on and reconstruct their circumstances. Though some critical theorists advocate the prioritisation of 'philosophically informed armchair theorising' (Burrell, 1980: 102), we would agree with Benson's emphasis on theory as an emancipatory guide and as a means for *empowering* a wider range of organisational participants. When empowerment is used by management theorists and practioners to describe 'enabling' employees to chase more customers or do three more jobs, the term joins a long list whose rhetoric is not matched by reality.

A critical use implies no particular form of politics or intervention, but rather empowering employees to make more choices and to act more effectively to transform workplace relations. It may be argued that this reproduces a one-sided partiality that is the reverse of the management orientation of mainstream theories. There is always that danger. But the existing realities and power relations in organisations will, for the foreseeable future, enable critical theory to maintain a certain distance and intellectual independence. Furthermore, any critical theory not testing its ideas through empirical investigation or practical intervention is ultimately arid.

NOTE

* This chapter has been adapted from, Thompson, P. and McHugh, D. (1995) *Work Organisations: A Critical Introduction*, Basingstoke: Macmillan.

REFERENCES

Albrow, M. (1973), 'The Study of Organizations – Objectivity or Bias? in G. Salaman and K. Thompson (eds), *People and Organizations*, Harlow: Longman.

Bartitz, L. (1960), *The Servants of Power*, Middletown: Wesleyan University Press.

Benson, J.K. (1977), 'Innovation and Crisis in Organizational Analysis', in J. K. Benson (ed.), *Organizational Analysis: Critique and Innovation*, London: Sage.

Bryman, A. (1984), 'Organization Studies and the Concept of Rationality', *Journal of Management Studies*, vol. 21: 394–404.

Buchanan, D. and Huczynski, A. (1985), *Organizational Behaviour: An Introductory Text*, London: Prentice-Hall International.

Burrell, G. (1980), 'Radical Organization Theory', in D. Dunkerley and G. Salaman (eds), *The International Yearbook of Organization Studies 1979*, London: Routledge & Kegan Paul.

Clegg, S. and Dunkerley, D. (1980), *Organization, Class and Control*, London: Routledge & Kegan Paul.

Donaldson, L. (1985), *In Defence of Organization Theory: A Reply to the Critics*, Cambridge: Cambridge University Press.

Fischer, F. and Sirriani, C. (1984), *Critical Studies in Organization and Bureaucracy*, Philadelphia: Temple University Press.

Habermas, J. (1971), *Toward a Rational Society*, London: Heinemann.

Huczynski, A. A. (1993), *Management Gurus*, London: Routledge.

Karmel, B. (ed.) (1980), *Point and Counterpoint in Organizations?*, Illinois: Dryden.

Littler, C. R. (1980), 'Internal Contract and the Transition to Modern Work Systems', in D. Dunkerley and G. Salaman (eds), *The International Yearbook of Organization Studies 1979*, London: Routledge & Kegan Paul.

Mills, A. J. and Tancred, P. (eds) (1992), *Gendering Organizational Analysis*, London: Sage.

Pascale, R. T. (1990), *Managing on the Edge*, Harmondsworth: Penguin.

Perrow, C. (1979), *Complex Organizations: A Critical Essay*, Illinois: Scott Foreman.

Peters, T. J. and Waterman, R. H. (1982), *In Search of Excellence: Lessons from America's Best-Run Companies*, New York: Harper & Row.

Randle, K. and Rainnie, A. (1994), 'Control, Contradiction and Complexity in a Pharmaceutical Research Company', paper to 12th International Labour Process Conference, Aston.

Reed, M. (1985), *Redirections in Organizational Analysis*, Tavistock: London.

Salaman, G. (1979), *Work Organizations: Resistance and Control*, London: Longmann.

Sandelands, L. E. and Srivatsan, V. (1993), 'The Problem of Experience in the Study of Organizations', *Organization Studies*, vol. 14, no. 1: 1–22.

Selznick, P. (1949), *TVA and the Grass Roots*, Berkeley, Calif: University of California Press.

Storey, J. (1983), *Managerial Prerogative and the Question of Control*, London: Routledge & Kegan Paul.

Watson, T. (1980), 'Understanding Organizations: The Practicalities of Sociological Theory', in D. Dunkerley and G. Salaman (eds) (1980), *The International Yearbook of Organization Studies 1980*, London: Routledge & Kegan Paul.

Woolf, J. (1977), 'Women in Organizations', in S. Clegg and D. Dunkerley (eds), *Critical Issues in Organizations*, London: Routledge & Kegan Paul.

9

STRUGGLE AND RESISTANCE*

Graeme Salaman

Hyman has noted,

> Work within capitalism is at one and the same time an economic and a political activity: it involves not only the production of goods and services but also the exercise of power. Patterns of power in relations of production reflect the differential distribution among individuals and groups of the ability to control their physical and social environment and, as part of this process, to influence the decisions which are and are not taken by others. This ability is typically founded on privileged access to or control over material and ideological resources. Thus ownership and control over the means of production involve immense power, since it carries the ability to admit or exclude those who depend on employment for their living.
>
> (Hyman, 1976, p. 88)

This chapter will discuss these 'patterns of power' and resistance. [. . .] [I]f union activity can be regarded as, in one form or another, political – i.e. having *some* concern for issues of control – this is not to deny that a great deal of intra-organisational conflict occurs outside the formal structure of union activity. Much organisational conflict, after all, occurs on a horizontal axis, between specialisms and departments. Usually such conflicts are not channelled through union negotiations. Furthermore, not all conflicts between low-level organisational employees and the owners and controllers of the organisation occur within the union framework. The relationship between formal union institutions and the concerns of organisational employees is by no means unproblematic. [. . .]

Nevertheless, clearly a large proportion of intra-organisational conflicts – especially those occurring on a vertical axis – are mediated through formal union activity and organisation. Indeed it could be said that all union activity reveals, in some degree, such conflicts. [. . .] In this chapter we shall focus on the organisational origins, and consequences of, processes of struggle and resistance within organisations.

The analysis [. . .]implicitly presents the organisational employee as a rather passive creature, controlled and dominated by his employers, meekly subjecting him or her self to a variety of organisational directions and sanctions. Clearly such a view is quite erroneous: organisational employees actively strive to avoid and divert control; they seek to maximise their own interests which they may or may not see as coincident with the organisation's, and they attempt to resist the domination of others while advancing or defending their own area of control and autonomy. [. . .]

Directors and assistant directors, socially conservative, fight with great passion for technical change and modernisation. At the same time, technical engineers, who would like to transform the present social order are very conservative about technical matters; they do whatever they can to keep their skill a rule-of-thumb one and to prevent efforts to rationalise it. This is the reason that they act as trouble-shooters, even if it means always running to patch things up, and that they oppose any kind of progress which could free them from certain of their difficulties. Their only solution has always been to ask for an assistant, and they are quite prepared to remain overworked if this demand cannot be met. What is the common thread among these diverse strategies? Each group fights to preserve and enlarge the area upon which it has discretion, attempts to limit its dependence upon other groups and to accept such dependence only insofar as it is a safeguard against another and more feared one, and finally prefers retreatism if there is no choice but submission. The group's freedom of action and the power structure appear to be clearly at the core of all these strategies.

(Crozier, 1964, p. 156)

These suggestions of Crozier's raise the major points of this chapter: organisations are characterised by constant and continuing conflict. Despite the major efforts of senior executives to legitimise the activities, structure and inequalities of the organisation and to design and install 'foolproof' and reliable systems of surveillance and direction, there is always some dissension, some dissatisfaction, some effort to achieve a degree of freedom from hierarchical control – some resistance to the organisation's domination and direction. Frequently this struggle is muted, mainly defensive and reactive, often individualised, spasmodic, intermittent. Frequently it is defined and presented as the result of trouble-stirrers, laziness, bloody-mindedness, inflexibility, or stupidity, as the result of the psychological pathology or inadequacy of the members. But in fact it is the systematic response to a form of organisation which is designed to achieve hierarchical control and domination of members' activities for the pursuit of objectives and interests which are not theirs, and with which they may be in conflict. The inevitable result of such organisational forms, and the interests they serve, is the alienation and 'refractoriness' of members.

Secondly, Crozier's remarks [. . .] emphasise that such struggles, such resistance, usually centres around the very process which generates it: the efforts of senior groups to control the activities of subordinates. These struggles are not only *rooted* in conflicts over power, they are usually *expressed* in terms of efforts to regain, defend or achieve, control or autonomy. Thirdly, conflicts within organisations reflect internal inequalities and contradictions or organisational structure which in turn reveal class-based interests. 'Bureaucracies not only rest upon classes,' writes Mills,

they organise the power struggles of classes. Within the business firm, personnel administration regulate the terms of employment, just as would the labour union, should a union exist: these bureaucracies fight over who works at what and for how much . . . within the firm . . . and as part of the bureaucratic management of mass democracy, the graded hierarchy fragments class situations. . . . The traditional and often patriarchal ties of the old enterprise are replaced by rational and planned linkages in the new, and the rational systems unite their powers so that no one sees their source of authority or understands their calculations.

(Mills, 1956, p. 111)

We can identify three bases of organisational conflict. The first is the result of 'distinctive functions' developing, or holding, their own culture, priorities and norms. The discussion below will consider examples of such conflicts, for example between academic and administrator, or sales and production departments. The second type of conflict occurs when organisational units have similar functions. In this case rivalry and competitiveness can develop. The third form of conflict is hierarchical conflict stemming from interest group struggles over the organisational rewards of status, prestige and monetary reward. Such conflict is particularly likely between lower-level personnel and their superiors, although such struggles are not confined to this group alone. In this chapter we shall encounter examples of all these types of organisational conflict.

We must remember that the final, demonstrated structure of an organisation is not the result of members' obedient execution of senior executives' (and their experts') directions as these are represented in bodies of rules, procedures and regulations, payment systems, budgetary limits, work design, technology, work flow, supervision etc. The actual structure of an organisation – i.e. its apparent regularity and predictability – is the result of members' reactions and resistance to, and interpretation and avoidance of, these formal limitations and restrictions. Many classic studies of the 'informal' side of organisations reveal the endless ways in which members *use* the formal organisational rules to produce results more to their own liking, and which demonstrate that *no* system of organisational control, however sophisticated and elaborate, can completely eliminate the discretion, however minimal, of the employee. In Crozier's terms, however thorough the organisation's effort to eliminate the discretion of the employee, some area of uncertainty will remain, and such uncertainty is the breeding ground for efforts to achieve some, however slight, self-control, some degree of autonomy. The final structure of an organisation – as compared to the mythical structure described so elegantly (and symbolically) on organisation charts – is the result of these negotiations, interpretations in which organisational members actively strive to resist some directions and controls while attempting to advance their own self-control. [. . .]

'Bureaucracy', remarks Gouldner, 'was man-made, and more powerful men had a greater hand in making it' (Gouldner, 1954, p.140). What's more, 'the degree of bureaucratisation is a function of human striving; it is the outcome of a contest between those who want it and those who do not' (p.237). Organisational rules and procedures and work design constitute efforts to resolve what senior executives regard as problems by achieving an increased degree of reliability. But the 'tools of action' retain their recalcitrance, and hierarchical intentions are seldom executed perfectly.

Blau's study of two government agencies shows some of the ways in which rules and procedures established by senior management to achieve a certain effect can produce unexpected consequences. He describes some of the consequences that followed the introduction of statistical records in an employment exchange. He notes how this procedure operated as a new form of control. And as such it created what he describes as a 'displacement' of goals. That is, it encouraged the members to orient their activities towards new priorities: 'An instrument intended to further the achievement of organisational objectives, statistical records constrained interviewers to think of maximising the indices as their major goal, sometimes at the expense of these very objectives' (Blau, 1963, p.46). Furthermore, Blau argues that the introduction of this sort of work measurement caused a reduction in cooperation and an increase in competitiveness within the work groups.

Blau regards bureaucratic rules as necessarily general and abstract: 'A bureaucratic procedure can be defined as a course of action prescribed by a set of rules designed to achieve a given uniformity. Agency-wide rules must be abstract in order to guide the different courses of action necessary for the accomplishment of an objective in diverse situations' (Blau, 1963, p.23). Because of this inherent generality rules must be interpreted, defined, and adjusted by the organisational member in the face of particular cases, clients, circumstances and situations.

Blau sees such modification as essentially functional, for otherwise the 'organisation could not have served the employment needs of the community' (Blau, 1963, p.35). This is a naive assumption. Organisational members use the inherent generality of organisational rules in exactly the same way as they exploit the inherent incompleteness of any structure of control and regulation – to achieve their own interests, advance their own self-control, defend themselves from what they regard as onerous, misguided or hostile constraints. They *might* because of their commitment to their own conceptions of occupational, expert or organisational goals, *use* the rules to achieve with greater efficiency and speed, ends which are not incompatible with the formal objectives of the organisation but this is simply a possibility, not an inevitability.

Gouldner has pointed out that one of the ironic characteristic organisational rules is that although they stem from attempts to control and regulate the behaviour of employees, they can be used as bargaining resources in the interactions between superiors and subordinates. Rules tend to describe the preferred behaviour. *In so doing they also stipulate minimal behaviours.* 'The rules served as a specification of a minimum level of acceptable performance. It was, therefore, possible for the worker to remain apathetic, for he now knew just how little he could do and still remain secure' (Gouldner, 1954, pp.174–5). Similarly, supervisors could use the enforcement of the rules as a bargaining counter between superiors and subordinates. When things are going well various rules may not be enforced: *formal* control may be replaced by *informal* cooperation.

Conflict and negotiation over organisational rules, work methods, technology and procedures characterise all organisations for such conflict is a 'normal' and endemic organisational feature. Even the rules themselves, introduced to reduce the recalcitrance of employees, are transformed, in organisational practice, into battlegrounds of adjustment and bargaining.

There are numerous axes of conflict within organisations. Some conflicts are personal and individual, not only in *expression* (for this is true of many structural conflicts and divergences) but in origin.

Competitiveness is a natural product of a form of organisation that encourages ambition, rewards individual achievement, but offers progressively fewer promotion possibilities. [. . .]

One common ground for intra-organisational conflict is functional differentiation. Organisational employees engaged on different organisational or occupational tasks and specialities frequently develop, or maintain, distinctive work-based cultures and interests. A great deal of organisational conflict occurs between these specialist groups, as they attempt to advance their interests – enlarge their establishment, improve their facilities, raise their budgets, increase their voice in the senior councils and so on. [. . .]

Within industry, such conflict frequently occurs between sales and production, with production planning playing an intermediate, conciliatory role. Production's efforts to make life predictable and satisfactory by ensuring long stable production runs, are likely to be at odds with sales' efforts to please customers by promising quick delivery, and a front place in the work queue. Each department is likely to regard itself as the key one, and will seek to maximise its interests, which are defined as coincident with the 'real' interest of the organisation as a whole.

[T]hese efforts to legitimise sectional interest and advantage will involve reference to general organisational objectives or symbols. So all departments within manufacturing industry show the importance of their departmental expansion or primacy by reference to general organisational efficiency, or customer demands. [. . .] To be able to define sectional interests as coincident with the general organisational interest is not only a reflection of the power of the section concerned; it is also a useful and plausible strategy in intra-organisational conflicts.

[. . .]

It must be noted that conflicts between departments and specialities within organisations can, like conflicts between ambitious individuals, actually serve the interests of the owners and controllers of the organisations. Firstly, such conflicts often centre around – however rhetorically – the over-arching organisational goal. More importantly, they distract attention from more basic conflicts between senior and junior levels within the organisation and divide and divert the work force. [. . .]

Elliott's account of conflicting occupational ideologies ('therapy' 'basic science' and 'early diagnosis') held by doctors and scientists in a hospital specialising in the treatment of cancer patients, and an associated cancer research institute, explores the relationship between specialist ideology and work experience and pressures. The therapy and basic science ideologies, Elliott notes, 'supported a tendency towards separation and polarization between the two groups (doctors and researchers)' (Elliott, 1975, p.280). Elliott discusses the origins of these ideologies in the organisational settings and histories, the work practices (especially the variable of patient contact) and occupational/professional memberships, cultures and careers of the two groups. He notes the potential for conflict inherent in these ideological differences and remarks: 'One importance of these ideologies is the part they play in deciding the distribution of resources and reflecting the interests of those concerned. . . .' (Elliott, 1975, p.286).

Pettigrew's analysis of relationships between specialist computer personnel furthers our understanding of the ideological and functional bases of intra-organisational, inter-specialist (or departmental) conflict. It concerns the efforts of a new speciality to define its task, protect its identity, develop a legitimating world view and occupational ideology, and expand its activities. These efforts are likely to produce a defensive reaction, from established, threatened specialities: 'As a defensive reaction, the more established group may accuse the expansionist one of incompetence and encroachment. The older group may also attempt to invoke a set of fictions about itself to protect the core of its expertise' (Pettigrew, 1975, p.260).

The temporal dimension to Pettigrew's analysis is particularly useful: his study of the expansion strategies of the new speciality, and the defensive reactions of established experts, each allied with particular patterns of belief and attitudes, is especially relevant to an understanding of intra-organisational conflict relations.

Even more frequent than conflicts between different specialities as they struggle for dominance, are conflicts between experts and bureaucrats, or staff and line. These conflicts, which have been discussed earlier, are often sharpened by the existence of associated differences and distinctions – of dress, age, cultural preferences, leisure habits, etc.

[. . .] [P]rofessionals in organisations attempt to defend their autonomy, resist the imposition of bureaucratic control and work patterns, and secure their own interests. These efforts normally centre around the definition of professional, expert work as inherently opposed to 'rationalised', specialised, fragmented and differentiated work processes, and the definition of professional work as innately resistant to external control, direction and surveillance. Conflict around these principles is common in organisations that employ professionals; even if, as noted earlier, the fact of such conflict should not be interpreted as implying a serious divergence between professionals' activities and senior executives' objectives, for other 'insidious' forms of control and training operate to minimise such divergence, such 'irresponsibility'.

Professionals justify their opposition to centralised control and bureaucratic work practices on the grounds of the efficiency and necessity of self-control, and the complexity and mysteriousness of the work tasks and skills. It is, however, possible to see such arguments as ideological, and as protecting professionals' privileged position and treatment. [. . .]

CONTROL AND RESISTANCE OF SUBORDINATES

The most common basis of intra-organisational conflict is that between superiors and their subordinates over issues of domination and the distribution of rewards. These conflicts are usually mediated by trade unions. The most common and pervasive conflict of this sort is between shop-floor members and their superiors, and between those with the poorest share of the organisation's rewards, the most fragmented and specialised and least autonomous jobs, and the more privileged members who control, manage and coordinate them.

Clearly, such conflicts can be revealed in a number of ways: formal and informal, organised and unorganised, group or individual. For example, Scheff's article, 'Control over policy by attendants in a mental hospital', shows some of the ways in which lower level organisational members can influence, avoid and determine policy decisions and organisational practice. The study documents the ways in which a vigorous and ambitious program of reform in the hospital was launched by the administration and 'largely frustrated' by the attendants. First the subordinate group had to be able to maintain solidarity and discipline among its own ranks. Such control is a frequent consequence of informal work groups. Secondly, they must achieve some control over senior organisational members, and thirdly they must use their informal power to achieve their conception of desirable and proper organisational practice. Typically, whatever its real nature, this conception will be firmly related to over-arching organisational or professional rhetorics.

The attendants gained their power [. . .] as a result of the structured vulnerability of the senior members and the solidarity of the subordinate groups. The vulnerability of the senior members – the physicians – followed from their *reliance*, or *dependence*, on the cooperation of the attendants. 'Typically,' Scheff writes, 'the doctor facing the ward staff was in a weak position, relative to the staff, because of his short tenure on the ward and his lack of training in administration . . . the typical ward physician was a newcomer. The ward staff, in contrast, was all but rooted to the ward' (Scheff, 1970, p.331). [. . .]

The discrepancy between the formal authority of the physician and the real power of his subordinates on whom he depended constituted a significant objective basis for lower-level control. The subordinates employed a variety of sanctions: withholding information; the manipulation of patients, so that the attendants withheld their 'gate keeper' role and encouraged the patients to question and accost the medical staff; outright disobedience; and the withholding of cooperation. Variants of these techniques are extremely common in organisations. [. . .] In fact each level of the organisation is always dependent on the cooperation of the subordinate level, for all jobs, however routine, require some 'common sense', some understanding of and commitment to, the organisation's objectives. No system of work design, or technology, or structure of rules and procedures, can achieve the transformation of man into a machine. But if cooperation is always required, it can always be withheld, even if this is achieved by liberal interpretation of, and compliance with, the rules.

Organisations as we know them are inherently inegalitarian structures involving, as basic elements, processes of superordination and subordination. These two features serve as the basis for conflict between the least advantaged and most controlled and the more advantaged controllers. It is true that some of the advantaged controllers are themselves controlled. [. . .] But this control is itself less onerous and frustrating, and is accompanied by a much larger share of the organisation's rewards. But for our purposes the distinction between lower-level organisational members – with no managerial or supervisory responsibility – and the controllers *en masse* is the critical one.

'The reason why hierarchy is so crucial for the organisation's leaders', writes Fox, 'is that it facilitates the making of decisions over which they can hope to exercise some control. Acceptance of the norms covering these relationships is therefore the key to the acceptance of all other norms' (Fox, 1971, p.34). This is why management invests so much energy in trying to establish the legitimacy of the hierarchic structure of the organisation, trying to obtain lower-level members' consent to the norms covering the hierarchical relationships of superiority and subordination. [. . .]

The degree to which lower-level organisational members are incorporated into and committed to an ideology which justifies the structure of the employing organisation and their place within it, varies. Such commitment is more likely with middle-level members who have some degree of normative commitment. However, we shall limit our attention to white-collar and manual worker organisational employees, since it is they who are most likely to resent the structure of their employing organisation and their position in it.

How do these members react to their situation? We must remember that bureaucracy is instituted so that owners and managers can retain overall control. But the control of the executive is less than perfect since 'workers in the pyramid have some power as well (for example, they can withhold information or simply 'work to rule', thus diminishing efficiency). But the workers' power is mainly defensive and open opposition always brings into play the most basic power relation: the capitalist's legal right to fire the worker' (Edwards, 1972, p.116). Workers' resistance and opposition to their organisational situation and treatment follows from the obvious disparity between their levels of reward and status and the privileged treatment and prestige meted out to managers, administrators, etc., inequalities which reflect and make up societal differences in income and wealth (see Hyman, 1972, pp.89–94) and which include the nature of the work itself, conditions, promotion chances, etc. It is also a result of their status as employees, as people who sell their labour as a commodity to organisations which utilise their labour for their purposes. But it must be remembered that such an arrangement is inherently insecure – within industrial concerns in particular, but increasingly also within hospitals, universities, training colleges, the armed services, government departments, etc. This insecurity is the result of the basic feature of organisational work – that it is constantly subject to the vagaries of market and economic forces which make it profitable or unprofitable, possible or impossible to hire or retain labour.

[. . .]

From the point of view of the senior executives of organisations, lower-level members never conform and comply completely. They never entirely lose their potential for recalcitrance. This is a major managerial problem. [. . .] As Henry Ford admitted – 'Machines alone do not give us mass production. Mass production is achieved by both machines *and* men. And while we have gone a long way toward perfecting our mechanical operations, we have not successfully written into our equation whatever complex factors represent man, the human element' (Ford, quoted in Walker and Guest, 1952, p.249). It is not for want of trying.

It is dangerous to generalise about the orientations and work aspirations and attitudes of all lower-level employees. There are bound to be substantial exceptions to any assertion. Nevertheless, some remarks can usefully be made. First, it is undoubtedly the case that the vast majority of lower-level members comply, in general, with organisational directions (though such compliance will possibly be perfunctory, partial, and unwilling); second, they do not *continually* oppose the hierarchical structure of their employing organisation, nor the principles which lie behind the design of their work, nor those which determine and justify their relatively low level of rewards, their working conditions, promotion opportunities etc. Numerous surveys of work satisfaction have argued for a surprisingly high level of acceptance of these aspects of work.

[. . .]

This low-key, begrudging acquiescence, however, is a long way from full-blooded resistance and opposition. [. . .] Most accounts of organisational life contain descriptions of the various ways in which members attempt to circumvent the official rules and regulations, seek to interrupt the organised flow of work, or avoid obtrusive procedures and systems. Sometimes these efforts are organised and explicit; more frequently they are based on group reactions and norms which justify and impose the alternative behaviours in the light of the agreed injustice and unreasonableness of the official procedure. Occasionally such responses are spontaneous, or individual.

[. . .]

How is it that low-level organisational employees show acceptance of their organisational position and treatment? Or to put it another way, why is it that the disadvantaged, subordinate members of organisations do not attempt more effectively to organise, collectively, radically to improve their locations, or to alter the structure of the organisation, and the distributions of rewards within it? Various factors are relevant. [. . .]

[. . .]

The fragmentation of the work force

[. . .]

The very fact of extreme differentiation of jobs and activities, and the associated variation in the distribution of rewards, status, working conditions, discipline, payment methods, holiday allowances and so on, [. . .] also serves to fragment the theoretical unity of subordinate employees. This fragmentation has horizontal and vertical elements. Vertically, organisational employees are differentiated by various aspects of privilege. It is true that middle managers too are controlled: but their control is less onerous, and their share of the rewards greater. Such privilege serves to attract the individual loyalty of the manager, especially when it is allied with a strong emphasis on individual success and career development. Organisational employees who apparently share the same, low, level within the organisation also demonstrate a marked awareness of distinctiveness, even of opposition. Partly this follows from differences within the organisation – of activity, department, function, shift. Frequently it is based on extra-organisational differences – of sex, race, locality, or age. Often these two types of factor are compounded. [. . .]

Organisational differentiation – the fragmentation of the work force – is presented as an inevitable consequence of organisational technology (in the widest sense) and the search for greater efficiency. In fact, however, it is also – possibly primarily – ideological. This follows from two interconnected processes: the splitting of basically similar employees into differentiated, often competitive, groupings; and the construction of a finely graded hierarchy of small differences in privilege and position which acts to distinguish one employee from another and to raise his commitment to the beneficial organisation, through bestowing differential degrees of prestige, organisational rewards and career opportunities.

[. . .]

Such processes of differentiation also occur among organisational employees at the same level. [. . .] This occurs through the differentiation of functions, the use of payment schemes, the division of employees into shifts and departments, and the use of competitive procedures. Within organisations it is not difficult to find employees who reserve most of their complaints for some basically rather similar group who supply them with parts, or perform some prior function to the product, or prepare the paperwork they must process, or whatever. [. . .]

The use of impersonal and insidious forms of control

This is closely related to the first mechanism, since conflict between groups and departments not only masks the ways in which both are constrained by hierarchical control, but is a function of it, as the remarks about overtime illustrate. This is a highly divisive form of control, through payment. By disguising control, or by making it appear as either inevitable and inexorable or a neutral function of constraints – technology, 'progress' or the market –, organisational employees must find it hard to locate the forms of control, understand their origin and articulate their opposition. It is a brave man who opposes 'progress', for all the harm it does him.

The forms of control discussed earlier – through technology, work design, regulations, personnel procedures and other insidious methods – not only achieve regularity, they disguise their own nature and origins, thus making resistance all the more difficult.

Ideology

These difficulties are compounded by the ideological underpinnings of modern forms of organisational control, which define the nature of the employment contract, the nature of the organisation, the necessity for organisational hierarchy, the neutrality of the organisation's objectives and activities, the justice and legitimacy of any individual's location within the system, and the benefits which all derive from organisational life.

Frequently these ideological efforts are sustained and buttressed outside the organisation. Individuals are prepared for their organisational roles by education and educational selection. 'Inappropriate' aspirations are 'cooled out'; excessively academic, or non-job-related schools or academic enterprises are disciplined; the shared benefits of consumerism and materialism (claimed products of organisational structure and process) are proclaimed; the individual achievements and superiority of managers, experts and executives are lauded; technology itself is worshipped and mystified. 'The prevailing forms of social control are technological in a new sense' writes Marcuse:

> [. . .] in the contemporary period, the technological controls appear to be the very embodiment of Reason for the benefit of all social groups and interests – to such an extent that all contradiction seems irrational and all counteraction impossible. . . . The intellectual and emotional refusal 'to go along' appears neurotic and impotent. . . . The impact of progress turns Reason into submission to the facts of life, and to the dynamic capability of producing more and bigger facts of the same sort of life.
>
> (Marcuse, 1972, p.23)

It is thus that the 'sheer madness' of forms of work organisation that result in employees wishing their lives away in the endless repetition of moronic activities becomes, miraculously, *reasonable*. [. . .]

Within the organisation members' ability to articulate their feelings of frustration and oppression is further obstructed by the contradictory nature of organisational life: that it involves both conflict *and* cooperation: differentiation and coordination. It is difficult to define as entirely external and oppressive a system of work which is highly interdependent and where the 'victim' of individual recalcitrance is frequently a fellow member of the organisation – the salesman who finds his customer disappointed, the manager who has worked nights to put the finishing touches to some planned reorganisation, the fellow Open University academic who is urgently demanding the completion of some material for *his* course. In this way, by establishing the social nature of organisational life, resistance is made all the more difficult, more costly, more 'irrational'.

Furthermore, it is also, in a sense, true that there is some area of common interest between all levels of the organisation – from the executives and owners, to the lowest level employees. If the organisation ceases to function all will be out of work. This will probably hurt some more than others, but it will have its impact on them all. But this is not the same as saying that the organisation is a cooperative enterprise in which all pull together for the shared good, because the very social system within which they operate, and which they serve to sustain, is based upon a basic conflict of interest, and work and control arrangements, and the distribution of rewards, within organisations reflect this basic conflict.

Nevertheless, 'Sheer force of habit also makes at least a minimum of day-to-day co-operation between employers and workers seem the norm. So for workers to break out of their everyday routine and engage in some form of overt conflict, a specific incident or grievance must usually generate the necessary momentum' (Hyman, 1972, p.103). This habitual cooperativeness, allied with the employees' unwillingness to obstruct the flow, the momentum, of production, deliberately to stand there and watch things going wrong must be seen in the context of the ultimate constraints of the market, financial viability and possibility, which are themselves defined as neutral and God-given. As something you can't do anything about – like the weather – and which cause an increase in work pressures within the organisation. As Marcuse says, you have to submit to the 'facts' of life, and in so submitting the facts are made more onerous, more oppressive, more powerful.

The employment contract

This is frequently presented as a fair, equal and free arrangement whereby employees agree to sell their labour power to the employers. The employee is protected in this exchange by his trade union. Therefore, this argument runs, within work it is immoral and unprincipled for employees not to abide by their contract, and to resist management's 'right to manage', to question the reasonableness of management decisions, oppose innovations, or alterations. [. . .] The employment contract is neither equal nor free, and the power of the parties to it are far from equivalent; there are numerous and massive obstacles to the employees gaining equal, legal, bargaining power; and the frequent restriction of bargaining to the financial aspect of the relationship is a reflection of its inherent imbalance.

Is this emphasis also evident among the work force? Are they prepared to sacrifice any interest in the nature of work, or in autonomy, for financial rewards? It is clear that organisational members vary in the emphasis they attach to various organisational elements and rewards. [. . .] And if people expect different things from their employer then it is clear that as long as the prime aspiration is met, they might be prepared to put up with otherwise highly depriving work experiences. They might develop their 'central life interest' outside of work. [. . .] In this way they could be 'bought off' from any interest in altering the structure of the organisation, their subordinate status, or the design of their work.

There are a number of problems here. First, what is the *salience* of the workers' claimed instrumentality? [. . .] Second, how stable is this priority? Isn't it entirely possible that the frustration and dissatisfaction these instrumental workers experience (for their instrumentality doesn't reduce their dissatisfaction, just establishes a price for it) might suddenly explode into action? And even if it is true that instrumentality is so deeply held that it 'operates like a local anaesthetic' (Daniel, 1969), then it is quite likely it will result in ever larger claims for the valued reward. As Fox has remarked [. . .]:

> Insofar as subordinates are – or can be brought to be – strongly committed to the value of a continuously rising material standard of life, managers may hope to strengthen their legitimacy by trying to meet subordinates' aspirations in respect of material rewards, welfare and fringe benefits. Since this is one of the appetites that grow by what they feed upon, it is apt to prove an unstable basis for authority.

(Fox, 1971, p. 41)

[. . .]

Even when organisational members restrict their aspirations to the financial aspects of their work they need not, by virtue of this alone, lose interest in control issues. Goodrich has noted that discipline and management – aspects of any organisation – are expressive of control, and of the 'frontier of control', that 'shifting line in a great mass of regulations'. Goodrich points out how a great many taken-for-granted union issues and concerns are directly to do with control – for example over dismissal, hours of work, demarcation, apprenticeship, craft regulations, hours of work, working conditions, methods of payment, and so on. [. . .]

Organisational members are [. . .] strengthened in their resistance to organisational control [. . .] by the frequent existence of informal work groups which transform and inspire individual reactions to frustration and oppression. [. . .] Informal work groups can be regarded as informal – but highly significant – efforts by organisational employees at all levels to pursue some or one of these goals.

Informal work groups represent a 'considerable structuring of the work situation . . . done by the worker themselves' (Katz, 1973, p.199). In many organisational situations, even where members are exposed to highly specific and detailed constraints, some unofficial culture will develop, with norms and expectations through which members carve out some area of autonomy and freedom. It has been argued that these informal cultures serve the purpose of supplying satisfactions denied by the formal organisation. Katz maintains that informal cultures and groups promote the affiliation of organisational members who are denied many or any areas of satisfaction in their work. Informal culture, he argues, 'permits continuation of working class style of life and provides ties of sociability' (Katz, 1973, p.191).

This is a rather naive, functionalist view: informal work groups are more likely to develop and support anti-organisational sentiments and behaviour than to strengthen members' commitment to the organisation through serving as an outlet for sociability and joking. Informal work groups – which means any organisational grouping which is not specified by senior members, and which contains its own distinctive culture – are always potentially active in their efforts to structure the work situation, the flow of work, the quantity of work and level of supervision, etc. [. . .]

The most famous study of an informal working group is that of workers in the Bank Wiring Room investigated by Roethlisberger and Dickson. These authors noted that the workers were subject to informal norms and expectations backed up by group membership and support. This informal control achieved internal similarity of levels of output, and protected them from external interference. The authors discuss the causes of the workers' restriction of output. They note that the workers explained it in terms of insecurity and anxiety: 'if output were too high something might happen – the "bogey" might be raised, the "rate" might be lowered, someone be laid off, hours might be reduced, or supervisors might reprimand the slower workers' (Roethlisberger and Dickson, 1964, p.532).

Roethlisberger and Dickson reject such explanations as based on confused, contradictory and groundless anxieties, but are prepared to grant that the workers are not simply 'ungrateful', or plain lazy, or deliberately and maliciously opposing management. They explain these sentiments as based on the workers' *ideology*, not on any *real* grounds (sic).

Although these authors deny that the behaviour of the workers they studied was a manifestation of any 'real' conflict between management and workers, other writers have been more prepared to see the origins and consequences of unofficial norms in terms of conflict of interest within the organisation. [. . .] Roy, in a fascinating paper, reports that workers cooperated with each other as fellow-members of a combat team at war with management, in ways which were completely at variance with the carefully prepared designs of staff experts and in flagrant violation of basic principles of shop-floor behaviour (Roy, 1954). His account of informal culture is particularly interesting for the emphasis it places on the constant, shifting 'frontier of control' between workers and time and motion men – each group attempting to outwit the other and to achieve, or circumvent, control.

Informal work groups and their associated cultures of resistance are by no means limited to shop-floor organisational groups. [. . .] Zimmerman's study, 'The practicalities of rule use' (1973), supplies further evidence of the existence and significance of informal work norms among white-collar and managerial organisational employees. Zimmerman argues, sensibly, that it is *never* justified to assume actual behaviour from mere knowledge of organisational rules; it is always necessary to know what rules mean to, and how they are used by, organisational employees in their organisational work. In particular, Zimmerman stresses the importance of understanding the variety of circumstances, constraints, meanings, taken-for-granted definitions and stereotypes which members typically consider in using organisational rules. For example, one major determining feature is members' own assessment of the real objectives of their work (which will usually be different from formal organisational statements of objectives). Organisational members frequently bend, ignore or re-interpret organisational procedures and authority in order to achieve the real object of their work. This process frequently relies upon the member's extensive knowledge of his clients, patients, or cases. [. . .] Becoming a competent organisational member means becoming familiar with and committed to these shared conceptions of work priorities, the meaning of rules and procedures, and the varying significance and salience of typical organisational problems. It means learning the informal interpretation of organisational procedures and applying them to group conceptions of purpose and group definitions of the organisation, its work, and its reality. [. . .]

[T]he power of individuals and groups within organisations is not restricted to their official authority. Officially, 'power or authority would tend to be hierarchic; each level would have just that amount of power necessary to carry out its responsibilities; ascendant levels in the hierarchy would have increasing power based on broader knowledge about the organisation and/or greater task expertise' (Wamsley, 1970, p.53, quoted in Hall, 1972, p.205). But reality isn't as neat as this; actual power within organisations is not simply the result of amounts of job-related authority allocated by the organisational executive. [. . .]

Crozier argues that the power of maintenance men in the organisation he studied followed from their power to handle the major sources of organisational uncertainty – technical breakdowns. The engineer, writes Crozier, has control over the last source of uncertainty remaining in a completely routinised organisational system' (Crozier, 1964, p.109). This view of the basis of organisational power has been developed by Hickson *et al.* (1973). These authors argue that the more a sub-unit within an organisation copes with uncertainty, the greater its power within the organisation; but they add that such power will increase if the subunits are not easily substitutable, and if the activity is particularly central to the overall activity of the organisation. The importance of this model of organisational power is not only that it reveals why senior organisational members go to such lengths to reduce the autonomy of low-level organisation members [. . .] so as to reduce the power of such members, but it also points to the relationship between the installation of procedures which are designed to achieve routinisation (by reducing reliance on judgement and discretion) and the elimination of lower-level members' power. To routinise by laying down procedures or by incorporating these procedures in machinery or the work design, increases enormously the substitutability of personnel, for the decision-making has been removed from the employee and invested in procedures, regulations, machinery. The new less skilled job will require less training and expertise. This way of reducing the power of sub-units involves legislating – through various systems – for ways of reacting to and coping with the uncertainty; another method involves reducing the uncertainty itself. This might mean, in the case reported by Crozier, installing a system of planned maintenance. It might mean reducing the variability of the organisation's raw material through pre-selection or other controls. The result of both procedures is the same – the reduction of the sub-unit's intra-organisational power by reducing its control over uncertainty. It is precisely because of this consequence of processes of automation, 'rationalisation', work study, mechanisation and routinisation that such processes are resisted by the employees concerned. And it is because of the power implications of the discretionary element of organisational work that senior executives tend to impose prescription and standardisation. But they won't succeed, because, as Crozier reminds us, it is not possible entirely to eliminate discretion. Despite centralisation, automation and formalisation, some areas of potential autonomy, or uncertainty, remain. And it is on these that members base their efforts to regain sufficient unpredictability to increase their organisational power. The organisation of work and the organisation of control are two sides of the same basic process of organisational domination.

[. . .]

NOTE

* This chapter has been adapted from, Salaman, G. (1979), *Work Organisations: Resistance and Control*, Longman, London.

REFERENCES

Blau, P. (1963), *The Dynamics of Bureaucracy*, University of Chicago Press, Chicago.

Crozier, M. (1964), *The Bureaucratic Phenomenon*, Tavistock, London.

Daniel, W. W. (1969), 'Industrial Behaviour and the Orientation to Work,' *Journal of Management Studies*, 6.

Edwards, R. C. (1972), 'Bureaucratic organisation in the capitalist firm', in Edwards, Richard C., Reich, Michael and Weisskopf, Thomas E. (eds), *The Capitalist System*, Prentice-Hall, New Jersey, pp. 115–19.

Elliott, P. (1975), 'Professional ideology and social situation', in Esland, Geoff, Salaman, Graeme and Speakman, Mary-Anne (eds), *People and Work*, Holmes McDougall, Edinburgh, pp. 275–86.

Fox, A. (1971), *A Sociology of Work in Industry*, Collier-Macmillan, London.

Gouldner, A. W. (1954), *Patterns of Industrial Bureaucracy*, Free Press, New York.

Hall, R. H. (1972), *Organisations: Structure and Process*, Prentice-Hall, Englewood Cliffs, New Jersey.

Hickson, D. J., Hinings, C. R., Lee, C. A., Schneck, R. E. and Pennings, J. M. (1973), 'A strategic contingencies' theory of intraorganisational power', in Salaman, G. and Thompson, K., *People and Organisations*, Longman, London, pp. 174–89.

Hyman, R. (1972), *Strikes*, Fontana Collins, London.

Hyman, R. (1976), 'Trade unions, control and resistance', in *People and Work*, an Open University Course, Open University Press, Milton Keynes.

Katz, F. E. (1973), 'Integrative and adaptive uses of autonomy: worker autonomy in factories', in Salaman, G. and Thompson, K. (eds), *op. cit.*, pp. 190–204.

Marcuse, H. (1972), *One Dimensional Man*, Abacus/Sphere Books, London.

Mills, C. W. (1956), *White Collar: The American Middle Classes*, Galaxy Books, Oxford University Press, New York.

Pettigrew, A. M. (1975), 'Occupational specialisation as an emergent process', in Esland, G. *et al.* (eds), *op. cit.*, pp. 258–74.

Roethlisberger, F. J. and Dickson, W. (1964), *Management and the Worker*, Wiley, New York.

Roy, D. (1954), 'Efficiency and "the Fix": the Informal Intergroup Relations in a Piecework Machine Shop', in S. M. Lipset and N. J. Smelser (eds), *Sociology: The Progress of a Decade*, Prentice-Hall, New Jersey.

Scheff, T. J. (1970), 'Control over policy by attendants in a mental hospital', in Grusky, O. and Miller, G. A. (eds), The Sociology of Organisations: Basic Studies, Free Press, New York, pp. 329–40.

Walker, C. R. and Guest, R. H. (1952), *Man on the Assembly Line*, Harvard University Press, Cambridge, Mass.

Wamsley, G. L. (1970), 'Power and the crisis of the universities', in M. N. Zald (ed.), *Power in Organisations*, Vanderbilt University Press, Nashville, Tenn.

Zimmerman, D. (1973), 'The practicalities of rule use', in G. Salaman and K. Thompson (eds), *op. cit.*, pp. 250–63.

SECTION 3: CHANGING ORGANISATIONS

INTRODUCTION

This section is about how organisations are changing. It is about whether they are changing, and about the origins and consequences of these changes. It will offer material on, and analyses of changes in work organisation. It supplies you with material with which to assess and analyse these changes in the light of the material you have read so far and the two approaches to organisational understanding outlined in the previous section.

Chapter 10: Re-inventing organisation man? – Paul Thompson and David McHugh

This chapter is also about attempts by senior managers to change the cultures of the organisation – i.e. to persuade their employees to be committed to the employing organisations' priorities, to share senior management's values, to be committed to the business. This chapter takes us back to a major discussion in chapter one. You will find this concern of employers to try to shape how their employees think – and their values, particularly their attitudes towards their work and their employer, familiar. Needle discusses these projects thoroughly, in the first chapter, where he noted that these projects originated with the work of Peters and Waterman in the early 1980s. He identified some potential difficulties surrounding these efforts. These 'corporate culture' projects represent attempts by managers to persuade employees to share managers' objectives and to 'feel that they are working for something worthwhile'. They are about 'the historic search for meaning or the holy grail of commitment in the study of organisations'. This chapter is a thorough assessment of the bases and claims of these projects.

We have already encountered the importance of employee commitment for managers and noted how the realities of work experience – as driven by competitive market pressures and the search for increasing levels of profit – often make such commitment precarious. If control is increased commitment often decreases.

Chapter 11: Organizational structuring and restructuring – Christopher Mabey, Graeme Salaman and John Storey

This is the first of three closely connected chapters which deal with current programmes of organisational restructuring. Chapter 11 looks at changes to the classical bureaucratic model and assesses their merits and implications. These changes take place within the organisation as traditionally defined and demarcated. They concern internal boundaries and structures. Chapter 12, on the other hand, looks at some of the ways organisations have been changing their boundaries as a major form of change: placing activities traditionally conducted within the organisation outside it; generating networks, forging strategic alliances with other companies, and so on. Chapter 13 looks at these programmes of organisational restructuring and assesses the empirical evidence of their impact. In the face of so many ambitious claims to radical changes in the nature of work and organisation, it argues that it is time to take stock of the nature and future of work and what options that creates for different kinds of workplace transformation.

Chapter 11 organises its analysis around two frameworks in figures 11.1 and 11.2. These offer a simple diagrammatic representation of current tendencies in organisational restructuring. Note that one form of change is change within traditional boundaries while the other depicts change outside or of these boundaries. But note also that the authors do not suggest that these changes necessarily imply improvement or progress. And the direction of change may not be linear; it may be cyclical.

Chapter 12: Beyond organizational structure: the end of classical forms? – Christopher Mabey, Graeme Salaman and John Storey

Chapter 12 continues the analysis of structural change initiated by the previous chapter. It is about forms of restructuring which change, move or cross traditional organisational boundaries. It addresses significant forms of current structural change. For example, market relationships are being established within the organisation where relations between departments and businesses within the organisation are defined *as if* they were market relations. This development is inspired by the currently influential conviction that the market is the best determinant of efficiency – a sort of purifying force. In a sense therefore the sorts of directions of change discussed in this chapter – increasing externalisation of control and relations; diversified activities; performance-based control; market mode of regulation – represent an attempt to resolve perennial organisational problems by replacing organisational solutions by non-organisational solutions – by externalising or transferring the problem and its solution outside the organisation itself.

Chapter 12 offers description and analysis of a number of forms of organisational change which cross or change organisational boundaries. However, note the cautionary comment in the first paragraph. Do not think that this chapter is suggesting a long term historical evolution of organisational forms (although management consultants would like to give this impression: every change is progress away from the deficiencies of history towards the wonders of the future). But note the passage: '. . . a historically-informed perspective on organisational studies would caution that apparent "trends" are often more like "cycles"'.

One of the strengths of chapter 12 is the way it evaluates the implications of each change in terms of its likely impact on the development of a long term strategic approach to human resources. The chapter is not simply descriptive although it does contain a great deal of material on current development in organisational restructuring. (The next chapter gives similar coverage of another major form of organisational change.)

Chapter 13: Hands, hearts and minds: changing work and workers at the end of the century – Chris Warhurst and Paul Thompson

This vigorous and sometimes somewhat polemical piece addresses all the forms of change discussed in this section – i.e. changes both in cultures and in structures, and the relationships between them. Once again it is organised as a form of dialogue. It starts with a discussion – which in effect is a brief summary – of the major forms of change currently taking place. The bulk of the chapter then consists of an assessment of these changes in terms of the extent to which they represent a radical or real change in the nature and experience of work. You will notice some interesting similarities and differences between this chapter and the two earlier discussions of structural change.

First, this chapter approaches structural change from the point of view of the employee whereas earlier chapters adopted a more depersonalised, structural approach. Also the tone of this chapter is different: it's slightly more emotional, possibly even polemical. If the earlier chapters seemed to go out of their way to be even-handed, this chapter is not afraid to be very decisive and definite. The overall tenor of chapter 13 is sceptical and critical. But note that it is critical in more than one way. It is critical in the sense that it does not accept the truth or validity of all of the pronouncements and predictions of the management gurus. (Note that one section is entitled: 'Don't let the facts get in the way of a good argument'.) But it is also critical in a more basic way in that this piece is clearly written from the critical radical approach to organisations. These authors are not people who believe that organisations are consensual institutions where all employees share objectives and priorities and are committed to the organisation. These authors have clearly read their Marx, Weber and Durkheim, and they are not going to be easily convinced about the plausibility of the optimistic prophecies of gurus about the workplaces of the future. It is clear that these authors believe that the design of work and organisation – although not determined, and not immutable – is nevertheless shaped by powerful economic, historic and social forces. It is going to be hard to change therefore. Furthermore these authors see the main pressure for change not as the achievement of some utopian new form of organisation but a very old fashioned one indeed: '. . . the increased competitive pressures on management to improve the quality and quantity of labour's input'. The question of course is to what extent new forms of work design and organisation can escape the contradiction noted earlier: that organisations are likely to react to competitive pressures in ways which will shape the experience of employees and reduce their commitment and their willingness to identify with their employer. At the same time the employer will try to engage the employees' commitment and energy.

Chapter 14: Failure – Richard Sennett

With this chapter we come full circle. It is the final chapter in this section, and with it we return to the issues raised in the first section – the meaning of work and how this varies (and how it is determined). If you think back to the first section the third chapter of that section showed some of the ways work arrangements and meanings can vary over time and place. The fourth chapter analysed the nature and meaning of the work of a large group of clerical workers in the US – and by implication elsewhere in the West. It did this by showing how this sort of work had lost many of the key features of an idealised form of work where work gave meaning and satisfaction, personal autonomy and control, 'no split of work and play': craftsmanship. The notion of craftsmanship was used as a powerful tool to explore the meaninglessness of white-collar work.

Mills' analysis, written in the 1950s, was aimed at a sort of work which has now reduced enormously in size – usually as a result of the sorts of change discussed in later chapters. To this extent it is dated. But the attempt to unravel the meaning of work experiences has not dated at all. In fact with recent developments and changes in organisations (treated in this section) such an analysis is all the more important. The final chapter in this section brings us up to date. It is concerned with the meaning of work – or rather the meaning of a loss of work. Mills was concerned with the impact of meaningless, skill-less work on the worker. Sennett's analysis is of the impact of loss of work on the worker. While Warhurst and Thompson were interested in the impact of restructuring and culture change on the nature of work and jobs, Sennett is interested in the impact of both organisational and job changes on the individuals concerned. This chapter therefore is about the human consequences of the processes described in this final section.

There are some similarities in style between Mills and Sennett. Both take a broad approach; both share a liberal concern with the social and personal implications of work issues. Both are crucially concerned with the ways public affairs – work structures and processes – impact on individuals' biographies. They are in a sense concerned with exploring the impact of the public, even the political, and the personal. Both, in E.P. Thompson's marvellous words, seek to rescue the victims of 'progress' from the 'condescension of history'.

Sennett's focus is firmly on the meaning of work – or rather loss of work. He is interested in how people make sense of loss of work – of failure. If Mills sets his analysis in the context of craftsmanship – the world the white collar workers have lost – Sennett sets his in the context of career. This is what they have lost. He suggests that they make sense of their experience by telling stories about what happened to them – developing narratives or accounts which 'make sense' of their experience. Crucially in these narratives they develop a new analysis of themselves and their responsibility for failing to master their situations and to take responsibility for themselves. The failure – redundancy – becomes a failure of self – not something done *to* them, but something they should have seen as a risk and avoided by taking responsibility for themselves. The failure is one of lack of enterprise, of being too trusting. So Sennett's piece is not simply and solely about the effects of restructuring on individuals' hopes and lives. It is also about how modern employees have imbibed an approach to themselves and their work. Remember the words of Warhurst and Thompson: '. . . if in the past managers had an employment relationship based upon mutual trust and commitment rather than contract with their companies, this relationship is now being replaced by a transaction based on mutual instrumentality involving a simple effort–reward bargain.' The ex-employees who speak in the Sennett piece blame themselves for failing to develop this instrumentality early and thoroughly enough. They had failed to realise the sea-change in employment relationships that was occurring. They had not 'learned the ropes'. But they have now. And this view of themselves, of their skills and personalities as products or resources to be marketed enterprisingly itself assumes and incorporates some of the core values of our time: that individuals, like organisations, must become marketable, must sell themselves, and the final section of the chapter raises questions about the wider implications of this. One could argue that this view of oneself may be a realistic and sensible strategy in the face of the experiences of organisational restructuring and its implications, but it also seems perilously near to what Marx would call alienation, or Durkheim anomie.

In a sense we have come full circle. In the first section Littler and Mills write of the ways that in modern societies, technology becomes seen almost as something sacred and unquestionable – as something outside of us which although we create it, dominates us. Remember Littler's quotation from Ellul: 'Technique (i.e. technology) itself selects among the means to be employed. *The human being is no longer in any sense the agent of choice.*'

This notion of powerlessness is precisely what the ex-IBM employees are seeking to understand and resolve. They do so by reference to a process Mills describes tellingly: 'In all work involving the personality market, . . . one's personality and personal traits become part of the means of production. In this sense a person instrumentalises and externalises intimate features of his person and disposition.' That is, as Sennett suggests, under modern conditions we explain and understand our personal problems and experiences at work including that of loss of work by reference to our failure to manage ourselves and our personality as if we were products to be marketed.

10

RE-INVENTING ORGANISATION MAN?*

Paul Thompson and David McHugh

In 1956, William H. Whyte wrote the influential *The Organisation Man*, a vituperative attack on the 'social ethic' shaping the values of those in the middle ranks of private and public corporations. This oddly named ethic was a collectivist nightmare which morally legitimated the powers of society against the individual. Amongst those blamed was Mayo and his obsessive concern for belongingness and group adjustment. Culture only became acceptable as an issue when it was associated with the necessity for managers to be sensitive towards national diversities in the 'collective programming of the mind' (Hofstede, 1980).

But by the end of the 1980s, organisation man was back in fashion. [. . .] Despite all the hymns of praise to corporations, the credit for reviving the issue largely goes to American academics and management consultants, notably Peters and Waterman (1982), plus Ouchi (1981) and Deal and Kennedy (1988) – all except Ouchi being connected to the McKinsey consultancy company. However, it was filtered [. . .] through a reading of the Japanese experience that located their success in the existence of strong cultures and 'turned on workforces'.

Corporate culture, which can be defined as the way that management mobilises combinations of values, language, rituals and myths, is seen as the key factor in unlocking the commitment and enthusiasm of employees. To the extent that it can make people feel that they are working for something worthwhile, it is projected as part of the solution to the historic search for meaning or the holy grail of commitment in the study of organisations. For work humanisation theorists such as Herzberg and Maslow, that search was connected to the provision of intrinsically satisfying tasks through job redesign. The ground has now shifted to the psychosocial benefits from identification with the company and its superordinate goals. There may be characteristics which make companies successful, as in the famous lists of Peters and Waterman or Goldsmith and Clutterbuck – autonomy, zero-basing, productivity through people – but corporate culture is the core and the glue that binds the increasingly diverse activities together. When the project is defined as developing a non-deified, non-religious 'spiritualism', it is to be expected that advocacy often takes on a distinctly evangelical tone, with managers and workers exhorted to love the company. [. . .]

More conventionally, there is an emphasis on culture *strategies*, with senior management taking the process of value-shaping seriously. But perhaps 'strategy' is the wrong word.

[. . .] [C]orporate culture is part of a proclaimed shift from the hard S's of strategy, systems and their quantifiable objectives, to the soft S's of style and shared values. So, is this another fad of pop-management or a doomed attempt to transplant culture-specific Japanese systems? Certainly, corporate culture is less prominent now as other panaceas such as business process re-engineering and TQM take centre stage. But it has by no means been entirely displaced. The management of culture is recognised as one of the central features of HRM, given that [. . .] employment relationships are seen moving away from bureaucratic hierarchy and low-trust industrial relations towards securing real commitment (Guest, 1987; Legge, 1989). Similarly, the battle to introduce private sector styles and methods into public services and the widespread adoption of mission statements indicates that the identification and transmission of values remains on the organisational agenda.

Nor should we underestimate the shift in management theory, and to a lesser extent practices, that has been going on. Changing people's emotions or what they think has mostly been off-limits to the dominant strands in OB. [. . .] Under systems of bureaucratic or unobtrusive control, what had to be changed was the structure of communication, rules or selection, along with provision of the appropriate rewards and sanctions.

Managerial and professional employees *were* subject to moulding and socialisation processes, though how seriously or effectively is open to question. But for all the unitarist rhetoric about goals, routine manual and clerical workers were not really expected to identify with the company. It was more a case of 'if you've got them by the balls, their hearts and minds will follow'. *Normative regulation* changes this: 'it is only with the advent of the "excellence" literature that management is urged to become directly involved in determining what employees should think, believe or value' (Willmott, 1992: 72). [. . .]

It is not the case that questions of attitudes were wholly by-passed in previous theory and practice. For example, the Neo-Human Relations tradition tried to develop ideas that could link individual aspirations to organisational goals through more open, participative and high-trust relationships (Legge, 1995). In turn this gave way to Organisational Development or OD, which was probably the most direct antecedent to the corporate culture movement. Bennis (1966) argued that the only way to change organisations was to change their cultures. [. . .] By the late 1970s the OD movement had suffered 'a collapse of professional confidence in itself' (Harrison, 1984: 12), and a dismantling of some of the largest internal company units. Whatever the practical limitations, NHR and OD did not satisfactorily deal with values and commitment from a managerial standpoint. Meanwhile, companies still advertise for OD managers, but who can plan and implement culture strategies. . . . This is the new ball game: OD as specific techniques within a broader organisational culture and human resource context, and this time targeted at workers as well as managers.

PRODUCT AND PERSPECTIVE

The corporate culture merchants

'In culture there is strength' is the ominous sounding new law of business life proclaimed by Deal and Kennedy (1988: 19). What such writers are actually talking about is a specific product: 'a culture devised by management and transmitted, marketed, sold or imposed on the rest of the organisation' (Linstead and Grafton Small, 1992: 332). But what is it that gives such strength? One of the most recurrent themes is *attention to employees*: ownership in a shared vision rather than changes in work or working conditions. The notion of 'pillars' occurs again, this time in creating a committed workforce. The British personnel writers Martin and Nicholls (1987) name three – a sense of belonging to the organisation, a sense of excitement in the job, and confidence in management. In general terms 'the notion of employee commitment is built on the internalisation of the norms and values of the organisation' (Kelly and Brannick, 1987: 19).

Interestingly there is explicit recognition of the benefits of *emotional* engagement: affectiveness more than effectiveness. As 'man is quite strikingly irrational' (Peters and Waterman, 1982: 86), employees can be appealed to through symbolism and the ceremonies and awards of 'hoopla'. In the new corporations it is the role of those at the top to act as symbolic rather than rational managers – as scriptwriters and directors of the daily drama of company life (Deal and Kennedy, 1988: 142). By symbolising the organisation internally and externally, heroes become a crucial component of the leadership process. For Deal and Kennedy, John Wayne in pinstripes is an appropriate role model. Leadership is invested with a large burden in cultural management, reflecting in part research which has identified the *founder's* influence in shaping values (Schein, 1985). [. . .]

In addition, the focus of such organisations is on disseminating values through stories, myths and legends about the company, its products and heroes, backed up by rites and rituals which reinforce cultural identification. The latter also helpfully facilitate the goal of a large dose of Skinnerian positive reinforcement, where *everyone* is made to feel a winner. Management in general is expected to use non-authoritarian styles to create a climate of trust. Some writers make a nod in the direction of feminism by referring to nurturing qualities and androgynous managers (Naisbitt and Aburdene, 1985: 207). Others are content to report the aim of shifting from an aggressive, confrontational and macho style at companies such as Ford and Rank Xerox (Giles and Starkey, 1987).

Though the package of corporate culture is new, some of the ideas are not. Pop management writers seldom discuss theoretical sources, but Peters and Waterman acknowledge that, 'The stream that today's researchers are tapping is an old one started in the late 1930s by Elton Mayo and Chester Barnard' (1982: 5). Human relations influences can most clearly be seen in the focus on managing the informal organisation; workers as irrational creatures of sentiment; and social needs to belong; whereas the shadow of Barnard looms over conceptions of the organisation as a co-operative social system and on the role of the executive in articulating and disseminating values and superordinate goals.

But there may also be deeper, less direct roots: 'it is in the various writings of Durkheim that a conceptual framework for discussions of corporate culture may be found' (Ray, 1986: 290). Ouchi is one of the few corporate culture writers to accept the need for a macro-sociological analysis that breaks from the interpersonal level favoured by many organisational writers. His article with Johnson (1978) draws directly on a Durkheimean framework which sees a modern division of labour involving a loss of moral community and mutual obligation, with a decline in the role of the family, church and other institutions. Durkheim believed that the necessary function of social control and cohesion could be played by professions and occupational groups, a theme echoed later by Mayo. Ouchi and Johnson argue that Japanese work organisations have provided the necessary primary relations. Ray (1986) extends the analysis by pointing out that the corporation is expected to take on the functions embodied in Durkheim's realm of the sacred. Hence the emphasis both on faith in the firm and binding rites and rituals. Most corporate culture books draw on such assumptions. Deal and Kennedy do so explicitly: 'corporations may be the last institutions in America that can effectively take on the role of shaping values' (1988: 16).

What is the *evidence* for the dual claim that strong cultures exist and that they constitute the primary reason for better or even excellent performance? Many of the same companies tend to appear across the range of US books – IBM, Procter and Gamble, Hewlett Packard, McDonald's, Delta Airlines. So do some of the 'baddies', notably Harold Geneen and ITT, who seem to get it in the neck consistently. In the UK the roll call includes Marks and Spencer, Plessey, Sainsbury, Burton and Schweppes. As for the information about the companies, the opening sentence of Deal and Kennedy begins, 'S.C. Allyn, a retired chairman of the board, likes to tell a story . . .' (1988: 3). With the partial exception of Ouchi, stories, vignettes and anecdotes about the dedication and commitment of corporate heroes and managers, or the devotion of ordinary employees, constitute a large proportion of the evidence presented.

Of course, they are not the only sources. Across the books, it is possible to find interviews with top management; testing the culture by conversing with the receptionist; profiles based on company documents; use of formal statements of objectives and philosophy and of biographies and speeches; and questionnaires filled in by chairmen asked to rank their firm according to 'excellence' criteria. Occasionally, as in Goldsmith and Clutterbuck, there is reference to interviewing people on the shop floor, but there is no sign of the results.

There is considerable positive reference to slogans such as Delta airlines 'the Delta family feeling'; IBM's 'IBM means service' and 'respect for the individual'; GE's 'Progress is our most important product'. Apparently *everyone* knows and believes in Tandem Computer's slogans such as 'It's so nice, it's so nice, we do it twice' (Deal and Kennedy, 1988: 9). McDonald's has an extraordinary quality assurance and level of care for its people (Peters and Waterman, 1982: xix–xx). The slogans of privatised utilities in the UK, such as BT's 'We answer to you', and the numerous statements of supermarkets and other companies about customer care could be put in a similar category (Legge, 1995). These kinds of statement about 'qualitative beliefs' are then linked to a second set of quantitative information detailing the superior financial and economic performance of the given companies over ten or twenty years. Strong cultures are the assumed link, but there is no direct evidence, or real discussion of other market or environmental variables. A rare statement of this kind comes from Deal and Kennedy, 'we estimate that a company can gain as much as one or two hours of productive work per employee per day' (1988: 15). No criteria or proofs are ever given.

Mini 'cases' are also developed in the popular literature – for example, of Hewlett Packard's 'HP Way'. Open-plan offices, open managerial styles, extensive formal and informal communication, and team and workforce meetings are just some of the mechanisms to generate the high commitment that is the key to quality and innovation. Stories about the heroic exploits of founders Bill and Dave reinforce a collective identity and organisational goals. Peters and Waterman found it impossible not to become fans. A more serious academic account of a similar organisation is given in Kunda's (1992) *Engineering Culture*. Most male engineers operate in what appears to be an informal, egalitarian, work and play hard environment, sustained by a commitment to job security and technical innovation. Slogans and metaphors permeate working life – 'do what's right', 'he who proposes does', 'having fun', 'tech is a bottom-up company', 'we are like a football team' – and there is a mini-industry of meetings, rituals and workshops that reproduce company culture.

Something like the 'HP Way' is a classic rhetorical device, a communicative symbol whose goal is primarily to mobilise organisational commitment and project community of interest. We are seeing this kind of corporate culture advocated as the solution to the problem of *global integration*. There are powerful globalisation tendencies in the international economy that are producing forces for standardisation within and between companies. Firms need to integrate an increasingly diverse number of activities and units, and, at the same time, there are pressures for them to adapt to the more rapid diffusion of 'best practice'. Many management theorists portray culture as the glue that binds those diverse units into cohesive and co-ordinated 'families'. [. . .]

HRM and the management of culture

If employees are the strategic resource, then *commitment* is the key to unlocking the untapped human capital. In turn this requires conscious development of the value base of companies, such as mission statements, and new and expanded means of communicating them; as well as the battery of participative measures such as team working and team briefing to generate the high-trust culture associated with 'soft' versions of HRM (Storey, 1989; Guest, 1989). The imputed strategic character of HRM thus facilitates the development of strong cultures by integrating policies of recruitment, reward and retention. Culture becomes a shorthand for a new ideology and rules of the game accompanying a shift from collectivism to individualism in the management of the employment relationship (Sisson, 1990). Collective bargaining and unions are bad words in the new world of *unmediated* relations between the organisation and the individual. An example of the new practices is that of direct communication with the workforce. [. . .] Hence the rash of briefings, videos, house magazines, open days and consultative forums. Trade unions are not given much of a part in strong culture companies. At best they are considered a recalcitrant junior member, and at worst an unnecessary obstacle. [. . .] In fact, such employment practices already constitute a significant part of strategies by a growing number of companies to make themselves union-free by removing or substituting for any employee desire for collective representation (Basset, 1989). Any independent, 'sub-cultural' source of alternative values, trade unions, profession or occupational groups is therefore an obstacle to the development of a unitary, cohesive culture.

Certainly there are prominent companies that fit this picture, notably the major US computer firms. IBM and Hewlett Packard carefully construct their employment practices to individualise employee's relations with the company. Prominent features of this approach are personal wage 'negotiation' and performance evaluation, immediate grievance accessibility to management, and an internal labour market which provides for mobility and job security. But is this typical? We know from case studies (for example, Martinez Lucio and Weston, 1992) and wider survey evidence such as the Workplace Industrial Relations Survey (Millward *et al.*, 1992) that HRM practices, in the UK at least, exist extensively in unionised workplaces.

Extending levels of identification between employee and organisation may be less distinctive than in the famous, often greenfield site examples, but research shows that many top companies have been engaging in widespread culture change programmes (Storey, 1992). More generally, especially for white collar and professional employees, measures designed to create a performance-conscious culture or environment have been spreading. [. . .] Within the overall process of managing a culture change, performance-related pay and new appraisal systems are often seen as a key element in transforming employee attitudes. [. . .]

CRITICS AND QUESTIONS

Questioning the novelty

The extent of strong culture companies is exaggerated. These are trends within some, but not all, organisations. Many companies, small and large, will carry on with 'weak cultures' and would not recognise a culture strategy if it landed on the managing director's desk. Indeed, the novelty of the phenomenon can also be overstated. Companies such as Cadbury and Marks and Spencer in the UK *do* have corporate cultures of a highly distinctive nature. Such companies have long used management styles based on 'sophisticated paternalism' which combine high levels of employment security and social benefits with careful screening of recruits, direct communication and in-house training, wrapped up in a 'philosophy' of respect for the individual (Miller, 1989). And all this before any thought of corporate cultures and human resource management!

Accounts by historians and sociologists show that we can trace paternalism back to older patterns. Joyce (1980) shows that from the mid-nineteenth century many Victorian firms, particularly those influenced by religious nonconformism, developed a social paternalism embedded in the interwoven fabric of work and community life. Though often associated with small firms, paternalism survived and changed form as size and scale increased, though family ownership still played a key role. At Lee's Tapestry Works on Merseyside between the wars, considerable efforts were made to develop 'a sense of belonging and a feeling of loyalty to the firm' (Johnson and Moore, 1986). There was an 'exceptional' family atmosphere, company saving schemes, a holiday camp, and partnership certificates issued to employees – or 'members' as they were called from 1931. [. . .]

Even after the war, many large workplaces generated employee identification based partly on stable employment, as well as being a focal point in and for local communities. A typical example is English Electric in Liverpool (Thompson, 1994). Worker identification with the firm was enhanced by almost all promotions coming from the shop floor, thus creating a strong internal labour market, though top management tended to be imported. The company owned houses and had its own hospital and dentist on site. There was an extensive company social life, including an annual sports day which catered for 10,000–12,000 children, a flower show, and a variety of clubs, dance and shows. These were all organised on a voluntary basis by a combination of management, staff and workers. The firm, though paternalistic, was not anti-union and officially recognised a number of appropriate trade unions. Though management did not always like it, they worked within an industrial settlement in which a system of bureaucratic controls over work and employment relationships empowered shop floor union organisation.

In the late 1960s, the company was taken over by GEC, their main competitor. They began to run down production and transfer products out of the place almost immediately. A new layer of senior management was brought in, with very different attitudes. Within a short time the whole social side of the factory apparatus was wound down. What happened at English Electric was indicative of the breakdown of the old culture paradigm under the impact of the first major wave of post-war restructuring of capital in the mid to late 1960s. Under the impact of this concentration of capital, firm mobility, mergers and acquisitions and the decline of company towns and occupational communities, old forms of identification tended to break down. British management responded in a variety of ways. There were many measures designed to tighten controls on the wage–effort bargain, for example the replacement of piecework by Measured Day Work. [. . .] A smaller minority tried progressive work redesign schemes such as work humanisation, but, 'Anyone who talked about employee "loyalty" and "all pulling together for the good of the firm" was regarded as a nostalgic crank who did not understand modern industry' (Ackers and Black, 1991: 30).

Paternalistic cultures became a minority phenomena though they continued to exist in different forms, often in smaller firms. [. . .]

Questioning the evidence

Given the reliance of the product on stories, myths and other forms of 'organisation talk', what executives and managers say in words or on paper tends to be taken as proof for the existence of string and distinctive cultures. There is little critical reflection on this. Martin and Nicholls are at least honest in admitting that:

> we cannot be sure of the extent to which the companies we studied were *actually* successful in creating that commitment or whether that commitment contributed to their success. All we can say is that the managers in question *reported* that their efforts to create commitment met with a positive response and produced a significant improvement.
>
> (1987: ix [our emphasis])

In addition, they present some useful, if brief and largely propagandising cases. As for the most of the literature, much of the time even corporate slogans are taken as virtually inconvertible evidence of culture and effects, because they are taken to be synonymous with superordinate goals.

With this kind of evidence, so much of it resting on bland management statements, unattributed quotes and plain assertion, it is tempting to dismiss the whole enterprise as a fairy tale. Drucker, the best-known management writer, pulled no punches in describing *In Search of Excellence* as 'a book for juveniles' and a fad that would not last a year (quoted in Silver, 1987: 106). The lack of rigour in research methodology has been a persistent theme of critics (Hammond and Barham, 1987: 8–14; Guest, 1992). Samples of companies – for example, those used by Peters and Waterman – were selected and treated in a cavalier and uncontrolled manner; dropping some from the original list and using evidence from others not in the sample at all (Silver, 1987: 113). The tenuous link between cultures, excellence and performance turned out to be highly fragile. Companies were included whose performance was far from excellent and a significant number subsequently ran into difficulties, as *Business Week* (1983) reported under a headline of 'oops!' An important book on IBM (Delamarter, 1988) – by a senior economist who had worked in the US Justice Department on the anti-trust case against IBM – pointed out that the company built up its dominance by undercutting its competitors in vulnerable market sectors and paying for it through excess profits from customers who had little choice. Commenting on *In Search of Excellence*, the author argues that

> According to the authors, IBM has benefited from a strong central philosophy that was originally laid down by its charismatic leaders, the Watsons. They present a simple, appealing model for IBM's success – excellence in management. But this view is dead wrong. IBM's success comes from the power of monopoly.
>
> (1988: xvii)

Follow-ups such as Peters and Austin's *A Passion for Excellence* (1985) have failed to quell the doubts, particularly as the same author has apparently decided (Peters, 1987) that there are now no excellent companies in the USA. The treatment of theory and evidence is similarly suspect, with eclectic and uncritical use of parts that suit particular arguments, even if they are not compatible with the general perspective. The use of Skinner in *In Search of Excellence* is a case in point. A further remarkable aspect is the failure to learn from their main inspiration, the human relations tradition. There is no sign of recognition of the central flaw that arose from the Hawthorne Studies, that intervention based on 'attention to employees' produces independent effects on performance. At least some of the hoopla and contrived events could produce a stream of Hawthorne effects of a short-lived and superficial nature.

Of course, expectations of high-quality evidence from popular management texts would be somewhat naïve. Is there anything more conclusive from broader accounts of culture change programmes, particularly those associated with HRM? Legge (1995) attempts to evaluate that research and finds it inconclusive due to a range of methodological and conceptual problems. There has been little research on the explicit links between culture and commitment, which would in many cases be premature anyway, given the need for an in-depth and longitudinal view of change. Even more importantly, both culture and HRM tend to have been treated as generic headings for a variety of interrelated changes, from which it is impossible to disentangle the key variable or variables. Although it is not surprising that, given the centrality of managers as focal points for the articulation and dissemination of values, many have absorbed the message, there is less evidence that this has worked its way fully through to the shop and office floor. Or, if it has, that the effects are on manifested behaviour rather than internalised values. This is a crucial distinction to which we will be returning later.

Questioning the concepts

The previous discussion illustrates the need for a complex understanding of culture. Too often the corporate culture debate has been working with impoverished conceptions of culture which mistake style for substance. A complex and realistic analysis would avoid treating culture as a catch-all for the soft aspects of management (Hammond and Barham, 1987: 10), or as a reified and monolithic phenomena. There is some recognition of *sub-cultures* on functional or gender lines, but not enough, and anyway these can be *managed* to produce a healthy tension within the corporate framework (Deal and Kennedy, 1988: 152–3). It is precisely this assumption that culture can be managed that is called into question by a range of critics that Willmott dubs 'culture purists'. Such critics take their cue from the influential paper by Smircich (1983) which argued that it is better to regard culture as something an organisation *is*, rather than something an organisation *has*. It is a process, not a checklist, and something continually being creatively remade by all participants, rather than fixed (Wright, 1994). As a result, in the context of a variety of often contradictory influences, cultural development is just not as amenable to direction or use as an integrative device as believed (Martin and Siehi, 1983: 53). Nor can it be simply fitted into overall strategic goals. [. . .]

Whether it can be managed or not, it remains the case that the complexity of organisational cultures has been neglected and employees treated as an 'empty space' within which values can be inserted. There is, 'a tendency in the organisational culture literature to treat workplace culture as independent of the labour process' (Alvesson, 1988: 3). Without a recognition that the labour process is fractured by a variety of social cleavages, organisational analysis will continue to neglect the dimensions of conflict, power and even consent. [. . .]

Given the numerous flaws, it is tempting to dismiss most writing on corporate cultures as simply the emperor's new clothes. [. . .] New ideas are required to motivate the troops and a 'gaggle of culture consultants', as well as human resource and personnel teams and others whose empires expand with the literature, are feeding at the honey pot. It appeals to managers because it proclaims that their activity and skills can produce the results, as Mayo once did in relation to early human relations. Silver (1987: 123) also argues that corporate culture is the latest attempt by management consultants to 'wrap each new technique in packaging slightly different from that of its predecessors'. If it is a fad, and one that vastly overestimates its capacity as a change mechanism, then the whole trend is destined to go the same way as others: 'Culture appears to have been reduced to the status of yet another concept, which, like many before it, has reached the decline stage of its "life cycle"' (Ogbonna, 1992a: 6).

But all this is bending the stick back too far. Willmott (1993) criticises the 'purist' position for moving from a judgement that the corporate culture literature is so deficient that it is unworthy of serious attention. Meek is an example, when she argues that if culture is embedded in social interaction, 'it can *only* be described and interpreted' (1988: 293, our emphasis). This may be underselling its potential as a control mechanism. [. . .]

CULTURE: COMMITMENT OR CONTROL?

Corporate culture writers like to present their prescriptions as an *alternative* to control (Naisbitt and Aburdene, 1985: 53; Kelly and Brannick, 1987: 8). But the perspective is riddled with glaring contradictions. We are told that 'in institutions in which culture is so dominant, the highest levels of autonomy occur' (Peters and Waterman, 1982: 105); while

Deal and Kennedy (1988) assure us that companies with strong cultures can tolerate differences (p. 153) and that outlaws and heretics are encouraged in companies such as IBM (pp. 50–1). At the same time the latter authors tell us that managers did not tolerate deviance from company values and standards (p. 14), and that middle managers as well as blue collar workers should be told exactly what to do (p. 78). The books are so anxious to convince us that these are anti-authoritarian, 'no-boss' set-ups, that we are expected to accept that calling workers 'cast members' (Disney) or 'crew members' (McDonald's) in itself banishes hierarchy and class divisions. In Silver's brilliant demolition of the excellence genre, he reminds us of the reality of McDonald's 'people-orientation': 'Behind the hoopla and razzle-dazzle of competitive games and prizes lies the dull monotony of speed-up, deskilled Taylorised work – at McFactory. And McFactory's fuel is cheap labour – part-time, teenage, minimum wage, nonunion workers' (1987: 110).

Reconceptualising the process in terms of new forms of management control is not entirely foreign to the more academic of the culture literature, which openly describes the process as a form of organisational control (Ouchi and Johnson, 1978; Martin and Siehl, 1983). Nor is it inconsistent with many of the statements from the more popular works, such as, 'Strong culture companies go into the trouble of spelling out, often in copious detail, the routine behavioural rituals they expect from their employees' (Deal and Kennedy, 1988: 15). Cultural or *normative* control is essentially concerned with the development of an appropriate social order which provides the basis for desired behaviour (Kelly and Brannick, 1987: 8). Indeed, in order to let people loose to be 'autonomous' they have to be pro-grammed centrally first, with a central role played by more intensive selection and training (Weick, 1987). Tandem Corporation's exhaustive selection process is likened to an 'inquisition' by Deal and Kennedy (1988: 12). [. . .]

Cultural controls also operate through expanding the sphere of social activities in the organisation. Communicating company goals can take place outside the workplace. Part of GM's Hydra-matic Division's QWL program includes week-long 'Family Awareness Training' sessions at education centres (Parker, 1985: 17–19). This does not refer to the employee's nearest and dearest, but to the notion of company as family. Once outside the normal environment and in circumstances where everyone is individualised, psychological exercise and techniques are used to break down old identities. GM questionnaires rate those with limited scores on loyalty to the company as having a low quality of work life. [. . .]

Some radical theorists go further than simply analysing culture in terms of control by arguing that corporate culture represents an alternative and dominant mode. The key theoretical influence is the work of Ray (1986), who utilises the Durkheimean framework discussed earlier. She points out that bureaucratic control though an attempt to integrate employees positively through internal labour markets and the reward system, is still control by incentive. [. . .]

Ray's analysis is complemented by like-minded empirical studies such as Alvesson's (1988: 1991) account of a medium-sized computer consultancy organisation in Sweden. The founders established an open and charismatic managerial style capable of generating strong emotional ties among the consultants employed. A particular problem for the management was that the work was by its very nature variable and flexible, and therefore could not be controlled by conventional means. It was also largely carried out at the client's workplace, potentially undermining the consultant's sense of identity with their own firm. This is compensated for by a large number of social and leisure-time activities with the emphasis on fun, body contact, informality and personnel support; which in turn build social and emotional ties and a sense of company as community. Some of these are consciously linked to presentations of corporate performance to enhance favourable perceptions.

Further support comes from research on the retailing sector. Employees have to be subjected to engineering the soul so that s/he can automatically deliver the quality service required by the new, more enterprising customer (du Gay, 1991a). Ogbonna and Wilkinson (1988) and Ogbonna (1992b) detail that engineering in a supermarket where management have initiated a substantially expanded staff training and development programme that ranges from the recruitment of 'like-minded' people to a 'smile campaign'. Supervisors claim that, 'We are able to detect when a check-out operator is not smiling or even when she is putting on a false smile . . . we call her into a room and have a chat with her' (Ogbonna, 1992b: 85).

Not only does this perspective counterpoise control through conventional rules and regulations to changing the way that employees think and feel, the latter is seen as 'considerably extending' the scope and penetration of managerial domination (Willmott, 1993: 522). Willmott makes a forceful case that in combining normative rules with the erosion of alternative sources of identity:

> Corporate culturism extends the terrain of instrumentally rational action by developing monocultures in which conditions for the development of value-rational action, where individuals struggle to assess the meaning and worth of a range of competing value-standpoints, are systematically eroded.
>
> (1993: 3)

Monocultures are designed to avoid contamination by rival ends or values and to the extent that they succeed, become the vehicle of nascent totalitarianism, accompanied by classic 1984-style doublethink of 'respect for the individual' in organisations where employees are seduced into giving up any autonomy. [. . .]

THE LIMITS TO CULTURE

In criticising culture purists, Willmott persuasively argued that we should take corporate culture seriously. But perhaps he has taken its significance and effectiveness *too* seriously. In arguing that the 'governance of the employee's soul' (1993: 517) is a key ideological element of a new global regime of flexible accumulation, he is in danger of over-extending the concept and maintaining a separation from traditional forms of control associated with Fordism, Taylorism and bureaucracy. Corporate culture should not be isolated as *the* defining feature of contemporary forms of control. Although Willmott rightly says that management is trying to extend the sphere of instrumental action to rules governing emotions and the affective sphere, traditional controls remain important in a number of ways.

Even within those organisations that do implement cultural controls, they are intended to complement, not eliminate, the need for bureaucratic, technical or other systems. In the supermarkets described earlier, employees are subject to surveillance by TV cameras in the managers' office looking for deviations from the desired behaviour, as well as controls through new technology that can record productivity – such as the EPOS (electronic point of sale) system. [. . .]

This continuing reality can be ignored or misunderstood by making culture into an overarching concept. For example, Wright talks of the 'culture' of Fordism which, 'is converted from a mission statement into detailed practices, dividing each task into tiny details and specifying how each should be done' (1994: 2). In contrast, the culture of flexible organisations rely on empowered, self-disciplined workers. Culture in this sense, however, should not be seen as *everything*, but rather as managerial attempts to mobilise values and emotions to support corporate goals. An expanded array of often traditional rules and sanctions is then used to enforce the new moral order and extend levels of identification between employee and organisation. We only have to return to our previous examples of

IBM and Hewlett Packard to see that their respective 'Ways' are sustained by careful structuring of the employment relationship around individualistic means and ends. [. . .]

Nor is culture necessarily the glue which links the parts of a global organisation together. For example, the contemporary large firm is increasingly built through acquisition, merger and collaboration, thus bringing together component parts with very different histories. Though it is not impossible to extend cultural controls across the diverse units and activities, evidence shows that integration through financial controls is more likely (Thompson *et al.*, 1993). In fact, there are a variety of means of integration available, as persuasively demonstrated by Duenas (1993). Drawing on case studies of a number of companies operating in global markets, he argues that only IKEA, the Swedish-based furniture dealer, operates a cohesive corporate culture that consciously transcends national and other cultural differences. [. . .]

Most companies will need or attempt some cultural dimension to the integration problem. In our research, most of the talk of culture and the need for 'Swedish behaviour' is, in our view, a kind of code for company-specific knowledge systems. Managers feel comfortable with talk of Swedishness, perhaps because it gives additional meaning and legitimacy. From this perspective, the prominence of Swedish managers in top positions in foreign subsidiaries is less to do with the superiority or distinctiveness of Swedishness than with the advantage such staff give in facilitating the smooth running of the 'global' management structure, with its attendant and often standardised knowledge system. [. . .]

What about the second element, the effectiveness of corporate culture as social engineering? Among radical critics there is a high degree of consensus on its limits, or at least to the extent to which commitment has been internalised. [. . .] Employees may be conceptualised as empty vessels in which to locate corporate values, but that is not how it works in practice. The research we have been discussing indicates that they may comply with demands for adherence to the language of mission statements, appearance and demeanour in the sales process, or participation in quality circles *without* internalising the values and therefore generating the 'real' commitment. Instead, employees may be aware that they are acting as a coping strategy (Ogbonna and Wilkinson, 1988), or go through the motions of cultural conformity while remaining sceptical that, for example, the 'Abba Way' was any different from the methods used by other international hotel chains (Thompson *et al.*, 1993). The dramaturgical theme is continued through employees developing a variety of means of disengagement or distancing from corporate values through cynicism, parody and irony. [. . .] Considerable evidence of cynicism and distancing was also observed by Kunda. Many employees used an alternative language to describe the culture – 'the song and dance', 'pissing contests', 'Tech strokes', 'burnout', 'doing rah-rah-stuff'; or rival slogans – 'I'd rather be dead than excellent', 'There is unlimited opportunity at Tech, for inflicting and receiving pain'. Much of this ambivalence was directed towards maintaining a private self, or showing that they understood the real politics and status processes underneath the official surface.

Does the predominance of behavioural compliance without commitment matter? Supporters may point to a time lag whereby behavioural precedes attitudinal change (Schein, 1985). But in the light of serious research, this seems optimistic. Are we back full circle to Perrow's view that to change individual behaviour, you do not have to change individuals? Some critics would appear to agree. Drawing on their research into customer care programmes, Harrison and Marchington argue that, 'management does not actually have to achieve value change among the workforce to successfully implement customer care' (1992: 18). The conventional armoury of management control and remuneration measures may be sufficient. Perhaps this does underestimate the distinctiveness of 'hearts and minds' programmes. Our disagreement with theorists such as Willmott is not whether *some* firms try to develop monocultures, but with the extent to which they can ever be successful. Willmott (1993a: 538–40) argues that the very process of roleplaying and cynical disengagement entraps employees in the insidious controls of the culture and confirms the appearance of tolerance and openness.

Such interpretations risk underestimating both the fragility of corporate culture and the creative appropriation, modification and resistance to such programmes. Corporate culture cannot eliminate the powerful informal group norms which are the bedrock of organisational life. Workgroups are just one of a number of sources of competing claims on commitment and loyalty. Attempts to prioritise an aggressive corporate identity may disrupt the delicate balance between these specific and superordinate allegiances. This is particularly the case in the public sector, where traditions of professional autonomy and an ethic of service are increasingly at odds with a new managerialism bent on central direction and enforcement of the bottom line (Anthony, 1990; Harrison and Marchington, 1992). [. . .] Resistance may also be generated by the selective or partial nature of participation in the culture and its attendant reward systems. Such programmes are aimed often only at the 'core' workforce, as Kunda's case study demonstrates: Class 2 workers, mainly clerical and temporary, received inferior benefits and were treated as non-persons, 'just not techies' as one manager put it (1992: 209).

This example reinforces the point that culture is sustained by material, institutional supports. Senior management may be taking greater risks with such initiatives because employees are being asked to invest more of their public and private selves, thereby raising the possibility of enhanced resentment when the promises of large-scale culture change programmes prove difficult to deliver, as at *British Airways* (Höpfl *et al.*, 1992). This is but one of the trends in corporate development which are working against the stability of cultures of company loyalty. [. . .] In addition, what the management pundits are calling 'downsizing' – the cutting out of middle layers of the company [. . .] is hurting most the 'organisation men, conditioned to look to large corporations as the fountainhead of security' (Thackray, 1988: 80). Even some of the high priests of the free market are beginning to despair at the effects of merger mania and the acquisition and asset-stripping of companies. The consequent breakdown of co-operation in the organisation can be seen in examples such as the 1989 strike and dispute about the selling-off of Eastern Airlines in the USA.

Loyalty, obedience and goal identification are not easy to sustain when companies are scrutinising their policy manuals to remove implied promises of job security or even terminate benefits:

[. . .]

CONCLUSION

In this chapter we have tried to set out both the significance of and the limits to attempts to re-invent organisation man. Given the theoretical faults and practical constraints, it is sometimes difficult to see why the product has been so influential, even outside the USA and UK. Undoubtedly, it fitted the mood of a certain period. Silver (1987) adds a wider ideological and political dimension to the explanation. He describes the excellence genre as 'Reaganism writ small', a glorification of entrepreneuralism and the capacity of the USA to stand tall again. It is certainly true that a clear sub-text of Peters and Waterman and Deal and Kennedy is that the discovery of excellent companies in the West means that all good things do not come from Japan. It is also true that the ideological content of most of the books often shows a sharp break with the old 'liberal' consensus. Deal and Kennedy say that the society suffers from too much uncertainty about values and that managers should have the conviction to set standards and not undermine them by being human (1988: 22, 56, 76). In Britain, similar links existed between the rise of corporate culture and a broader ideology celebrating the market and the spirit of enterprise (du Gay, 1991).

But it is not simply a sign of a particular times. For all the absurdities of content and presentation, the corporate culture literature has touched on genuine issues that, as we argued at the start of this chapter, were partly neglected in the past. These need looking at in a context free from the merchandising process. For the tragedy is that we have a lot to learn from studying organisational cultures (Frost *et al.*, 1985; Pheysey, 1993), particularly as culture mediates all change processes. Creating a culture resonant with overall goals is relevant to *any* organisation, whether it be a trade union, voluntary group or producer co-operative. Indeed, it is more important in such consensual groupings. Co-operatives, for example, can degenerate organisationally because they fail to develop adequate mechanisms for transmitting the original ideals from founders to new members and sustaining them through new shared experiences.

Such an emphasis by no means rules out studying specifically *corporate* cultures as management strategies. But this has to be within the plurality of cultures and interest groups in the workplace. Luckily there are rich sources to draw on, such as Salaman's (1986b) study of the occupational culture of the London Fire Brigade; [and] accounts of making-out on the shop floor (Nichols and Beynon, 1977; Burawoy, 1979). Organisation 'man' may be back on the agenda, but the cultural agenda cannot only be set in the board-room.

NOTE

* This chapter has been adapted from, Thompson, P. and McHugh, D. (1995) *Work Organisations: A Critical Introduction*, Basingstoke: Macmillan.

REFERENCES

Ackers, P. and Black, J. (1991), 'Paternalist Capitalism: An Organization in Transition', in M. Cross and G. Payne (eds), *Work and the Enterprise Culture*, London: The Falmer Press.

Alvesson, M. (1988), 'Management, Corporate Culture and Labour Process in a Professional Service Company', paper presented at Conference on the Labour Process, ASTON–UMIST.

Anthony, P. D. (1990), 'The Paradox of the Management of Culture or "He Who Leads is Lost"', *Personnel Review*, vol. 19, no. 4: 3–8.

Basset, P. (1989), 'All Together Now', *Marxism Today*, Jun.

Bennis, W. (1966), *Changing Organizations*, New York: McGraw-Hill.

Burawoy, M. (1979), *Manufacturing Consent: Changes in the Labour Process Under Monopoly Capitalism*, Chicago: University of Chicago Press.

Business Week (1983), 'A Work Revolution in US Industry', 16 May.

Deal, T. and Kennedy, A. (1988), *Corporate Cultures: the Rites and Rituals of Corporate Life*, Harmondsworth: Penguin.

Delamarter, R. T. (1988), *Big Blue: IBM's Use and Abuse of Power*, London: Pan Books.

du Gay, P. (1991b), 'Enterprise Culture and the Ideology of Excellence', *New Formations*, vol. 13: 45–61.

du Gay, P. and Salaman, G. (1991), 'The Cult[ure] of the Customer', *Journal of Management Studies*, vol. 29, no. 5, 615–33.

Duenas, G. (1993), 'The Importance of Intercultural Learning in the International Transfer of Managerial and Organizational Knowledge', paper for the *11th EGOS Colloquium*, Paris, July.

Frost, P. J., Moore, L. F., Louis, M. R., Lundberg, C. C. and Martin, J. (eds) (1985), *Organizational Culture*, Beverley Hills, CA.: Sage.

Giles, E. and Starkey, K. (1987), 'From Fordism to Japanisation: Organizational Change at Ford, Rank Xerox and Fuji Xerox', paper presented at Conference on: *Japanisation of British Industry*, UMIST.

Guest, D. E. (1987), 'Human Resource Management and Industrial Relations', *Journal of Management Studies*, vol. 24, no. 5: 503–21.

Guest, D. E. (1989), 'Personnel and HRM: Can You Tell the Difference?', *Personnel Management*, Jan.: 48–51.

Guest, D. E. (1992), 'Right Enough to be Dangerously Wrong: An Analysis of the In Search of Excellence Phenomenon', in G. Salaman (ed.), *Human Resource Strategies*, London: Sage.

Hammond, V. and Barham, K. (1987), *Management for the Future: Report on the Literature Search*, Ashridge Management College.

Harrison, R. G. (1984), 'Reasserting the Radical Potential of OD', *Personnel Review*, vol. 13, no. 2.

Harrison, E. and Marchington, M. (1992), 'Corporate Culture and Management Control: Understanding Customer Care', *Paper to Employment Research Unit Annual Conference*, Cardiff Business School, Sep.

Hofstede, G. (1980), *Culture's Consequences: International Differences in Work Related Values*, Beverley Hills CA.: Sage.

Höpfl, H., Smith, S. and Spencer, S. (1992), 'Values and Variations: The Conflicts Between Culture Change and Job Cuts', *Personnel Review*, vol. 21, no. 1: 24–38.

Johnson, A. and Moore, K. (1986), *The Tapestery Makers: Life and Work at Lee's Tapestry Works*, Birkenhead: Merseyside Docklands Community Project.

Joyce, P. (1980), Work, Society and Politics, London: Methuen.

Kelly, A. and Brannick, T. (1987), 'Personnel Practices and Strong Organizational Cultures in Ireland', paper presented at Conference on: *Japanisation of British Industry*, UMIST.

Kunda, G. (1992), *Engineering Culture: Control and Commitment in a High Tech Corporation*, Philadelphia: Temple University Press.

Legge, K. (1989), 'Human Resource Management – A Critical Analysis', in J. Storey (ed.), *New Perspectives in Human Resource Management*, London: Routledge.

Legge, K. (1995), *Human Resource Management: Rhetorics and Realities*, London: Macmillan.

Linstead, S. and Grafton Small R. G. (1992), 'On Reading Organization Culture', *Organization Studies*, vol. 13, no. 3: 331–5.

Martin, J. and Siehl, C. (1983), 'Organizational Culture and Counterculture: An Uneasy Symbiosis', Organizational Dynamics, Autumn: 52–64.

Martin, P. and Nicholls, D. (1987), *Creating a Committed Workforce*, London: Institute of Personnel Management.

Martinez Lucio, M. and Weston, S. (1992), 'Human Resource Management and Trade Union Responses: Bringing the Politics of the Workplace Back into the Debate', in P. Blyton and P. Turnbull (eds), *Reassessing Human Resource Management*, London: Sage.

Meek, V. L. (1988), 'Organizational Culture: Origins and Weaknesses', *Organization Studies*, vol. 9., no.4: 453–73.

Miller, P. M. (1989), 'Strategic HRM: What it Is and What it Isn't', *Personnel Management*, Feb.

Millward, T., Stevens, M., Smart D. and Hawkes, W. R. (1992), *Workplace Industrial Relations in Transition, The ED/ESRC/PSI/ACAS Surveys*, Aldershot: Dartmouth.

Naisbitt, J. and Aburdene, P. (1985), *Reinventing the Corporation*, London: Macdonald.

Nichols, T. and Beynon, H. (1977), *Living With Capitalism*, London: Routledge & Kegan Paul.

Ogbonna, E. (1992a), 'Managing Organizational Culture: Fantasy or Reality?', *Human Resource Management*, vol. 3, no. 2.

Ogbonna, E. (1992b), 'Organization Culture and Human Resource Management: Dilemmas and Contradictions', in P. Blyton and P. Turnbull (eds), *Reassessing Human Resource Management*, London: Sage.

Ogbonna, F. and Wilkinson, B. (1988), 'Corporate Strategy and Corporate Culture: the View from the Checkout', *Personnel Review*, vol. 19, no. 4.

Ouchi, W. G. (1981), *Theory Z*, Reading, Mass.: Addison-Wesley.

Ouchi, W. G. and Johnson, J. B. (1978), 'Types of Organizational Control and Their Relationship to Emotional Well Being', *Administrative Science Quarterly*, vol. 23, Jun.: 293–317.

Parker, M. (1985), *Inside the Circle: A Union Guide to QWL*, Boston: Labor Notes.

Perrow, C. (1992), 'Small Firm Networks', in N. Nohria and R. G. Eccles (eds), *Networks and Organizations*, Boston, Mass.: Harvard Business School Press.

Peters, T. J. (1987), 'There Are No Excellent Companies', *Fortune*, 27 April.

Peters, T. J. and Austin, N. (1985), A Passion for Excellence, New York: Random House.

Peters, T. J. and Waterman, R. H. (1982), *In Search of Excellence: Lessons from America's Best-Run Companies*, New York: Harper & Row.

Pheysey, D. (1993), *Organizational Cultures: Types and Transformations*, London: Routledge.

Ray, C. A. (1986), 'Corporate Culture: the Last Frontier of Control?', *Journal of Management Studies*, vol. 23, no. 3: 287–97.

Salaman, G. (1986), *Working*, London: Tavistock.

Schein, E. H. (1985), *Organizational Culture and Leadership*: A Dynamic View, San Francisco: Jossey-Bass.

Silver, J. (1987), 'The Ideology of Excellence: Management and NeoConservatism', *Studies in Political Economy*, 24, Autum: 105–29.

Sisson, J. (1990), 'Introducing the Human Resource Management Journal', *Human Resource Management Journal*, vol. 1, no. 1: 1–11.

Smircich, L. (1983), 'Concepts of Culture and Organizational Analysis', *Administrative Science Quarterly*, 28: 339–58.

Storey, J. (ed.) (1989), *New Perspectives on Human Resource Management*, London: Routledge.

Storey, J. (1992), *Development in the Management of Human Resources*, Oxford: Blackwell.

Thackray, J. (1988), 'Flattening the White Collar', *Personnel Management*, August.

Thompson, P. (1994), 'Corporate Culture: Myths and Realities, West and East', paper for Conference: *Convergence versus Divergence: the Case of Corporate Culture*, Dunáujváros, Hungary.

Thompson, P., Jones, C., Nickson, D., Wallace, T. and Kewell, B. (1993), 'Transnationals, Globalisation and Transfer of Knowledge', paper for the *11th EGOS Colloquium*, Paris, Jul.

Weick, K. (1987), 'Organizational Culture as a Source of High Reliability', *California Management Review*, vol. xxix, no. 2: 112–27.

Willmott, H. (1992), 'Postmodernism and Excellence: The De-differentiation of Economy and Culture', *Journal of Organizational Change*, vol. 5, no. 1: 69–79.

Willmott, H. (1993), 'Strength is Ignorance; Slavery is Freedom: Managing Culture in Modern Organization', *Journal of Management Studies*, vol. 30, no. 5: 515–52.

Wright, S. (1994), 'Culture in Anthropology and Organizational Studies', in S. Wright (ed.), *Anthropology of Organizations*, London: Routledge.

11

ORGANIZATIONAL STRUCTURING AND RESTRUCTURING *

Christopher Mabey, Graeme Salaman and John Storey

[. . .]

INTRODUCTION

Organizational structuring and re-structuring are fundamental to the idea of a strategic approach to managing human resources. It can credibly be suggested that the shifts towards Strategic Business Units, the break-up of large internal labour markets, privatization, outsourcing and delayering have done more to fundamentally redraw the contours of relations at work than any number of new selection, training, payment or appraisal devices.

[. . .] The main aim of this chapter [is to explore] how organizational structuring and re-structuring impact upon strategic human resource management. In pursuit of this aim, [this chapter] will examine the potential for organizational re-structuring; the dimensions of structure which are amenable to change; the types of structure which have been designed; the principles underlying design and re-design attempts; and we will also explain the key developments by presenting a new classification of organizational designs.

Recent years have been witness to a bewildering array of examples of extensive drives to re-structure. For much of the twentieth century there seemed to be an inexorable concentration of power in large corporations. Huge conglomerates were created which embraced diverse and even unrelated businesses. Examples included Hanson Trust, Trafalgar House, Unilever, GKN and BTR in the UK and, in the United States, companies such as General Electric with turnovers larger than the gross national products of many nation states. Such industrial behemoths developed HRM strategies based around internal labour markets with job ladders, seniority rules, internal training and development systems and similar devices. In the public sector too, huge bureaucracies were created with the nationalization of the utilities in the late 1940s and also the creation of the National Health Service in 1948 which had many of the features of a classic bureaucracy.

In order to help manage the large organizations, multi-divisional structures were created. Such structures were designed to allow whole-company strategic issues to be handled at the central 'corporate' level while devolving other major business decisions relating to marketing, business positioning and the like to the divisional level. [. . .] Tall structures were created with as many as 20 plus levels between the chief executive and the shopfloor operative. Managerial control of employees at all the multiple levels was based on a mixture of direct command and budgetary accountability. Hierarchy, command and control were the governing principles of employee management.

More recently, much of this trend would seem to have been thrown into reverse. We have seen many large multi-business organizations broken up. Examples include Hanson, Coates-Viyella and ICI. At the same time, the growth of larger and larger firms and larger work establishments has halted as the large bureaucracies have 'downsized'. Along with the smaller scale have been ushered-in a whole battery of 'new' managerial methods. Flexible organizations, responsive organizations, lean organizations, process organizations, re-engineered organizations, delayered, 'flatter' organizations; empowered, cross-functional teams – these are just a few of the more significant attempts in recent times to *restructure* the organization of work. Changes of these kinds constitute a key element in human resource strategies and also, in turn, they carry important additional human resource implications.

In this chapter, [. . .], we seek to put some much-needed conceptual order on this array of measures and to explore the relationships with SHRM.

ORGANIZATIONAL STRUCTURES AND SHRM: THE BACKGROUND

Central to the very idea of HRM are the ideas of flexibility, responsiveness, 'ownership' of organizational problems by as many employees as possible, empowerment and the winning of commitment. On the surface at least, each one of these appears to be the objective of contemporary restructuring attempts. Organizations in recent years have sought to enhance business and customer-oriented behaviours and priorities through the creation of Strategic Business Units (SBUs). They have sought to induce flexibility through cross-functional teams. Cost competitiveness has been pursued through slimmed corporate centres, the cutting away of 'overhead' and a cut-back in service functions by requiring production units to embrace a much wider range of functions and responsibilities. The tendency throughout much of the twentieth century for corporations to become larger and larger seems to have been halted, and in many countries to have been reversed. A veritable 'war' has been waged against bureaucracy. [. . .] In numerous cases they have first deemed it necessary to slim. But the restructuring that has excited attention in recent years goes well beyond mere adjustments in size and tinkering with the classical form. The logic impelling many of the restructuring movements we have witnessed in the past decade or so has been little less than the attempt to subvert the bureaucratic form.

Kanter (1991) showed just how pervasive organizational re-structuring has been throughout the world. Nearly 12,000 managers from twenty-five countries were surveyed and the results revealed widespread experience of downsizing, reorganizations, mergers and acquisitions and divestitures. The prevalence of re-structuring extended across national boundaries. Notably however, restructuring based on downsizing and redundancy was especially associated with Anglo-Saxon countries and Eastern Europe.

To a large extent the aspirations and principles underlying the recent structural changes seem to reflect those which also underpin the ideas of HRM. There are even the same hard and soft logics at play. From an organizational re-structuring point of view the 'hard' aspects are to be found in the drastic cuts in 'head-counts', the 'downsizing' and the 'outsourcing'. The soft side of the rationale is to be found in the ideas of 'empowerment' the 'learning' that is required to cope with multiple demanding tasks, and the 'teamworking' that is invoked. Both sets of facets appear to constitute, above all, a critique and of escape from bureaucracy.

Organizational structuring and re-structuring are intimately intertwined with many aspects of human resource management. Different structures carry implications for career opportunities, for job design and job satisfaction, for learning and development opportunities, for power distance, work content and skill levels.

The interconnections between organizational structures and human resource management strategies are however complex. Integral to the logic of the large organizations, which grew after the end of the Second World War, was the method of what Edwards (1979: 26) described as the 'bureaucratic control' system. This strategy was based around internal labour markets and the winning of employee commitment through the prospect of long-term career advancement, job security, welfare packages and seniority pay systems. The elaborate job ladders were underpinned by company-provided training and development. Where they existed, trade unions also supported these firm internal labour markets. Such arrangements were, in many ways, also well suited to the principles of human resource management. The material elements were in place to encourage a psychological contract based on commitment; extensive investment in training and development made sense; the system ought to have encouraged careful recruitment and selection, systematic appraisal and elaborate performance management systems. To this extent the fit between this organizational model and human resource management was rather promising. But there were limitations. The bureaucratic form tended to foster complacency and the link with customers became tenuous. As competitive conditions changed these systems found it hard to adapt. Bureaucracy was used to command and control. Initiative was stifled. Hence, in these ways the *departure* from the bureaucratic control system could be interpreted as actually rather more in tune with the principles of human resource management than would its preservation. But, as we will see in the next chapter, this has to be heavily qualified because the nature of the departures made have often been such that the resulting employment systems have been in some tension with HRM.

AN ANALYTICAL FRAMEWORK

We have already noted the almost bewildering array of forms which organizational re-structuring has taken in recent years. Mergers and take-overs are reported alongside de-mergers and corporate break-ups. Decentralization seems to be a perpetual process: a phenomenon surely only made possible by a series of moves which amount to increased centralization. More dramatically, in recent times there seem to have been some radical departures in the direction of networking and outsourcing – and even a good deal of talk about 'virtual organizations'. How is it possible to make sense of this apparent chaos? It can be fairly observed that not only has the field lacked a thorough exploration of the linkages between structuring and SHRM but, in addition, there has also been a notable failure in conceptual and analytical thinking in keeping pace with, and helping to explain, these myriad experiments.

To assist the analysis in this and the ensuing chapter a conceptual framework can be suggested, which arises out of the juxtaposition of different dimensions which appear to have been critical in recent re-structuring attempts. These are shown in figures 11.1 and 11.2. For the purposes of locating the various types of re-structuring which have taken place within conventional organizational boundaries it is necessary to refer to figure 11.1.

Figure 11.1 uses three cross-cutting dimensions. On the top horizontal axis is the dimension of centralized to decentralized; on the vertical axis is the dimension from 'directive' to 'autonomous'; and on the horizontal axis at the base of the figure is the

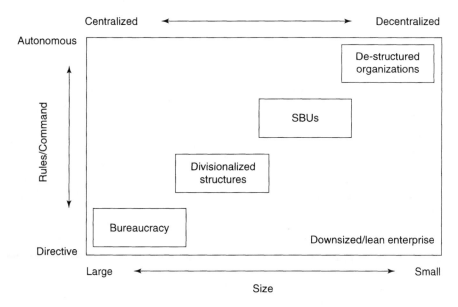

Figure 11.1 **Types of restructuring within organizational boundaries**

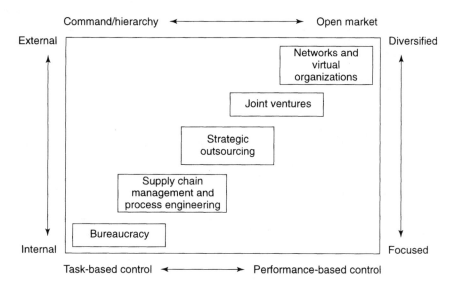

Figure 11.2 **A spectrum of relationship structures beyond conventional organizational boundaries**

dimension relating to size. For illustrative purposes, a selection of different organizational arrangements are shown. At the bottom left, the bureaucratic form is located to suggest a centralized, directive mode. Ascending the ladder and moving to the right, one progressively moves to divisionalized arrangements, to the use of strategic business units (SBUs) and then to autonomous, empowered teams.

So far, we have referred to forms of re-structuring which have occurred within the confines of conventional organizational boundaries. But many of the recent experiments have transgressed and even broken free of these boundaries. These types of re-structuring are located on a separate figure (see figure 11.2). This uses four dimensions. The first, running along the top of the figure, illustrates the spectrum from internal hierarchical command relations at one end, to open market relations at the other. The second dimension, located at the bottom of the figure depicts the contrast between task-based control and performance based control. The third dimension is located on the left-hand side vertical axis and it shows the spectrum from internal relationships to external. And the fourth, on the right-hand side of the figure contrasts diversified forms with more focused forms.

Using these cross-cutting dimensions it is possible to reveal a patterned ordering in the variety of organizational types which have proliferated in recent years. Thus, for example, starting at the bottom left of the figure, the bureaucratic form of organization can be seen as characterized by an emphasis on internal relationships, a hierarchical command structure and a mainly task-based set of control criteria. Progressing up the ladder, supply chain management and process engineering, strategic outsourcing, joint ventures, and networks are shown to represent, and result from, varying degrees of shift along each of the dimensions.

Other types of initiatives in re-structuring can also be located on such a frame-work. For example, the experiments with the idea of the 'internal market' in the British National Health Service where previous hierarchical arrangements were displaced by purchaser and supplier relations, can be located part way along the bottom and right of this figure.

These frameworks are useful in mapping the conceptual possibilities. It is also hoped that they help clarify where the many and varied forms 'locate', when considered in relation to each other and in relation to certain key dimensions. The figures do not suggest that any type of form is 'better' than another; they are not prescriptive. Nor do these figures suggest any historical 'progression'. In order to assess 'appropriateness' and to interpret possible 'trends' it is necessary to examine more closely the various design principles. This is what we will do when we have reviewed the different types of structure shown in the figures. In this chapter we focus on the various re-structuring methods that have been attempted within organizational boundaries (as shown in figure 11.1). In the next chapter we turn to examine the re-structurings which extend beyond conventional organizational boundaries (as shown in figure 11.2).

Bureaucracy

The contours of 'bureaucracy' (from the French word 'bureau', broadly translatable as 'rule by office') were drawn and analysed by Max Weber, around the end of the nineteenth century and the early years of the twentieth century. He was interested in describing and assessing the historic shifts in Europe from traditional authority regimes to the (then) new principles of formal rationality rather than in prescribing paths to 'efficiency' per se. While there is considerable doubt about whether Weber himself was endorsing the model, there were plenty of others who did (and who also assumed that Weber did too). At the same time, while many (particularly American scholars of complex organizations) have used the term in a positive, prescriptive sense, the popular everyday usage has been of a contrary nature – i.e. bureaucracy has a pejorative tone. In this usage it symbolizes unnecessary delay, red tape, ritual, and the stifling of individuality. However, the accelerated growth of large formal organizations throughout most of the twentieth century prompted social scientists to attempt a more dispassionate analysis of its characteristics and consequences (for example, Crozier 1964).

The key attributes of bureaucracy in the descriptive, social science, sense can be summarized as follows:

1 A clear division of work with stipulated boundaries to responsibilities; officials are given authority to carry out their assigned functions.
2 Referral by role occupants to formal (written) rules and procedures which ensure predictability and routinization of decisions.
3 A well-defined hierarchy of authority.
4 Appointment to posts arranged not through patronage or bribery but on the basis of technical competence.
5 A system of rules with formal (written) documentation of actions and decisions.

The model in its totality gave rise to impersonality – this was one of its intended characteristics. It had the advantage of overcoming nepotism, favouritism and arbitrary decision making. The principles seemed well suited to the administrative needs of the new democratic states and the emerging large industrial enterprises. This apparatus of legal rule stands in contrast to that which operated under patrimonial rule where custom, personal recruitment and obligation were the governing principles. In place of arrangements whereby posts could be appropriated and reward could derive from the revenue of the office, the typical alternative under bureaucracy is to reward the official by monthly salary based on a full time position and then by a pension following a lifetime career.

Three sets of 'unanticipated consequences' and 'dysfunctions' of bureaucracy have been pointed out by various organizational analysts (March and Simon 1958; Selznick 1949; [. . .] Merton 1957). The first derives from the emphasis on control. This can prompt rigidity of behaviour and defensive routines. The second focuses on the implications for the behaviour of subunits. Division of task and responsibility can elevate departmental goals above whole system goals – that is, lead to suboptimizing behaviour. And thirdly, as a result of the impersonality of rules the minimal acceptable standards can become transformed into targets and behavioural norms. Rules and procedures can also become ends in themselves.

[. . .]

Bureaucracy in perspective

However, despite this catalogue of problems and dysfunctions it has been frequently pointed out (for example, Robbins 1990) that throughout the world the largest organizations are essentially still bureaucracies. They remain so despite the competing ideas because they meet their goals through this type of structure. In the light of this it is evident that the phenomenon of bureaucracy cannot be easily dismissed or written off. On the contrary it demands close attention. Despite the chronicling of problems and dysfunctions, and despite the oft-heralded death of bureaucracy, this form of organization has proved to be remarkably resilient. Inroads have undoubtedly been made: delayering has sometimes reduced the number of hierarchical levels, flexible job designs have replaced narrow job specifications, teamwork has displaced clear individual accountability, empowerment has substituted lengthy specifications of formal rules. And yet, in the face of these numerous experiments, initiatives and change programmes, big and small, many of the features of the classic bureaucratic form reassert themselves and await treatment by the next initiative. One reason for this resilience may be the inherent 'stickiness' and inertia in organizations. Another possibility could be that bureaucracy actually carries certain advantages and therefore, even when assailed, organizational members find reason enough to reinstall or at least defend its existence.

One important strand in the drive against bureaucracy has been the ideological shift which urged the primacy of the market. This logic led to extensive deregulation and the consequent pressure on large organizations which had previously enjoyed oligopolistic conditions. It also manifested itself in the pressure to depart drastically from internal transactions and management in favour of actual or near-market 'contracts'. This type of market-based contractual relationship inevitably removed the need, the cause, and the opportunity to persist with each of the characteristic elements of bureaucracy described above. An associated development has been the relative decline of internal labour markets as the basis for managing employees be they managers or non-managers. In turn, the consequence of this shift from internal labour market techniques to an increasing reliance on external labour market methods has been a shift in the nature of human resource management methods deemed to be appropriate under these new circumstances. Thus, career planning and career management may not be required for large numbers of staff. Direct supervision, induction, training and development, socialization, appraisal, and even reward problems can potentially all be avoided by the primary contracting organization.

[. . .]

Downsizing and lean production

Faced with rapidly changing environments many employers have responded by downsizing and in the process have also retreated from long term commitments to employees, which the internal labour market model allowed and facilitated. Kodak, IBM and General Motors are examples of the kind of large blue-chip corporations which formerly exemplified the bureaucratic model but which, in restructuring, have dismantled many of the elements of that model. In the United States it is estimated that over one million middle managers lost their jobs as organizations flattened organizational structures. The strategy of many companies over the past few years has been to reduce their size; 'take costs out of the business'; increase productivity by having fewer people undertake the same or even more work; and re-focus activity on the core business. Senior executives were rewarded for so doing: share prices tended to rise when these steps were taken and top management salaries increased. Table 11.1 shows some of the key changes in organizational size.

[T]he broad trend between 1979–1991 as shown in Table 11.1 reveals a significant increase in the share of employment accounted for by the smaller firms and a decrease in the share of employment accounted for by the larger ones. Thus, micro-businesses (with between 1–10 employees) increased their employment share from 20 per cent in 1979 to 28 per cent in 1991. Meanwhile, businesses in the 1,000 plus employment category

Table 11.1 Trends in organizational size measured by numbers of employees in the United Kingdom

	1979	1986	1991
1–2	7	11	11
3–10	13	17	17
11–19	8	6	6
20–99	12	14	16
100–499	18	17	17
500–999	8	7	6
1000+	35	29	27
Totals per cent	101	101	100

Source: Adapted from D. J. Storey (1994: 21).

experienced a decrease in their share – falling from 35 per cent in 1979 to 27 per cent in 1991. It would, however, be dangerous to extrapolate this trend into the future. More recent data from the Department of Trade and Industry (DTI 1997: 32) reveals that during the period 1995–96 the share of employment of all the size bands between 1–99 fell, while the size bands with more than 100 employees all increased their share of employment. Overall, the fact remains, however, that when compared with the bulk of the post-1945 period when employment policies were generally predicated on the assumption that the larger firm was the dominant model, recent years have seen a shift to an employment pattern in which small and medium sized environments have become far more important.

It has been suggested that when properly implemented the 'lean organization' concept should involve a phased journey from cutting back on non value-added activities and downsizing to a reformed stage where activities smoothly interconnect in a more efficient manner. However, Purcell and Hutchinson (1996) found that most organizations which embarked on this process remained at the first stage – i.e. simply downsizing rather than 'maturing' into a state that could allow proper use of just-in-time and total quality management (TQM).

[. . .]

The backlash was perhaps bound to occur. People have asked at what point does the downsizing and externalizing have to stop and what impact has there been on other corporate strategies such as TQM? Stephen Roach the 'downsizing guru' has reportedly 'recanted' and has argued that corporations have taken this strategy too far. How compatible is the numerical flexibility with teamwork? How will training and development occur? Where insecurity prevails, people may be less inclined to train others, and where people have been encouraged to behave as independent competitive operators they too may be less inclined to share knowledge, information and ways of working. This may all trigger a vicious circle: lack of trust by employer and worker, disallowing long term commitment and trust, and therefore promoting reliance on further externalization.

Devolved management: divisionalization and strategic business units

Perhaps the most obvious way to respond to the catalogue of problems associated with bureaucracy is to seek in one way or another to 'decentralize'. This is a well trodden path. Indeed, it seems to have occurred so frequently that one can only suspect that there is some cycle of decentralization and (re)centralization at play. Be that as it may, for the past 20 years or so the cycle would seem to have been very much on the downswing – that is, in favour of decentralized units. The tendency began with a wholesale switch to divisionalized structures, first in the United States and then more widely – especially in Britain. Later, by the 1980s, the mood swung further and 'strategic business units' became the fashion. Business units became pronounced in companies such as ABB and GE.

So far did this go, that as Hamel and Prahalad noted, 'In many companies, one cannot speak meaningfully of a "corporate strategy" because the corporate strategy is little more than the aggregation of the independent strategies of stand alone business units. Where the corporate role has been largely devolved, corporate officers have no particular responsibilities other than investor relations, acquisitions and disposals, and resource allocation across independent business units' (Hamel and Prahalad 1994: 288). Naturally, there are drawbacks to this arrangement – synergies and the advantages of the big company are lost. Opportunities remain unexploited and the potential to use core competencies across units is undermined. Hamel and Prahalad argue that senior managers should 'seek to identify and exploit the interlinkages across units that could potentially add value to the corporation as a whole' (1994: 289). Aspiring to this however is one thing, achieving it is another. It will require special measures to ensure that corporate effort, rather than business unit goal achievement, is rewarded.

Meanwhile, delayering has continued, at least in some companies. General Electric, a company with over 200,000 employees, has delayered and now has businesses with as few as three or four layers of management between front line workers and the chief executive. A corollary of such delayering is often the devolution of more HR responsibility to lower levels of line management.

Research by Hall and Torrington (1998) on the issue of 'devolving' HR to line managers suggests that unless line managers also secure the incentive of budgetary responsibility for HR interventions, then the realization of the aspiration will remain problematic. On the other hand, if line managers do get this responsibility there is the danger that they will manage human resources with short-term priorities and that the achievement of strategic HRM will be even further away. 'It is paradoxical that devolution has been seen as part of a move to enable personnel practitioners to play a greater strategic role and yet the logical consequence of devolution is to make the implementation of the strategy extremely difficult' (1998: 52).

'De-structured' organizations

By this term we mean to cover the collection of types of structural innovations variously described as high performance organizations, knowledge creating companies, empowered teams, ad hoc, boundaryless, and process-based organizations – among other similar terms. Despite the range of titles, the underlying ideas are similar: they point to a departure from traditional bureaucratic forms with their formal rules, hierarchy of office and vertical communication, and circumscribed role responsibilities and celebrate instead the breaking down of internal barriers and formal structures. The new watchwords are teams (preferably cross-functional), lateral communications, the minimization (if not outright removal) of hierarchy, and the sparse use of rules. Informality and the exploitation of expertise, wherever it may lie in the corporation, is the essential idea. With some variance in emphasis, the same basic tenets can be found underpinning the so-called 'high performance work systems' and the 'knowledge creating companies'.

Ashkenas *et al.* (1995) title their influential book, *The Boundaryless Organization* and sub-title it *Breaking the Chains of Organizational Structure*. This book presages a new order for organizations as they shift from rigid to permeable organizational structures and processes. For example, Motorola is reported to have 'taken years out of its new product development cycle by replacing its traditional functional processes with fully accountable cross-functional teams composed of engineers, marketers, manufacturing experts, financial analysts and others (1995: 2). According to Ashkenas *et al.* the 'emerging organization' of the twenty-first century will act differently. Specifically, 'behaviour patterns that are highly conditioned by boundaries between levels, functions, and other constructs will be replaced by patterns of free movement across those same boundaries. No longer will organizations use boundaries to separate people, tasks, processes and places; instead, they will focus on how to permeate those boundaries – to move ideas, information, decisions, talent, rewards and actions where they are most needed' (1995: 2–3). This amounts to a 'paradigm shift' towards boundaryless structures.

Even these authors accept however that some boundaries are necessary. Boundaries help to give focus. They do not want to imply, they maintain, a total free-for-all. Rather, the permeability of boundaries will increase. Information, resources, ideas and energy must pass through the 'membranes'. The analogy is the living organism. They claim that already 'almost all organizations have experimented with some type of change process aimed at creating more permeable boundaries' (1995: 5). Sometimes this is impelled as a result of a crisis: for example at General Motors, IBM, Sony, Volkswagen, Lloyds of London, Citicorp and many others. These once great and seemingly unassailable institutions did not 'stumble' because of lack of planning, lack of investment or lack of technology. (General Motors probably invested more in automation than any other company in the world while IBM research investment was above the industry norm.) The general explanation was that they were faced with a rate of change that was beyond their capacity to respond. This is because they found, too late, that they lacked the flexibility and agility; their structures were too rigid.

The lessons here are said to point to a new paradigm. The organizational attributes which formerly conferred advantage can, under the new conditions, constitute disabling impediments. In summary form the contrast can be depicted in the two lists below.

Old Success Factors
- size
- role clarity
- specialization
- control

New Success Factors
- speed
- flexibility
- integration
- innovation

Source: Askenas *et al.* 1995: 7

A rather similar narrative is presented by proponents of the idea of the 'knowledge-based' company. For example, according to Nonaka and Takeuchi (1995), the source of corporate success under contemporary conditions resides in the ability of a company to create new knowledge, disseminate it throughout the organization, and embody it in new services and products. Japanese companies such as Canon, Matsushita, NEC, Kao and Sharp have been identified as special in their use of knowledge management to create new markets and develop many new products.

As with Ashkenas *et al.*, Nonaka and Takeuchi contend that the knowledge creating company is 'not a machine but a living organism'. Its competitive edge comes not so much from processing objective information, as from tapping the tacit and highly subjective insights of large numbers of employees. It draws out their insights, hunches and intuitions. The foundation stone for this type of company is one which is resonant with the fundamentals of HRM: 'The key to the process is personal commitment, the employees' sense of identity with the enterprise and its mission'. The managerial role in this new type of structure is far distant from the command and control activity of old. It is in many respects the antithesis of bureaucracy and of the classical administrative principles. The manager's role is also very different: managers need to project ideals as much as ideas; they need to articulate a vision of where the organization ought to be; they need to handle images and symbols. There are other diametric departures from classical principles. The value of a person's contribution is determined not by their location in the hierarchy but by the significance of the information which he or she provides to the knowledge creating system.

The knowledge creating company does not only entail shifts in managerial roles. The rest of the structure needs to alter too. Everyone has, to some extent, become a knowledge worker. Personal knowledge needs to become available to others – this indeed becomes a central activity of the knowledge creating company. Here Nonaka refers to the idea of a spiral of knowledge – essentially from tacit to explicit and as this is disseminated and internalized by employees, to further growth in tacit knowledge and so on. To convert tacit knowledge into explicit knowledge requires finding a way to express notions that are not amenable to conventional, explicit, clearly-defined instructions. On the contrary, it requires the use of figurative language, metaphors, analogy and symbols. These can permit project teams and others to grasp something intuitively and then to find their own interpretations of what it could mean in practice for new products and technologies.

A further organizational characteristic is what Nonaka refers to as the 'principle of redundancy.' This is manifested in the sharing of overlapping information across different activities in order to enable them to find their own implications. It is expressed also in the way Canon organizes its product development using competing groups which develop different approaches to the same product idea and then debate the relative advantages and disadvantages. Yet another device is strategic rotation of managers and other personnel across different functions, products, and technologies. The intent is to make the organization's vast repository of knowledge more fluid, rather than see it locked up in distinct units. At Kao, reports Nonaka, all employees are expected to hold at least three different jobs in any ten year period. A further device to exploit 'redundancy' is the free access to company information. This allows different interpretations to emerge of the new knowledge.

So much for the range of structural types and the restructuring examples. Having gained some appreciation of these the next step is to reflect more fully on the dimensions which are amenable to design and also the kind of factors which govern the exercise of choice in one direction rather than another.

MAKING CHOICES ABOUT ORGANIZATIONAL STRUCTURE

This final section of the chapter examines the basis on which choices are made about organizational structuring. By the same token, we seek explanations for the different forms. As we have seen, there are numerous structural forms which are in co-existence. Moreover, development can move in opposite directions: for example, there can be centralization and decentralization, mergers and demergers can occur, companies can acquire and divest. Why do these things occur? What principles, if any, are brought to bear?

'Structure' sounds rather static. It might be thought that senior managers would only contemplate a change in structure if and when they were faced with a crisis. Yet in many cases organizations must continually (and do) rethink and redesign structure in order to achieve their strategic goals. Competitive conditions are changing at an accelerated rate and organizations need to make appropriate responses, or even more ideally be one of the drivers of these wider changes. Companies such as IBM, ICI, Unilever, have all recently reorganized in order to achieve new objectives. Redesigning organizational structure is one of the ways (arguably one of the more strategic and far-reaching) in which managers can intervene in order to mobilize behaviour to attain desired goals. 'Structure' then might be seen as not only a pattern of relationships between roles and sub-units and as a means of co-ordination but may also be regarded as a framework for planning, organizing, directing and controlling.

In simple terms it can be said that while strategy describes *what* to do organizing defines *how* to do it. The constituent elements of organizational structure include the set of formal tasks assigned to individuals and departments; formal reporting relationships, including lines of authority, decision responsibility, number of hierarchical levels, and span of managers' control; and the design of systems to ensure effective co-ordination of employees across departments. However, the factors influencing choice are many and varied. As we will see the emergence of particular structures may not always be explained so easily, as if it were the exercise of 'choice' in the sense of a free, calculated rational weighing of alternatives.

First, we can note the factors which could be said to constitute 'rational' considerations. These include the desire to hold individuals and sub-units accountable for the use of resources and the achievement of targets. Lines of reporting and the use of job descriptions are the kind of devices used for this purpose. Another criterion is usually to ensure the flow of communication. Senior managers will usually want structures which enable a clear and direct flow of communication from top to bottom and possibly may also want to facilitate upward communication as well. Yet while wanting to issue instructions which are received and understood and be able to hold named individuals as accountable, senior managers will also usually not want the structures they create to stifle all sense of initiative and motivation. Hence, many instances of organizational design will include some measure of autonomy in order to elicit these desired behaviours and attitudes. In the possibly more sophisticated companies structures may also be adjusted in order to facilitate learning and the building of future organizational capability. Thus, for example, boundary-breaking or at least boundary-spanning measures such as cross-functional and cross-unit teams may be established so that parts of the organization can learn from other parts.

Second, it has to be realized that particular structural forms can also arise for reasons other than the technical reasons suggested above. Top managers may judge it safest simply to follow the 'industry recipe' – i.e. the normal pattern for their sector. In a similar vein, some changes in structure may come about because of prevailing fashion. Sometimes this fashion is further fuelled by the work of management consultants and gurus. Thus there are waves of 'merger mania'; periods when downsizing is the norm and is expected of incoming chief executives. Then there are political reasons why structural changes may take place. Powerful 'barons' who head-up important territories or who are responsible for particular products may need to be appeased and to that end organizational design may be moulded around that need. Power struggles can occur between SBUs which seek to use optimal supply chain rationalities, and divisions which have assets to protect, such as sales or capital investment or jobs.

Third, various contingent factors such as technology have been argued as exerting an influence on organizational structure. Rarely, if ever, is this a determining factor, but the scale required in technological investment, in say an oil refinery, is likely to have some influence on the nature of the organization which is formed in order to exploit those technological assets profitably. In recent years new technologies have begun to influence organizational structures and to a large extent, open them up: the mobile phone, PCs, lap top computers, modems and networked databases. Such technology has allowed tele-working and home-working for some. For those remaining in offices the causal influence of the technology-structure link has often been reversed: i.e. the new demands for project teams has prompted a reshaping of office technology. Open plan office space, removal or reduction in hierarchical space standards and the private 'ownership' of space has declined in favour of 'temporarily occupied' space.

Similarly, in a global marketplace, the need to 'act local' (be responsive to local conditions) and yet take advantage of the benefits of a transnational organizational resource is also likely to influence organizational structure. Organizational 'size' as a possible contingent factor has long been a topic of contention. One would expect that, other things being equal, larger organizations would have more complex and formal structures. None the less, even size is not a determining factor: some large organizations have managed to create informal arrangements while some smaller organizations have created more formal systems. In part, the variations are related to different contingencies faced in different industries. For example, in pharmaceutical industries, regulatory requirements ensure that 'good manufacturing practices' are followed and this in turn impels a certain measure of routine, formal procedure, accountability and record keeping. Also, in retail banking the duplication of routine activities in multiple small and dispersed locations tends to produce broadly similar structures across each of the main clearing banks.

In practice, managers are usually faced with a need to balance a series of diverse and sometimes conflicting considerations. Centrally, there is a need for balance between *differentiation* and *integration*. Formal organizations are notable for the way in which they divide-up tasks and responsibilities (differentiation) and yet also require some mechanisms for co-ordinating and controlling in order to pull these separate activities together (integration). Also, structures need to ensure some congruence between policies and priorities. If, for example, the organization is seeking to foster 'high commitment' this is unlikely to be attained by a tight command and control structure or with structures which limit discretion and autonomy [. . .]

A classic dilemma is between structuring on the basis of management function or on the basis of products (see figure 11.3). Under the former, each function such as production, marketing, finance, and sales has its own hierarchy. It is particularly favoured by small and medium sized enterprises. The emphasis is upon technical quality and cost control. On the positive side it is the least complex of structures; it allows economies of scale; enables in depth skill development, achievement of functional goals and clear accountability. On the negative side it is slow to respond to environmental change, is poor at encouraging horizontal co-ordination and communication and is not conducive to innovation. It also tends to encourage a restricted view of organizational overall goals. Product-based structures are more likely to be found in large organizations and in environments of moderate to high uncertainty. They are more able to respond to unstable environments, and the units should be better able also to tailor themselves to clients' needs. On the other hand, such structures tend to involve some duplication of resources, they fail to fully exploit economies of scale in functional departments and, if fully deployed in a pure form may sacrifice in-depth technical competence.

		Structure	
		Mechanistic	Organic
Environment	(Unstable)	Poor fit ✗	Good fit ✓
	(Stable)	Good fit ✓	Poor fit ✗

Figure 11.3 Fitting structure to environment

Matrix structures are supposed to allow some balance between these types. They should allow a focus on both economies of scale and product development, permit a balance between the demands of customer focus and functional specialization; and should be suited to complex decision situations. The weaknesses of matrix structures are that participants experience dual authority and this can lead to frustration and confusion. There is usually a higher degree of political behaviour with time-consuming and frequent meetings. Decision making may be slow with large coalitions entering the fray. It has been suggested that to help ameliorate these conditions one dimension of the matrix should normally take the lead and that senior management levels should be staffed with persons with collaborative styles and a high tolerance for uncertainty and ambiguity (Johnson and Scholes 1993).

Another factor shaping the way in which 'choices' are made about structure is the prevailing set of images which key actors hold about the nature of organizations. We have noted above how both Ashkenas and Nonaka were keen to cast aside the idea of organizations as machines in favour of organizations as living 'organisms'. The power of such images has been explored in some depth by Morgan (1986). He extends the range of ideas or 'metaphors' we tend to hold in our attempts to make sense of organizations. The importance of these images is that they frame and shape not only the way managers think about organizations but also, in consequence, the options perceived as available for redesign. New design possibilities emerge he suggests if conventional thought patterns are broken. For example: given the globalization of business, the increase in international travel, the spread of the multinational and even transnational enterprise and, not least, the international exposure of major consultants and gurus, it might be expected that organizational structures in different countries will become increasingly alike. This argument, the so-called 'convergence thesis', has been advanced by many commentators – most notably by Bartlett and Ghoshall (1992), Humes (1993) and Ulrich and Lake (1990). However, important differences in structural forms have been found to persist between different countries.

CONCLUSIONS AND SUMMARY

In this chapter we have examined the importance of organization structure and explored a number of the main types of structure. These types were located on an analytical framework using the three cross-cutting dimensions of centralized/decentralized; large/small; and autonomous/directive. Using this framework four main types of structures were identified and discussed: bureaucracy, divisionalized structures, strategic business units, and 'de-structured' forms. The characteristic features of the main types and their human resource management aspects were explored.

The chapter then moved on to a closer examination of the kind of factors which senior managers might bear in mind when making decisions about structuring and re-structuring. At the same time, we drew attention to the fact that organization structures were often emergent phenomena and that rational, technically-based weighing of alternative forms and their relative merits were often not the source of the structures which exist. Accordingly, various contingencies were identified and the influence of industry trends and organizational politics were also brought into the explanation.

This chapter has focused primarily on aspects of structuring which take place within the confines of conventional organizational boundaries. However, as we noted in the course of the chapter there are also instances of important re-structuring initiatives which cut across organizational boundaries. [. . .]

NOTE

* This chapter has been adapted from, Mabey, C., Salaman, G. and Storey, J. (1998) *Human Resource Management*, Oxford: Blackwell.

REFERENCES

Ashkenas, R., Ulrich, D., Jick, T., and Kerr, S. (1995) *The Boundaryless Organization: Breaking the chains of organizational structure.* San Francisco, CA: Jossey-Bass.

Bartlett, C. and Ghoshall, S. (1992) *Managing Across Borders: the transnational corporation.* Cambridge, MA: Harvard Business School Press.

Crozier, M. (1964) *The Bureaucratic Phenomenon*, London: Tavistock.

Edwards, R. C. (1979) *Contested Terrain: The transformation of the workplace in the twentieth century*, London: Heinemann.

Hall, L. and Torrington, D. (1998) 'Letting go or holding on – the devolution of operational personnel activities', *Human Resource Management Journal*, vol. 8, no. 1, 41–55.

Hamel, G. and Prahalad, C. K. (1994) *Competing for the Future.* Boston, MA: Harvard Business School Press.

Humes, S. (1993) *Managing the Multinational: Confronting the global–local dilemma*, Hemel Hempstead: Prentice-Hall.

Johnson, G. and Scholes, K. (1993) *Exploring Corporate Strategy*, Hemel Hempstead: Prentice-Hall.

Kanter, R. M. (1991) 'Transcending businesses boundaries: 12,000 world managers view change', *Harvard Business Review*, vol. 63, no. 3, 151–64.

March, J. G. and Simon, H. A. (1958) *Organizations*, New York: Wiley.

Merton, R. (1957) *Social Theory and Social Structure*, Chicago, IL: Free Press.

Morgan, G. (1986) *Images of Organizations*, London: Sage.

Nonaka, I. and Takeuchi, H. (1995) *The Knowledge Creating Company*, Oxford: Oxford University Press.

Purcell, J. and Hutchinson, S. (1996) 'Lean and mean?' *People Management*, vol. 10, October 1996.

Robbins, S. J. (1990) *Organization Theory*, New Jersey: Prentice-Hall.

Selznick, P. (1949) *TVA and the Grass Roots*. Berkeley, CA: University of California Press.

Semler, R. (1994) *Maverick!* London: Arrow.

Storey, D. J. (1994) *Understanding the Small Business Sector*, London: Routledge.

Ulrich, D. and Lake, D. (1990) *Organizational Capability: Competing from the Inside-Out*, New York: John Wiley.

Weber, M. (1947) *The Theory of Social and Economic Organization*, New York: Oxford University Press.

12

BEYOND ORGANIZATIONAL STRUCTURE: THE END OF CLASSICAL FORMS?*

Christopher Mabey, Graeme Salaman and John Storey

[. . .]

INTRODUCTION

[. . .]In this chapter we [. . .] examine those forms of organizational restructuring which cross organizational boundaries as conventionally understood. In recent years there would seem to have been a quite remarkable degree of interest in forming new sorts of structures which reach out to engage associates, partners and even competitors in the wider marketplace. These new arrangements have taken various forms but most prominent seem to have been joint ventures, strategic alliances, networks and outsourcing arrangements. Mirroring these developments have been those writings which reflect upon the 'breaking' of organizational boundaries (see for example, Quinn 1992; and Ashkenas *et al.* 1995).

The focus in conventional organizational analysis was overwhelmingly upon internal organizational structures. Organizations were seen as systems with fairly distinct boundaries. However, increasingly, attention is being paid to the connections made across organizational boundaries. Alliances, federations and networks are seen as increasingly important. Information and communication technologies carry the capacity to transcend organizational boundaries and allow work to be done in new ways on a distributed basis. The past identity of an organization, resting as it did on a physical place and associated perhaps with distinct products, is becoming less important and even less valid.

Much of the work on the extra-organizational forms has been undertaken by economists. The human resource dimensions of these developments have been very much under-explored. It is intended that this chapter should help to illuminate this hitherto under-developed agenda. We will identify the human resource management dimensions of each major structural initiative as we proceed through each section; then, in the final section, we address the implications for the *strategic* potential in HRM presented by these structural developments.

AN ANALYTICAL FRAMEWORK

Part of the problem to date has been the lack of an adequate conceptual mapping of the myriad developments. In this chapter we will use the framework [. . .] reproduced below (see figure 12.1). It should be emphasized that the main purpose of figure 12.1 is to locate the diverse initiatives on a conceptual map. Hence, the various forms which are creating so much new interest are located in reference to four key dimensions. They indicate a progression towards increasing externalization of relations; to diversified activities; to performance based control; and to an open-market mode of regulation (see the dimensions on all four sides of figure 12.1). Although many observers would, and many indeed do, assert a definite *trend* in the direction of the top-right of the figure, the evidence does not entirely point in one direction. Moreover, a historically-informed perspective on organizational studies would caution that apparent 'trends' are often more like 'cycles'. In this chapter we reserve judgement therefore on this point. As we will report in the body of the chapter, there are some instances where decisions are being made which indicate that at least some companies are re-internalizing rather than externalizing. None the less, for the past few years it would be fair to say that the general thrust (possibly as much expressed in sentiment and aspiration as in concrete action) has been in the direction away from the conventional bureaucratic mode in the bottom-left and more towards the various forms in the upper-right direction.

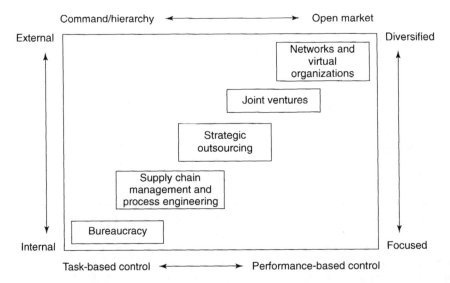

Figure 12.1 A spectrum of relationship structures beyond conventional organizational boundaries

We will start at the bottom left of figure 12.1 and work up the ladder to the top-right. The phenomenon of bureaucracy was discussed in the previous chapter and it is not necessary to revisit it here. It is, however, useful to place it in the figure as a compass point. In this chapter we begin the analysis therefore with the second step – supply chain management and process re-engineering.

SUPPLY CHAIN MANAGEMENT AND PROCESS RE-ENGINEERING

A radical innovation in the way in which companies regard their structural arrangements has been the rise in popularity of the idea of dismissing function and products as structural principles in favour of a rigorous focus on supply chains and processes. A supply chain and process analysis can extend through, and beyond, organizational boundaries. The starting point is an analysis of the value-adding activities. Following this an attempt is made to identify and eliminate the non value-adding components.

Such a zero-based analysis is claimed to be very far-reaching in its implications for organizational structures and human resource management. Thus, 'everything that has been learned in the twentieth century about enterprises applies only to task-oriented organizations, everything must be rethought' (Hammer and Champy 1992). In this statement the originators of the business process re-engineering concept make clear their radical intent. They prescribe and foresee nothing less than the total displacement of classical structures. The central idea of re-engineering is that in order to survive under the new competitive conditions, companies must re-orient themselves around their core processes – the start to finish sequence of activities which create customer value. The human resource management implications are extensive. Re-engineering, it is claimed, means the end of narrow jobs, the end of supervisory management, of traditional career paths and much more. Above all, it represents an outright challenge to practically all of the classical principles of organization developed throughout the twentieth century and as described in the preceding chapter.

Many commentators have reacted to these dramatic claims with the counter-charge that it is really nothing more than a managerial 'fad'. They see it as an example of successful marketing by clever consultants and gurus. It may, however, be something rather more substantial. Arguably it represents a critical response to fundamental changes in the nature of competition and changes in information technology. Supply chain and process re-engineering, in this view, is one of the more crucial and revealing reactions to these historic changes in the wider environment of business. The label itself may indeed become less fashionable but the underlying ideas are, none the less, likely to be sustained – albeit in some repackaged form. Accordingly, it is worth examining the central ideas and propositions of Business Process Re-engineering (BPR) as illustrative of contemporary concerns about organizational structuring.

We can describe the key elements of process re-engineering as expressed by the most notable original exponents: Hammer and Champy (1992), Hammer (1996) and Davenport (1993). These expositions of re-engineering struck a resounding chord with managers in many countries. The triggers for it are increasing affluence, more discriminating consumers, competition from the Far East, and developments in information technology which have generated the capability for firms to meet the market challenges in more flexible and sophisticated ways. Davenport (1993) in fact subtitles his book 'Reengineering Work through Information Technology'.

Thomas Davenport, was a consultant with Ernst & Young. In his book *Process Innovation* he writes:

> In the face of intense competition and other business pressures on large organizations in the 1990s, quality initiatives and continuous, incremental process improvement, though still essential, will no longer be sufficient. Objectives of 5% or 10% improvement in all business processes each year must give way to efforts to achieve 50%, 100% or even higher improvement levels in a few key processes. Today, firms must seek not fractional, but multiplicative levels of improvement – 10x rather 10%. Such radical levels of change require powerful new tools that will facilitate the fundamental redesign of work.

(Davenport 1993: 1)

How are these things to be done? Process innovation combines the adoption of a process view of the business with the 'application of innovation' to the key processes. The objectives are drastic cost reductions, and major improvements in quality, flexibility and service levels.

The key elements of process innovations are said to be:

- a 'fresh start', 'blank sheet' review.
- a process rather than functional view of the whole organization.
- cross-functional solutions.
- step change.
- the exploitation of information technology.
- attention to work activities on and off the shop floor.
- adoption of a customer's view of the organization/producing value for customers.
- processes must have owners.

Hammer (1996) in *Beyond Reengineering* explains how the 'process-centred organization' differs from traditional functional structures. The origins are traced to the late 1980s when a few advanced companies such as Ford, Taco Bell and Texas Instruments began programmes of business improvements which differed in kind from the usual run of the mill variety. They engaged in radical changes and redesigned their processes from a clean sheet of paper basis. The changes which they initiated have allegedly 'transformed American industry beyond recognition' (1996: xi). By bringing processes centre stage, re-engineering rendered redundant the accumulated wisdom of a hundred years of management thought.
    [. . .]
The take-up of re-engineering world-wide has been very extensive. In Britain, for example, it has been reported that a remarkable 70 per cent of large organizations have embarked on what their own managers say was a BPR programme. In America the transition to process-centred organizations began slowly in the early 1990s with organizations such as Xerox and Texas Instruments, but in a short time the trickle became 'a flood': Ingersoll-Rand, Shell, Levi Strauss, Ford, GTE, Chrysler 'are all concentrating on their processes' (1996: 8).

The will to undertake radical departures stemmed from the immensity of the problems faced by the traditional corporations. GTE, the telecommunications company, found that its customer service unit was able to resolve customer problems on first call in less than 2 per cent of occasions; Pepsi found that 44 per cent of invoices it sent to retailers contained errors; Texas Instruments discovered that its Semiconductor Group took 180 days to meet an order for an integrated circuit which a competitor could complete in just 30 days; Aetna Life & Casualty took 28 days to process an application for homeowners insurance of which only 26 minutes were real productive time. Radical remedies were required and achieved, and the key was a switch in focus from task improvement to a focus on process.

But what is a 'process' and how does it differ from a task? A task is said to be 'a unit of work, a business activity normally performed by one person. A process, in contrast, is a related group of tasks that together create a result of value to the customer' (Davenport 1993: 5). A process, [. . .] is 'a structured, measured set of activities designed to produce a specified output for a particular customer or market. It implies a strong emphasis on *how* work is done within an organization, in contrast to a product focus's emphasis on *what* . . . a process is thus a specific ordering of work activities across time and place with a beginning, an end, and clearly identified inputs and outputs: a structure for action' (1993: 5).

Most companies, even large ones, are said to be able, if they try, to reduce their generic processes to less than 20 – for example Xerox has 14, Dow Chemicals has nine. These major processes include product development, customer order fulfilment and financial asset management. Business organizations for the past two hundred years have been based on tasks and the basic building block of organizational structures has been functional departments constituted by similar tasks.

Human resource management considerations

Under these circumstances the first human resource management task is to ensure that everyone in the organization and across its wider reaches is aware of these processes. Shifting from a traditional mode of operating to a process-based one is no easy task. Employees fear that a process re-engineering initiative means job losses and extensive change. They are usually correct on both counts. Even years after the introduction of such a change employees may harbour resentment and blame the consultancy firm that was used. The implications for future commitment-winning measures can be problematical. Second, HR needs to help in the changing of mind-sets and behaviours which are required under such a radically different organizational form. One such crucial change is the abandonment of the task specialization we discussed in the previous chapter as a hallmark of bureaucracy.

In a process organization, workers engaged in operating a machine will need to see themselves, maintains Davenport, as there not merely to run the machine but to contribute to the 'order fulfilment process'. Hence, if production-flow backs-up, these operatives will be expected to investigate and then seek to resolve the problem. Such behaviour will simply be part of the new job. Indeed, language is so important to process re-engineering, say the gurus, that 'worker' should really be replaced by the term 'process performer'.

An additional step from an HRM point of view is that process measures are important in order to track performance and for planning improvements. This is allied to process management which entails a continual focus on process improvement and process redesign. A process centred organization entails and requires 'a fundamental reconceptualisation of what organisations are all about. It permeates every aspect of the business: how people see themselves and their jobs, how they are assessed and paid, what managers do and the definition and hence strategy and positioning of the business' (Hammer 1996).

New roles are required. 'Process performer' roles have already been noted; in addition, there is a need for 'process leaders', 'process owners' and 'process managers' whose jobs are to engage in process design and redesign, coaching and advocacy. This last means it is the process owner's job to obtain the necessary financial and other resources to meet the process needs; and to occupy a seat on the 'process council' (which is a forum of process owners and heads of remaining support services to discuss the business as a whole). Such a body is seen as necessary to avoid functional silos being replaced by 'process tunnels' or process protectorates.

This kind of process focus implies jobs that are much enlarged: jobs which require understanding, insight, autonomy, responsibility and decision making. Supervision is not supposed to be required. Hammer (1996) talks bluntly about 'the end of the organisation chart'. There are no departments or departmental managers, and very little hierarchy. Significant instead are 'centres of excellence'. These are to be thought of as in-house versions of professional associations. They are supposed to enable skill formation and continual development. In addition, they are intended to provide channels of communication which enable the sharing of knowledge and expertise. Because there are no managers, the best performers in a process organization do not become diverted into watching over others; they are freed-up to do what they do best. Corporations he says must adjust their reward systems accordingly. The old deal (or psychological contract) was based on obedience, loyalty and diligence in exchange for long-term security. The new deal exchanges initiative for opportunity.

These new entities are not only more co-operative internally, they are also inclined to be co-operatively interactive with external organizations too. Internal and external walls are broken down. Partnership here is not driven by goodwill as such but rather by 'enlightened self interest. The goal is not to change the way companies feel about their trading partners but the way they interact with them. Better interaction may well serve to modify feelings as a later consequence of mutual benefit received. But the tangible things, the underlying hard systems of operations, must be changed first' (1996: 173). It goes beyond outsourcing; it entails a co-operative endeavour where the partners excel together or sink together. Compartmentalism ultimately is not even possible at the level of the firm.

A more fundamental concern is that the model is based on a unitary view of the firm. In a telling section Hammer criticizes those corporate heads who so readily nowadays mouth the mantra of the primacy of 'shareholder value'. This is not what business enterprises are about he maintains, rather they are there for 'customer value'. While his main justification for this is couched in terms of the lack of guidance afforded by the former and the comparative clarity of needed behaviours under the latter, the underlying issue is never properly addressed: how does the worker/process performer come to identify so strongly with this enterprise? While it may be the case that a customer focus could be more persuasive than a sole concentration of shareholder value, it hardly seems sufficient to sweep away centuries of labour – employer conflict.

The role of coach, Hammer suggests, is critical for the organization's success.'No matter how well designed a process is, it's the people who make it work' (1996: 117). And so in one sentence we arrive at the heart of the matter. The process alone cannot deliver. 'In the long run the quality of an organisation's coaching is a key determinant of whether it succeeds or fails. Process design alone is not enough. As more companies learn how to create state of the art processes, the advantage will belong to those with an institutionalised capacity for staffing these processes with well-selected and well-trained people' (1996: 118). In the end it all comes down to the skill of the coach to train and to readjust mind-sets so that process performers are willing to focus on 'customer value'. And thus it is that some rather deep-seated issues and conflicts are conjured away in the mysteries of the learning organization, the persuasive power of the coach and the unitary intent of the team.

STRATEGIC OUTSOURCING

'Outsourcing' refers to the situation when a company subcontracts to another supplier work that it was previously performing in-house. Strictly speaking, therefore, it does not denote all forms of purchasing from suppliers, though the distinction between being a former producer of the service or product and simply being a purchaser is in practice very blurred. Essentially, however, outsourcing entails the externalizing of production and services. It is a manifestation of the classic 'make or buy' decision. The phenomenon has, as yet, generally found little recognition in the human resource management textbooks. In recent times it has been one of the more popular ways to cut costs and to refocus on core competencies. One graphic sign of the trend was that by the mid-1990s the labour agency Manpower Inc. had displaced General Motors as the largest employer in the United States. And a study of businesses and government agencies in the US showed that 44 per cent of the executives surveyed said they are doing more outsourcing than they did five years ago and 47 per cent said they expect to increase the amount of work they outsource in the future (Kelly 1995). Likewise, IT-related outsourcing revenues are estimated to be growing at 14.4 per cent annually (Bruno 1995).

In practice, there are many different types of outsourcing activity and usage. Some of the instances are piecemeal and opportunistic with little strategic character. Office cleaning is an example in most circumstances. The commissioning client has low vulnerability in relation to this kind of service, and likewise the contribution to competitive advantage is not likely to be high. But for other services the outsourcing decision might arise from a very close analysis of the value chain and this can permit strategic use of outsourcing. An example would be the link between certain Marks & Spencer suppliers where the reliable level of quality provides competitive advantage, and where the service is at the high end of the vulnerability scale. Determining just what is core can, however, be problematical. For example, Nike outsources all of its manufacturing; Apple Computers outsources 70 per cent of its components; while GM has outsourced its car-body painting activities.

The reasons for the growth of outsourcing are many. In a complex, fast-moving market it is a speedy way to gain access to specialist services. Alternatively, it can be a means to reduce costs by sourcing from low-cost producers, many of whom are likely to be non-unionized. In this regard, advances in information and communication technologies have played a part in that companies headquartered in high-wage cosmopolitan areas can outsource routine billing etc. to remote stations almost anywhere in the world.

Problems of scrap can be drastically reduced or even eliminated as defective components can simply be rejected. Outsourcing also enables flexibility in that supply can be more readily turned on or off – at least in theory. In some instances it is merely, however, a device to respond to pressures of 'headcount control' – i.e. a means, on paper at least, to show that the critical measure of direct employee numbers is being kept under control. But, according to the more cutting-edge theories of 'winning' companies, the outsourcing phenomenon is, above all, a manifestation of enterprises clearing-out peripheral distracting activities, in order to focus on core functions and core competencies. Quinn (1992) argues that companies should concentrate on those 'core competencies' (these, he says are usually intellectual or service activities) in which they can be best in the world. The other activities should be outsourced.

Human resource management considerations

In addition to the commonly outsourced services such as catering, security, IT services and the like, various HR functions can themselves be outsourced. To date, the most popular candidates have been training, retirement planning, outplacement services, relocation, counselling and various forms of consultancy. American Express, for example, has out-sourced its retirement plan and benefits system. IBM created a spin-off company called Workforce Solutions in 1992. It outsourced its own HR staff functions to this company and Workforce Solutions can sell its services also to other customers.

There are consequences for organizational structures and human resource management, though it seems likely that the full consequences have not as yet been fully grasped or even researched. Organizational hierarchies are much flatter, there is reduced scope for inter-functional activity and therefore a lower need for co-ordination. The priority management task becomes not the handling of physical and capital assets but the management of intellectual processes and the management of staff who are not direct employees of the company. Negotiation of contracts with the providers becomes critical. There are issues of confidentiality, risk sharing, continual improvement and so on. Even where there are clear opt-out clauses for non-compliance the management of the actual occurrences may prove difficult.

A critical strategic human resource management issue is the potential loss of expertise in certain areas which may be difficult to recover. There is a danger of a serious 'hollowing-out' of the organization. The modern tenets of organizational learning, corporate culture and shared visions may all be put in some jeopardy if this occurs. Likewise, the sources of innovation needed in order to keep pace with rapidly changing markets may be put in jeopardy if a company is heavily reliant on strictly delineated services from a host of outside suppliers. Arranging the wherewithal to forestall this problem is an important HR challenge under conditions of extensive outsourcing.

The HR function could potentially assume a key role when outsourcing occurs. In fact HR departments reportedly already play a role in some 65 per cent of all company outsourcing cases in the United States (up from about 35 per cent in the past five years). So while the search and selection team ideally involves a top executive, the respective department manager and a legal expert, human resources often plays a critical role as facilitators and co-ordinators of the entire process. 'It is a natural role for human resource professionals to play because of their communication and administrative expertise' (Sunoo and Laab 1994: 70). A recent study of six UK building societies found, however, that five of them did not even have a formal policy towards outsourcing, only the Derbyshire had such a policy which enabled it to make plans for the identification and protection of core competencies (Jennings 1996).

Part of the human resource management function is to attract and retain people who have the appropriate skill sets required under the new conditions. A series of decisions to buy rather than to make, taken individually, may make economic sense, but collectively they may undermine the ability of a firm to compete. Using research conducted in North America, Europe and Asia, Bettis (1992) describes and illustrates how inappropriate outsourcing is promoting the continuing decline of many western firms. He extends the argument on a larger scale to the industry and country level.

While not all contracted staff are in the vulnerable, low-pay category, there has been some widening of inequalities as the remaining few permanent staff enjoy higher earnings, fringe benefits and better access to skill acquisition. This presents a further challenge to the maintenance of an organization which is low on formal control structures but is supposed to score high on shared values.

Drucker (1993) argues that companies will eventually outsource all functions that do not have a career ladder up to senior management. He contends that corporations, once built to last like pyramids, will be more 'like tents'. In this new world, managers he maintains, must take responsibility for their own career development by exploring their own competencies and making good competency deficiencies. Moreover, he suggests that information will replace authority as the executive's primary tool.

JOINT VENTURES, MERGERS AND ALLIANCES

Joint ventures and strategic alliances have become a common feature of the US business horizon. In the UK also, joint ventures and alliances have been very popular. For example, BT alone has more than 70 joint ventures and overseas distribution arrangements. Some pharmaceutical companies form as many as 20 to 30 new alliances per annum.

Through joint ventures, organizations are able to achieve a number of objectives. Large companies using their marketing expertise and systems can bring new products developed by smaller companies to market rather faster than a small company acting alone. For example, the joint venture between Hoechst and Schering to acquire a majority stake in Plant Genetic Systems, a small genetic research enterprise. Additionally, large companies may seek a joint venture in order to gain a foothold in new product areas and to acquire new expertise rapidly. This has been the case with large agrochemical companies which have allied with small- and medium-sized biotechnology companies. A third reason for joint ventures is to enable the partners to reduce their cost base by pooling resources. Companies have often cut their staffing levels and reduced their distribution costs. A fourth factor is that certain developing countries such as India and China may disallow inward investment which is not tied to some form of joint venture with a domestic concern. Salomon Brothers, the American investment bank, and Dresdner Bank of Germany, have both entered into joint ventures with Chinese financial companies as a result. Likewise, Royal Dutch/Shell invested in a power-generation plant in India in a joint venture with Essar Group, an Indian industrial company.

Despite these attractions and the frequency of occurrence, failure is high. In the United States approximately half of all alliances forged in the early 1990s were considered failures. In Europe too, a high failure rate of companies involved in international joint ventures has been noted (Harper 1995). One of the most frequently-cited causes of such failures has been that the organizational and HRM issues were not adequately addressed.

Human resource management considerations

The human resource management aspects have usually been neglected by companies embarking on new alliances and joint ventures. There are, however, a few exceptions. Merck, for example, in the US, has a high reputation for the way it uses the HR role in managing joint ventures. Numerous joint ventures, both national and international in character have been entered into by Merck and in each case the HR staff have been involved from the outset. Staffing solutions are devised, procedures and policies drawn up. Communication and education are given an especially high priority in order to ensure that the partners not only understand each other but can learn from each other. The overall HRM challenge involves blending corporate cultures, compensation schemes and overcoming staffing problems.

A variant on the joint venture is an arrangement whereby companies enter into co-operative arrangements to invest in and share common services – such as a local training facility. In a more formal way this is exemplified by the Shared Service Centre (SSC) established for the BBC by a joint-venture company formed by Coopers & Lybrand and EDS, the US systems group. A 10-year contract has been signed under which staff will eventually work for the joint-venture company – but on BBC premises. The shared service centre has allowed the finance function the opportunity to offer career development to two quite different groups of staff. 'High quality finance staff are not going to spend a lifetime pushing debits and credits. We want to build skills in the value-added areas,' claimed the Finance Director. In time other companies may use the SSC as it effectively becomes an outsourcing centre. For the present time it is located inside the BBC. Shared service arrangements have also been launched by General Electric, Seagram, Bristol Myers Squib and Whirlpool. Essentially an SSC does all those tasks that do not need to be kept close to the heart of a business. Placing an order with a supplier is a decision that must be taken at the centre – but the payment of the bill and recording of the transaction can be done at the SSC.

Meanwhile, the staff working on processing transactions find themselves in a larger single organization with greater career opportunities. There has also been a need to put in place management structures to ensure the main customer/contractor is able to keep a measure of strategic control. [. . .]

NETWORKS AND VIRTUAL ORGANIZATIONS

An organization such as Benetton is characterized by its organized network of market relations based on complex forms of contracting. It operates a retail system based entirely on franchising. On the other hand, its sourcing for garments is based on a putting-out system which has a long history. Nowadays, information and communication technology allows the total complex system to operate with rapid feedback system enabling it to operate with the absolute minimum of stock. In this system it is the wider network rather than the organization which is the interesting unit of analysis – indeed arguably Benetton, as such, is not an 'organization' at all in the conventional sense (Clegg 1990). Organizations such as Coca Cola and Visa, despite their strong world-wide presence, are likewise not traditional organizations. [. . .] It is very hard to pin down the 'ownership' of these forms as some of them have no fixed assets. Some commentators maintain that they really are 'virtual organizations'.

A 'network organization' has been defined as an economic entity that operates through a cluster of compact business units, driven by the market, with few levels of decision making and a willingness to outsource whatever can be better done elsewhere (Snow 1992). It can be expected that new management functions will be needed – for example, brokers, architects, lead-operators, and caretakers.

This free-flow across organizational boundaries can reach a stage when the organization per se becomes undefinable and unrecognizable – what Davidow and Malone (1992) have described as the 'virtual organization'. [. . .]

Human resource management considerations

The underlying logic of network organizations as presented by their advocates and practitioners is that 'know-how' and resource capability are now critical factors, and these are increasingly difficult to locate within the boundaries of a single organization. Know-how and capability are increasingly distributed across a network of different business and contractors. But if this is so, the human resource management challenge to identify, retain, develop and appropriate such scarce resources are immense.

Part of the know-how resides in the identification of the parties and the capability to bring them together. In 'the boundaryless organization' there are huge uncertainties about who, if anyone, is managing these processes. External boundaries are barriers between firms and the outside world, including customers and suppliers, but also government agencies, special interest groups and the community at large. In traditional organizations there are clear demarcation lines separating 'insiders' from 'outsiders'. Role expectations were relatively clear. Management dealt with the former group and had mechanisms and techniques to help them do this. But these traditional methods are of doubtful validity in the network situation.

Under the network arrangement, there are contracts of a more commercial nature. Equally, there are connecting lines based on repeat business, trust and reputation. Mind-sets and attitudes have to change considerably. Traditional methods of negotiation, competition, win-lose, information withholding, power plays and the like, may cause difficulties.

Increasingly, boundary maintenance behaviour is seen as having dysfunctional consequences. When the boundaries are dissolved or drastically reduced, customers and suppliers may be treated as joint partners. Employees, as such, may be hard to identify. A range of parties may be expected to help the firm solve problems and to innovate. Effective network organizations need to make permeable the external boundaries that divide them from their customers and suppliers. The key concept here is that of the value chain. This is the set of linkages which create services and products of value to the end user. In the traditional view each company is supposed to maximize its own success with disregard for that of others. The overriding idea is that of competition. Under the new value chain concept the idea is to loosen external boundaries so as to create a win–win situation across the whole value chain.

Under the network concept co-operative relations between organizations are given high priority. As the cost of innovation increases, as complexity increases and everything changes so much faster, many companies have come to the conclusion that they simply cannot work alone. Business partners, customers and suppliers are urged to work together to co-produce value. This entails reconfiguring roles and relationships. The use of co-operative arrangements of a network kind has long been well developed in Japan. The *keitsu* consists of cross-locking companies often straddling very different sectors. They have shares in each others' equity but there is no governing holding company.

The successful value chain companies co-operate in both strategic and operational business planning. Network organizations require managers and staff to change their assumptions and behaviours. Instead of developing plans and strategies independently, planning needs to be co-ordinated and even shared with other participants in the network. Information therefore must not be hoarded and protected, but shared to allow joint problem solving. Moreover, measurement and auditing systems need to be co-ordinated.

Organizational members therefore need to adjust their mind-sets so that the well-being of the whole value chain is kept in mind and enhanced. For example, GE Appliances collaborated with key suppliers. Together they can plan for and respond more quickly to changes in the production schedules. Production, inventory, sales, specification and scheduling data can be co-ordinated. A monthly data package is shared with 25 main suppliers. An organization may be considered well linked into its value chain if it scores high on a set of measures of joint development in marketing plans, product development planning, production and inventory planning, distribution planning and information systems planning. And for the management of resources and capabilities the indicators would be shared resources as opposed to separate resources in the areas of technical expertise, financial expertise, management skills, information systems and training, and development.

How and why does a company become a core organization in a network's value chain? The main identifying feature of a core organization is that it 'manages the network' – a role that is not, however, legally recognized. The actual process of managing such a network is a difficult one and it requires skills for which, as yet, little or no formal training is usually offered. Boyle (1993) examines the role of the core as a user organization, as the provider and/or user of goods and services, and as the link organization. He sees the possibility of the role of the core organization changing over time as exemplified by Esso's shift away from being a petrol station franchiser to becoming a link organization by moving into forecourt convenience stores.

It is argued that the capacity to command and co-ordinate service activities, supplier networks and contract relations has become an important strategic weapon and scale economy for many successful enterprises (Quinn 1990). Because the role of service technology in providing added value is becoming predominant, strategies are increasingly being built around core service skills, rather than products. Examples of success achieved by such 'integrated' companies, according to Quinn, include Toys 'R' Us, Apple Computer and Honda.

According to these and other proponents of networks, the human resource management implications include the involvement of as many employees as possible so that they become familiar with customer and supplier needs. This can be done through inviting customers and suppliers to meetings where outlines of plans, goals and problems can be explained; by sending employees on customer and supplier field trips to encounter the detailed operations of day-to-day work; collecting and collating customer and supplier information. An additional stage can involve experiments with collaboration through, for example, organizing cross-value-chain task forces and sharing technical services. And a more ambitious step involves companies integrating their information systems and reconfiguring roles and responsibilities in the light of the collaboration achieved across the networks.

The immensity of these challenges has led some corporate chiefs to revert to old-fashioned command and control solutions. Thus, Lord Weinstock's successor at GEC has said that he wants to move away from 'the joint venture culture' and towards direct investment and control by GEC managers. In the late 1980s and early 1990s, partnership with rivals and others had been one of the central pillars of GEC's strategy. Now, it appears, this strategy is being largely abandoned in favour of attempts by the group to build global businesses on its own. Likewise BA's chief executive has said he expects to employ as many people in the future as he does now. And Microsoft's business might seem more suited to virtual operation, yet it has 20,000 employees focused on developing its own software products. [. . .]

IMPLICATIONS FOR STRATEGIC HUMAN RESOURCE MANAGEMENT

The host of structural developments reviewed in this chapter, such as strategic outsourcing and joint ventures, have sometimes been argued as offering a major opportunity for human resource management to raise its strategic profile. This case rests partly on the observation that the many failures in initiatives of this kind have been traced to the shortcomings in human resource management and therefore this presents a strategic opportunity. It also rests in part on the point that many of the challenges thrown up by such initiatives put a premium on strategic thinking about human resource issues.

There is, however, an altogether different case that can be made: this suggests that these structural developments are highly inimical to a strategic approach to human resource management and that they rather express and impel the short-term financial denominator management approach in place of the sustained, numerator approaches extolled, for example, by Hamel and Prahalad.

There are a number of reasons why these developments might impede a firm's strategic potential. Outsourcing and other moves to market-based contractual arrangements are likely to reduce the investment by the organization in long-term skill formation activities. This is likely to apply as much to management development as it is to employee development and training more generally. There are still uncertainties about the possible loss of intellectual capital when extensive outsourcing occurs. An organization which contracts for services other than peripheral matters such as cleaning, catering and security may, even though it initially gains a cheaper and perhaps more specialized service in the short-term, lose the capability to undertake an activity close to its core.

This set of reservations is of course not an argument for simply retaining the large bureaucracy and its internal labour market solutions. What seems to be required is a new type of strategic management within the context of the new form of 'boundaryless' or extended 'organization'.

CONCLUSIONS AND SUMMARY

This chapter has traced the extent to which the traditional model of organizational structuring has come under attack. A proliferation of new organizational forms has signalled a revolution in the management of organizations. The old organizational model was also associated with particular sets of human resource practices. But the relationship between the two does not translate into a simple mapping of one onto the other. The bureaucratic structure was associated on the one hand with command and control, hierarchy and rigid job boundaries – all things which in large measure the human resource management movement was trying to overturn. Classical organization principles and Tayloristic job design with high division of labour and low trust were diametrically opposite to the high commitment intent of HRM. And yet, on the other hand the bureaucratic form and HRM can be interpreted as sitting together rather well. In so far as the large bureaucracies such as British Telecom and the major clearing banks offered life-time employment, career ladders, extensive training and development, career planning, above average pay and benefits and other appurtenances of the internal labour market, the correspondence between many of the features of HRM and this organizational type was rather propitious. Indeed, it was when some organizations began to dismantle the internal labour market model and abandoned lifetime careers, made large numbers redundant, cut back on training and development and outsourced or subcontracted significant parts of their activities that the real threat to HRM became rather clearer.

Thus it can be seen that classic bureaucracies harbour a *dual potential*. They can emphasize the rigid rules, multiple hierarchical levels and impede horizontal communication along with a command and control approach to worker management. Or, they may emphasize the psychological contract of security for long-term commitment and loyalty along with an infrastructure of training and development and corporate identity. In so far as the classic form has not been entirely abandoned these dualities remain.

But, as we have seen in this chapter, there have also been many very significant departures from this classic form. The alternatives have been numerous. Descriptions and prescriptions of these have proliferated. And, to a large extent, the alternatives are still unfolding. No one has a firm fix on the emergent form. Various key attributes have been championed: prominent front runners have been the process-oriented company, the network, joint-ventures and strategic alliances, the boundary-less organization and the virtual organization. We have argued in this chapter that there are some significant overlaps in these conceptualizations. For example, Ashkenas *et al.*'s (1995) concept of 'boundarylessness' both within and between enterprises shares very many features with Davidow and Malone's (1992) 'virtual organisation'. Likewise, Nonaka and Takeuchi's (1995) description and proselytizing of the features of 'the knowledge creating company' shares a great deal in common with Senge (1990) on 'the learning organisation', Quinn (1992) on 'the intelligent enterprise', and even Hamel and Prahalad (1994) on the vital strategic importance of building core competencies.

Thus, similarities and overlaps abound. Each management consultant and would-be guru is seeking to crystallize a complex set of developments into a central idea which can be made appealing, be packaged and sold. The variations around certain underlying themes should not therefore be too surprising. This is not to say, however, that the whole set can simply be dismissed as manipulated 'fads'. The numerous accounts of the nature of 'the new organization' are capturing, albeit it in a selective and partial way, critical features of important trends in organizational (re)-formation. They detect, record and chronicle initiatives in a select group of leading-edge firms. This knowledge they formalize into frameworks and concepts. They go on to project the beginning of a new trend based on their limited data. And beyond that they prescribe these frameworks and devise audit tools which indicate the gap between where client organizations currently are, and where they 'need' to go. The new forms are finally packaged into practical step-by-step action points to help managerial clients enact the new organizational form. But behind all this, and in a sense clouded by all of the prescriptive packages, are certainly the signs of actual change. Corporate restructuring has been the norm in large organizations at least.

But, as we have seen, there is no inevitability about the drive to more and more outsourcing or to the creation of virtual organizations. GEC, BA, Microsoft and Benetton have all shown signs of bucking the trend. Benetton, with 6,000 direct employees, has recently made a massive investment in one of the most advanced manufacturing complexes in the world. The processes which it does outsource tend to be those which do not suit centralized textile production – a practice of very long standing.

Moreover, there are significant variations in the use of these new forms across different countries. For example, despite the availability of the same telecommunications technology the use of teleworking in Japan is only one-quarter of its use in the UK. Similarly, according to a study conducted by the Centre for Economic Performance at the LSE, there are marked differences in the degree to which German and British companies have undertaken restructuring. Downsizing and delayering has been far more prominent in the UK than in Germany. Over the past ten years over three-quarters of British companies have reversed their diversification; in contrast German companies have been reluctant to pursue refocusing strategies. Joint-ventures and strategic alliances though have been a common feature strongly favoured by 47 per cent of companies in both countries.

The nature and character of these changes are, however, still somewhat uncertain. We may doubt whether they are in fact expressive of any single trend. At least two very different tendencies can be detected. On the one hand, there are indeed some instances of firms restructuring in a manner which allows them to locate and exploit knowledge and intellect far more effectively than in the past and to utilize it as a strategic resource. But on the other hand, a great deal of the restructuring which has taken place has been more to do with simple cost-cutting and the externalizing of costs and risks. In the latter instances, it might even be said that far from being 'new' developments in organizational structuring they reflect the outsourcing patterns of nineteenth-century capitalism (Edwards 1979; Littler 1982).

It seems likely that neither of these 'models' will entirely capture the future. Market segmentation will continue to find reflection in markedly different organizational forms. Nor are they perhaps quite so starkly opposite as they are usually depicted. Even 'knowledge-centred' organizations are likely to want to externalize as many costs and risks as possible. Thus, it would be too simplistic to categorize the two 'new' forms as 'good' or 'bad'. Consultants selling their favoured packages have a clear interest in so doing, but a more objective analysis suggests that the emerging organizational forms are not to be quite so easily pigeon-holed in value terms. None the less, there will continue to be different emphases and mixes of positives and negatives. Some organizational forms will be more attractive than others. Hence, awareness-raising of the range of possibilities and of the ways to achieve the more enlightened outcomes are worthwhile missions for the organizational analyst.

Key points

- There are numerous indications that very significant departures have been made from the classical bureaucratic form. New organizational structures have been the clearest manifest sign of radical change in human resource and business strategies.
- Despite the proliferation of labels such as cluster organizations, network organizations, knowledge-centred organizations, and the like, there are many common elements in the various models which have been advanced. The underlying ideas and principles which have been most frequently catalogued as expressive of the New Organization include the stress on responsiveness, speed and flexibility; the primacy of knowledge, intellectual capital and hence learning; and the boundary-breaking character of these new forms – including vertical barriers, internal horizontal barriers between functions, and external horizontal barriers between the 'organization' and suppliers and customers.
- While developments of these kinds are invariably described in highly positive terms by the consultants and gurus, not all instances of the new flexible organizations can be quite so easily judged as good. In the real world, many of the initiatives to break down traditional bureaucracies have focused almost exclusively on cost-cutting of various kinds. These have included massive job cuts, outsourcing, and the creation of lean and mean organizations. Internal labour markets have been dismantled and replaced with part-time, casual and other contingent workers.
- The future of organizational structures is therefore likely to be characterized by multiple forms. It seems unlikely that bureaucracies will entirely disappear – indeed there may even be some reversal of outsourcing for example. Equally, the new network forms will vary between those trading on specialized knowledge and those trading on least cost deriving merely from near-nil commitment. The long-term sustainability of many of the enterprises in the latter category is open to question.

NOTE

* This chapter has been adapted from, Mabey, C., Salaman, G. and Storey, J. (1998) *Human Resource Management*, Oxford: Blackwell.

REFERENCES

Ashkenas, R., Ulrich, D., Jick, T., and Kerr, S. (1995) *The Boundaryless Organisation*, San Francisco, CA: Jossey-Bass.

Bettis, R. A. (1992) 'Outsourcing and industrial decline', *The Academy of Management Executive*, vol. 6, no. 1.

Boyle, E. (1993) 'Managing organizational networks', *Management Decision*, vol. 31, no. 7, 23.

Bruno, C. (1995) 'Outsourcing mania', *Network World*, vol. 12, no. 51, 1–42.

Clegg, S. R. (1990) *Modern Organisations: Organisation Studies in the Postmodern World*, London: Sage.

Davenport, T. (1993) *Process Innovation: Reengineering Work through Information Technology*, Boston, MA: Harvard Business School Press.

Davidow, W. H. and Malone, M. S. (1992) *The Virtual Corporation: Structuring and Revitalising the Corporation for the 21st Century*, New York: HarperCollins.

Drucker, P. (1993) 'The post-capitalist executive', *Harvard Business Review*, vol. 17, no. 3, May–June.

Edwards, R. (1979) *Contested Terrain: The Transformation of the Workplace in the Twentieth Century*, London: Heinemann.

Hamel, G. and Prahalad, P. K. (1994) *Competing for the Future*, Boston, MA: Harvard Business School Press.

Hammer, M. (1996) *Beyond Reengineering*, London: HarperCollins.

Hammer, M. and Champy, J. (1992) *Reengineering the Corporation*, London: HarperCollins.

Harper, J. (1995) 'Mergers, marriages and after: how can training help?' *Journal of European Industrial Training*, vol. 19, no. 1, 24–9.

Hendry, J. (1995) 'Culture, community and networks: the hidden cost of outsourcing', *European Management Journal*, vol. 13, no. 2.

Jennings, D. (1996) 'Outsourcing opportunities for financial services', *Long Range Planning*, vol. 29, no. 3, 393–8.

Kelly, B. (1995) 'Outsourcing marches on', *Journal of Business Strategy*, vol. 16, no. 4, 38–42.

Littler, C. R. (1982) *The Development of the Labour Process in Capitalist Societies*, London: Heinemann.

Nonaka, I. and Takeuchi, H. (1995) *The Knowledge Creating Company*, Oxford: Oxford University Press.

Quinn, J. B. (1990) 'Beyond products: Service-based strategy' *Harvard Business Review*, vol. 68, no. 2, 58–64.

—— (1992) *Intelligent Enterprise: A knowledge and Service Based Paradigm for Industry*, New York: The Free Press.

Senge, P. (1990) *The Fifth Discipline: The Art and Practice of the Learning Organisation*, London: Century Business.

Snow, C. C. (1992) 'Managing 21st century network organizations', *Organizational Strategy*, vol. 16, no. 4, 38–42.

Sunoo, B. P. and Laab, J. J. (1994) 'Winning strategies for outsourcing contracts', *Personnel Journal*, vol. 73, no. 3, 69–78.

13

HANDS, HEARTS AND MINDS: CHANGING WORK AND WORKERS AT THE END OF THE CENTURY*

Chris Warhurst and Paul Thompson

IMAGES OF CHANGE

Charles Handy (Handy 1995) has argued that we do not have 'hands' in today's organisations. The popular view is that organisations are opting, by choice or necessity, to engage with hearts and minds instead. It sits slightly oddly with a recent report on the fastest growing US occupations in the decade from 1994, which include home and health service aides, varieties of therapists, corrections officers and security guards. It seems that the future is care or constraint. Actually, there is a considerable amount of common ground among popular business and academic commentators about what the trends in work and workplace are. That commonality starts from a relabelling of the big picture. We are now living in a post-industrial, information or knowledge economy. [. . .]

The rise of the service sector and the decline of manufacturing is associated with a technological dynamism epitomised by announcements of the end of the *machine age* and the emergence of an *information age* (Hamel and Prahalad, 1996), within which work is no longer about the production of tangible goods but concerned with the centrality of knowledge and manipulation of symbols (Drucker, 1986). This abrupt, and dramatic, shift in the nature of the economy and work requires an equally categorical response from organisations in terms of their structures and practices. Success for organisations, Quah insists, rests not on 'having built the largest factory . . . or the longest assembly line . . . [but] on knowing how to locate and juxtapose critical pieces of information, how to organise understanding into forms that others will understand' (1997: 4).

Beneath the over-arching descriptions the engine of change is held to be driven by two interrelated transformations in the technical division of labour and the structure of the organisation. Like many commentators, Robert Reich argues that the workplace is no longer a pyramid or bureaucracy, but a 'web of enterprise'. Such webs have an internal and external dimension.

In terms of the overall structure, ownership and control, use of advanced information technology allows the firm's boundaries to become blurred, even to the point of the much-vaunted 'virtual organisation'; while its functions are increasingly disaggregated into complex mixtures of profit centres, franchises, small firms and subcontractors. As disaggregation is combined with downsizing and delayering, we will move, according to Charles Handy (1995), towards a 20–80 society with only a small core directly employed by the organisation. A growing number will become 'portfolio people' offering their skills to a collection of clients and customers, and leading flexilives between home and workplace. Reich echoes this when stating that few people in the 'high-value enterprise' will have steady jobs with fixed salaries (1993: 90).

Internally, the web will result in the replacement of hierarchies by networks. Put another way, the old vertical division of labour will be replaced by horizontal co-ordination. This is driven by the nature of knowledge work itself, which is essentially concerned with problem solving, problem identifying and strategic brokering between the two processes. The key employees of the information age will therefore be what Reich calls 'symbolic analysts' who trade globally in the manipulation of symbols, such as engineers, consultants and advertising executives. Such work is too complex, domain-specific and esoteric to be subject to vertical control. Instead, and facilitated by information technology, co-ordination can be based on collaboration between technical and professional groups who retain authority over their own work (Barley, 1996). Indeed, knowledge workers, working for their own interest rather than that of the company, are 'less inclined to think of themselves as loyal soldiers and more inclined to think of themselves as sought-after faculty members' (Hamel and Prahalad, 1996:238). With the diffusion of information and resources, and control of knowledge workers by managers illusory, the 'corporate campus' requires a form of management that is 'more collegial than supervisory shar[ing] information, delegat[ing] responsibility and encourag[ing] upward and horizontal communication' (Despres and Hiltrop, 1995:19).

Such horizontal co-ordination is replicated at lower levels through the increased use of teamworking to involve workers in problem solving and continuous improvement. Frenkel et al. (1995:786) note that, 'The trend away from routine work towards more creative, information and people-focused activity . . . leads management to cede more control over the work process to employees and requires management to ensure reciprocated trust.'

For such commentators, the implications for managers and workers are immense. Old-style command and control management is out, to be replaced by co-ordination based on managing ideas. Much of middle management can be eliminated because they were co-ordinating functions which have disappeared or processing knowledge which can be directly accessed. Once perceived as the indispensable functionaries of organisations; the standard bearers of rationality, technocratic efficiency and the embodiment of a corporate ideology that says managers know best, they are now no longer seen as the solution to organisational problems.

Within such reconfigured organisations the old tension between professional autonomy and bureaucratic control will diminish. Even at the bottom, empowered production and service employees will be 'working smarter not harder'. For those workers who can contract into the new workplace through their education, experiences and amenability, the workplace of the future offers new possibilities for creative expression, greater satisfaction, more security and enhanced personal growth (Osterman, 1991). Assets rather than liabilities, these employees can make 'major contributions of strategic and long-term importance' to their companies (Despres and Hiltrop, 1995:13).

Future knowledge workers of all kinds will be selected, rewarded and promoted according to competencies, values and individual performance rather than seniority, formal skill or rate-for-the-job. Stable career patterns will be a thing of the past. Rather than climb the reduced rungs of the organisational ladder, knowledge workers will hawk their skills around organisations, moving 'toward the centre of an occupational community rather than the pinnacle of an organisation' (Barley, 1996:47). In this respect, having a 'job' reverts to its etymological origin in that it once again refers to a task or piece of work rather than permanent employment.

Handy (1995:6–7) describes the outcome as 'fewer jobs for better people in the core', while admitting that 'there will be many casualties in the new dispersed organisations' among those who cannot add value. Such unfortunates will be pushed to the organisational and social margins. Recognition that all is not likely to be well in the garden is welcome, but how realistic is this overall picture of the 'new' workplace?

DON'T LET THE FACTS GET IN THE WAY OF A GOOD ARGUMENT

Optimistic predictions of the development of work and the workplace are nothing new, and claims of an emerging knowledge economy are in a tradition of proclamations of third waves, information societies and computopia. Certainly, occupational shifts have been and are taking place, with a long-term rise in non-manual employment (Routh, 1987). Within this trend, the creation of new tertiary occupations and the expansion of older ones, for example in financial services, medicine, education, leisure and technical services, is particularly notable. So is the growth of the retail sector. Britain may never have been a nation of shopkeepers, but the continued expansion of multiple stores is pushing employment in the retail distribution and service sector close to 4.5m, only just behind total manufacturing (*Labour Market Trends*, 1996).

However, official classifications of the occupational structure focus upon the form of jobs rather than the content of labour. If we examine lists of so-called knowledge workers – ranging from librarians to musicians, bankers, insurance workers (Handy, 1995: 4) – the sheer banality of the description links become clear. That workers are now more highly educated does not necessarily indicate a higher level of knowledge inherent in the jobs in which these people are employed. Kumar (1996) is right to suggest that the rise in credentialism results in a misleading appearance of the growth of more knowledgeable workers – a point further complicated by the growing tendency to relabel job titles so that travel agents become travel consultants, or plumbers become heating engineers.

This phenomenon seems widespread. The *OECD Jobs Study* (1994) notes that there are now a substantial number of workers and managers throughout the developed economies who are vastly over-qualified for their jobs. In addition, the survey shows that particularly in the US, an 'unbundling' process can be identified in which the jobs created are in no small part accounted for by manufacturing restructuring through subcontracting and outsourcing. Here again, the fragility of the accounting process that delineates industry and service sectors is highlighted. In analysing the decline of manufacturing and increase in service jobs, the study points out that 'temporary workers, classified as service workers, were hired by manufacturing firms who were trying to retain flexibility and cut costs. If these temporary workers working in manufacturing firms were counted as manufacturing workers, the loss of manufacturing jobs since 1991 would be cut by two-thirds' (157–9).

Of course there have been more serious attempts to capture the extent of skill change from survey data. Reporting on the ESRC's *Social Change and Economic Life Initiative*, Gallie argues that, 'the upward shift in the occupational structure did indeed reflect the expansion of higher skilled jobs, even when a different range of indicators of skill were used' (1991: 349). This may indeed be the case and it is surely time to move beyond the dominant 'optimists versus pessimists' scenario reproduced by Gallie. The expanded range of indicators moved beyond conventional categories, such as qualifications and training, to the question of whether individuals considered their current job to have had a significant increase or decrease in levels of skill and responsibility compared to five years ago. But it remains the case that such methods provide a very blunt instrument for telling us much about what is happening to different types of work, particularly when employees may be comparing their present job to a completely different one! With this in mind, we move to an examination of changes in the labour process of each major sector of waged work, engaging with key issues and debates along the way.

ROUTINE WORKERS – LOOK NO HANDS?

Despite Handy's 'no hands' scenario, the content of much contemporary work remains highly routinised. Despite his emphasis on the key role of symbolic analysts, this is recognised by Reich (1993), who estimates that repetitive and highly specified production and in-service jobs account for 55 per cent of the US economy. Statistics from the US Bureau of Labor Statistics show that those who could be classified as 'symbolic analysts', that is those who in some way manipulate symbols and ideas, comprise only seven per cent of current employment in the US (Henwood, 1996). Indeed, proponents of the knowledge economy fail to appreciate that most tertiary sector growth has occurred not in knowledge work but in the low-paid 'donkey work' of serving, guarding, cleaning, waiting and helping in the private health and care services, as well as hospitality industries.

We find that much of the 'knowledge' work, for example in financial services, requires little more of workers than information transfer. This includes the inputting of customer details on to pre-programmed screens and software, as Leidner (1993) shows in his examination of work in the insurance industry. Non-standard responses and requests are referred to supervisors or 'exceptions claims handlers'. Much of the growth in service work has been in the more explicitly 'interactive' categories such as telesales or call-centres. [. . .] For Ritzer, this is an extension of his McDonaldisation thesis. This version of the carefully calculated, simplified and predictable 'McJob' adds in the familiar Taylorist element of incorporation of workers' skills – this time verbal and interactive rather than manual – into a management 'technology': 'just as management has long "conceived" what employees are supposed to do, it now "conceives" what they are supposed to say and how they are supposed to say it, and in both action and interaction employees have little choice but to "execute" management's demands' (1997:11). While there have been some pretty silly applications of Ritzerian imagery – the 'McUniversity' springs immediately to mind – this argument has real force. Companies like to argue that it is the human element that now adds value to the provision of services. Hence the appearance of a 'quality' agenda in sectors such as hotels and hospitality. But there is a contradiction at the heart of the service encounter. The very uncertainty that inevitably accompanies the human element, in itself often provided by relatively unqualified labour, drives management to try and *standardise* the encounter as a means of ensuring 'quality' or at least consistency (Thompson *et al.*, 1996).

The routinisation of clerical and white-collar work has been a long-observed phenomenon. [. . .] Despite gleaming new buildings and open-plan offices, employees 'endlessly repeat familiar routines' around rigidly structured tasks and performance schedules. A manager in one of the organisations referred to clerical work as 'basically a production line process'. This corresponds with the view of an increasing number of commentators that service work is now characterised by an 'industrial logic' (Segal-Horn, 1993). But this carries an assumption that factory work has some traditional or immutable character. What if that 'logic' is different?

Changing the logic: innovation and its limits

It is not necessary to accept an epochal shift argument to recognise the increased competitive pressures on management to improve the quality and quantity of labour's input. This *has* led many companies to put into question aspects of the traditional Taylorist division between thinking and doing, as well as the rigidities characteristic of a Fordist production regime.

This argument has been around since the mid-1980s, if not earlier, but the practice did not necessarily match the rhetoric. For example, quality circles and employee involvement were characteristic of early stages of work transformation, but were not intrinsically built into a different technical division of labour. The introduction of teamworking in a context of an expanded array of lean production techniques, facilitates a much more substantial restructuring geared towards innovation and continuous improvement. This is not a return, or indeed advance, to craft or professional labour given that task structures largely remain unaltered. But the collective skill of the group requires an increased emphasis on cognitive and behavioural abilities geared towards multi-skilling, problem solving and decision making. [. . .]

So far, so (relatively) consensual, given that there are only a few diehards clinging to the view that nothing really has changed and that it is still just the same old capitalist labour process. But it is a curious feature of contemporary debate that the same developments can be interpreted to form entirely different views of the nature of the future workplace.

We have already seen the relatively optimistic account managerial commentators – ranging from advocates of HRM, to enthusiasts of lean production and the information age – have produced of the nature of modern work and organisations. It is surprising just how much their radical equivalents share that agenda, at least in terms of an acceptance of some kind of paradigm break, as well as shifts away from traditional forms of bureaucratic control and division of labour towards the high commitment workplace based on dispersed, delegated authority, combined with electronic or cultural controls.

With their accounts of captured subjectivity and labour trapped in totalising institutions combined with new, oppressive forms of regulation and surveillance through JIT, TQM and corporate culture, it is as if contemporary management theory has produced its own dystopian offspring. [. . .] As McKinlay and Taylor (1997:3) observe, such writers 'have inverted the euphoric rhetoric of HRM to produce gloomy analyses of emerging factory regimes in which workers lose even the awareness of their own exploitation'. They note the pervasive and particular influence of Foucault, and it is true that British universities at least are producing generations of graduate students who can spot a panopticon, a disciplinary practice or a power/knowledge discourse at fifty paces. While critical of (mis)interpretations of Foucault, McKinlay and Taylor's own empirical work on Phoneco's plant in Scotland appears to travel well down the dystopian path: 'It is difficult to overstate Phoneco's ambition in its attempt to go beyond the rhetorics of flexibility, commitment and quality: to achieve nothing less than the total colonisation of the EasterInch workforce' (1997:9). At the heart of the shopfloor strategy was the introduction of peer review, a form of 'mutual control' where employees accept responsibility for self-discipline and assessment of each other.

[. . .]

So, which is the 'factory of the future'? Or are they simply different lenses on the same thing? To answer this question it is necessary to start from a recognition of the need for forms of analysis that can capture the balance between continuity and change, convergence and variability. Take the issue of knowledge as an example. It is important not to lose sight of the elements of continuity. All workers are, of course, knowledgeable about their work – and always have been. At the turn of the twentieth century owner-managers were keenly aware of the knowledge workers possessed and how important that was to the development of their companies. As Jacques reveals in his sweeping historical account of management knowledge, it has long been management's job to make capital out of the originality of what labour knows and does. Indeed, 'It could be said indeed that the knowledge of workers was a key concern at this juncture in the development of industrial capitalism, providing the "constitutive problem" of capital–labour relations throughout the twentieth century' (1996:143). The knowledgeable worker is therefore not a post-industrial phenomenon but rather an integral part of the development of industrial capitalism. However, if throughout this century management has attempted to appropriate this knowledge or accommodated the residual knowledge of workers in the form of informal working practices, now management is keen to introduce organisational structures and practices which facilitate initiative in the form of creativity and learning.

With this in mind, it might be useful to jettison the overly-broad notion of *knowledge workers* in favour of a more realistic appreciation of the growth of *knowledgeability in work*. The managerial instruments to register and if possible capture employee knowledge have some innovative forms in teamworking and off-line problem-solving groups. But we should not lose sight of the role played by the development of traditional Taylorist techniques. Wright and Lund (1996) chart the introduction of new engineering standards systems – which they dub 'computerised Taylorism' – which result in real-time monitoring of highly variable work processes in Australian grocery distribution. As the ex-work study engineer, Oswald Jones (1997) demonstrates, more sophisticated forms of work measurement necessarily underpin a TQM-style regime, though workgroups are increasingly encouraged to contribute to job analysis. This kind of activity has been dubbed 'democratic Taylorism' by the more honest and critical advocates of lean production (Adler, 1993; Adler and Cole, 1995). The idea that Taylorism is itself innovative or can contribute to innovation should come as no surprise to any student of industrial history who has followed the earlier path-breaking work of the Gilbreths, Henry Gantt and many others. But the point is lost on those who present Scientific Management as a static, historically-bound system.

A recognition of continued variability in workplace trends is also important. The banal but simple truth is that there is no simple or universal direction. Look in detail at case study research across companies and countries and we find the usual suspects of mediation by institutional factors; notably national industrial relations systems and labour markets, as well as strategic choices by firms themselves. This should be obvious, but runs counter to the investment in high theory and epochal breaks by those whose job description is to draw the 'big picture', resulting in too many commentators continuing to insist on a coherent transformation package.

For example, whether one focuses on the technical, governance or normative dimensions of teamworking, research reveals that companies vary significantly in the extent to which their practices focus on or facilitate flexibility, normative attachments or delegated responsibilities. [. . .] In fact, the very same skill requirements in leaner production can lead to a preference for different labour inputs in particular countries or companies. With respect to the UK, readers will be unsurprised to know that there is evidence that British managers frequently choose to use the current state of the market and weakening of union strength to redefine their skill needs away from craft to semi-skilled labour (Thompson *et al.*, 1995). As Ackroyd and Proctor (1996:11) note, 'there is little evidence that the emasculation of traditional skills is being counter-acted by the emergence of new comprehensive systems of education and training to produce the "polvalent employee". What evidence there is of new forms of training points towards the use of cut-down 'on-the-job' company-based skill appraisal and training schemes.'

Agreements for workers to acquire more skills and knowledge are often circumscribed by management as Clark's (1995) detailed case study example of Pirelli Cables illustrates. A massive financial investment in Aberdare, South Wales, was intended to produce the 'all singing, all dancing' factory of the future with full task flexibility and worker autonomy. However, flexibility was within rather than across occupational groups and managerial action to cap the acquisition of 'skill modules' further constrained progress. Shop floor innovation is also constrained by continuing evidence that most managements simply do not trust their workforce. British companies are still less likely to initiate and implement progressive human resource policies than other European companies, according to academic sources such as the *Second Company Level Industrial Relations Survey* (Edwards *et al.*, 1996) and consultants (Ingersoll Engineers, 1996).

[. . .]

If much management remains *traditional*, it should also make us more wary of claims of radical departures in control technologies. Some organisations have invested in expanded means of monitoring and surveillance. But while digital smart cards that track employee movements on site and discreet video surveillance that allows managers and security personnel to remotely view workers make good publicity and lecture material, the 'electronic ball and chain' (as one trade union official put it), remains the exception (Lyon, 1994). Social scientists have a particular susceptibility to being dazzled by the potential of technological or other managerial devices without fully investigating how or even whether they are being utilised. There are indeed enhanced controls operating in the contemporary workplace, but they are more likely to be based on monitoring and evaluation through processes such as internal benchmarking, customer appraisal or financial targets.

Underneath all the rhetoric about new-wave management, the most important trend appears to be people working harder. Pressures on the effort bargain are, of course, a constant feature of market relations. But the combination of increased competitive pressures for cost reduction on private and public sector organisations, with expanded means for reducing and recording 'idle time', are leading to substantial work intensification, whether through reductions in manning levels and job demarcation, or other means (Elger, 1991; Nichols, 1991). The nature and effects of such intensification are consistent themes in the studies in this volume. But the hollow laugh received when mentioning the word 'empowerment' in most organisations is the true test that employees at many levels experience this 'great innovation' less as the opportunity to exercise extra discretion and more as the necessity to undertake more tasks. The extent to which people feel change fatigue and 'worn down' by increased expectations in downsized structures is registering firmly in popular consciousness. Even in Japan – *karoshi*, or death by overwork, has become a matter of policy debate (Kyotani, 1996). Actually, there is more consensus on this issue than might appear. Most managers would be far too embarassed by the evidence of their own eyes and ears to repeat the 'working smarter not harder' mantra. These days 'lean and mean' is an accepted, if regretted, part of the organisational landscape (Harrison, 1994).

Captured hearts or hardened arteries?

If minds are more engaged and bodies are tired, what about the third of our managerial objects – hearts? There can be no argument that many organisations have been trying to engender more commitment, no doubt influenced by the popular managerial nostrum that being competititive today requires more than instrumental compliance. What managers refer to as 'buying into the message', academics prefer to relabel the 'internalisation of values'. On one level this is the most controversial area of current change, both because issues of subjectivity are the most complex to theorise, and because of the strength of claims by corporate culture theorists and radical commentators alike the new regimes have succeeded in reshaping the affective domain.

This apparent success is, of course, heavily disputed (see particularly Thompson and Ackroyd, 1995). [. . .] There are two widely acknowledged aspects to this process. The first – that of emotional labour – has moved from the rather exotic illustrations of Hochschild's (1983) studies of airline attendants and debt collectors to mainstream studies of retail and service work in a variety of settings. As we observed earlier, the interactions between employees and customers are likely to be highly scripted, but the former are increasingly exhorted, indeed trained, to manage and mobilise their feelings in pursuit of higher quality and increased productivity. That may be linked to a wider process in which employees are encouraged to be 'enterprising subjects' – more self-reliant, risk-taking and responsible as part of a contemporary discourse of organisational and political change (du Gay, 1996 [. . .]).

The second aspect focuses on the extension of normative controls, this time not restricted to the service sector. Management is increasingly specifying an extended repertoire of attitudes and behaviour deemed appropriate to job performance. To use the example of teamworking again, once this range of expanded 'skills' needed to become a 'team player' has been identified – for example co-operativeness and positive attitudes – logic is likely to dictate that they seek some means of measuring and regulating them. Workers are often well aware that efforts are being made to 'change your personality' (McKinlay and Taylor, 1997; and see Marks *et al.*, 1997). Hence the concept of normative controls is rightly used to help understand new forms of appraisal and selection.

Controversy nevertheless remains concerning the salience and effectiveness of both aspects of the 'winning hearts' process. Here we side with the sceptics. The high profile examples are more topical than typical. After all, there are few companies with as ambitious an agenda of head-fixing as Phoneco. This is compounded when cultural engineering is elevated from an aspect of managerial activity into *the* driving force of workplace transformation, when new managerial discourses simply *displace* old corporate realities as the focus of attention.

It is too easy in this area to confuse managerial ambition with outcome. But even where it gets beyond the mission statement or other change texts, engaging with employees' feelings and values is likely to be the most fragile of all managerial activities. In part this is because many, perhaps most, employees do not buy very far into the message. Case studies reveal considerable scepticism about the 'new' managerial agenda. Jones notes of a TQM programme 'Hotpoint employees view these US-inspired changes with the cynicism of workers who recognise another management scam designed to ensure that they work harder' (1997:19). Even the most dystopian studies often reveal the rather more muddied realities when managerial schemes are filtered through employee attitudes and self-organisation. For instance the sting in McKinlay and Taylor's fascinating tale of Motorola is that the company with the grandest ambitions to 'govern the soul' found intense opposition to the disciplinary purposes of the system: 'Quietly and systematically peer review was dismantled by a combination of workforce resistance and tactical choices by a plant management under intense pressure for output' (1997:12). If we switch to a different reading of subjectivity, survey data, often generated by companies themselves about employee attitudes to change and change programmes, also tend to make for gloomy corporate reading (Coopey, 1995; Marks *et al.*, 1997). For example, in 1993 the results of the Royal Mail attitude survey indicated that 70 per cent of the employees were unhappy at work. 'Uncertainty' over privatisation, reorganisation of the service, new technology and worries over job security – all contribute to rock-bottom morale' (Summers, 1993:8).

Academics can debate from now until the end of time whether this scepticism and distancing is 'authentic' resistance, or whether, as the Daleks used to proclaim – 'resistance is futile'. But it seems clear that in terms of what management set out to do, employees often *dis*engage and treat expanded demands as a form of additional calculative performance. Of course, employees are often responding to the gap between managerial words and deeds rather than rejecting the aims of better service and enhanced competitiveness, as other case studies amply demonstrate (Rosenthal, Hill and Peccei, 1997). Mobilising subjectivity is consistently put under strain by internal and external tensions. For example, [. . .] employees frequently react adversely to being told to 'act natural' whilst being subject to the plethora of measuring and monitoring techniques to enforce compliance to standardised scripts or managerial controls. Equally, Flecker and Hofbauer illustrate how external demands on individuals generate 'superfluous subjectivity' which means that in managerial attempts to capitalise subjectivity, 'workers' orientations, aspirations and ingenuity are neither tailormade nor reserved' for organisational utility.

Subjectivity is a difficult subject matter to research with accuracy and sufficient complexity, and academics should always be careful about the strength of the claims they make (Thompson and Findlay, 1996). But we would make one cautious observation in reviewing these issues and debates. When management asks workers to be 'really' committed and emotionally engaged, it is likely to be asking for impossible outcomes from workers whose conditions of labour lack the necessary characteristics of autonomy and trust that would lead to making those 'investments'. This may well be different for employees further up the occupational ladder, to whom we now turn.

TECHNICAL AND PROFESSIONAL LABOUR

A reading of the popular and academic literature indicates that technical and professional workers are best placed to benefit from these changes to the workplace. Certainly these 'new professionals' who represent the archetypal symbolic analysts or knowledge workers, such as scientists, engineers and marketeers, have expanded massively as an occupational group in the recent period (*OECD Jobs Study*, 1994). They now form the largest occupational group in the UK and indicate the highest projected growth rates towards the end of the century in the US (McRae, 1996). Their labour, as with salaried managers before them in the old 'new middle class thesis', provides the creative entrepreneurialism that can best assure the accumulation of capital in the twenty-first century.

More concretely, these workers, with their superior qualifications, creative work content and operational autonomy are the typical pre-'information age' knowledge workers. Moreover, 'technicisation' – that is, an infusion of theoretical knowledge into previously tacit knowledge-only jobs – would further indicate that the nature of work for service and production workers is changing as abstract thinking and theorisation attain increasing centrality (Frenkel *et al.*, 1995). Technical labour is inherently uncertain and ambiguous, requiring an artful management of 'creative, and rather intelligent and autonomous individuals' (Jain and Triandis, 1990:xiv). The most immediate outcome of this management is reciprocated trust relations and an operational autonomy through which they can determine the techniques and timing of much of their work. As the earlier outlines of the management and organisation of the 'new workplace' indicated, it is precisely this form of operational autonomy that is advocated for all workers by commentators of the knowledge economy. In this sense technical and professional labour's experience of work could be argued to be the *new benchmark* for all employees in the workplace.

Suggestions that technical and professional labour represents the new model worker, however, rests on a gross over-simplification of their current working experience and organisational status. The extent of the autonomy of these workers can be exaggerated. The dominant characteristic features of their labour does not exclude these occupational groups from management intervention or control, nor is professional status with its characteristic terms and conditions of employment immutable. Although still relatively highly paid (see, for example, *Labour Market Trends*, 1996), in organisations with less defined boundaries, the claim to and strategies of ensuring occupational closure and exclusivity expected by professionals is undermined. Horizontal coordination which combines flexibility with the pooling and sharing of information, can produce a trend towards 'de-professionalisation' because, as Kanter argues, 'the organisation that produces a great deal of innovation must by definition be less category-conscious' (1983:32). [. . .]

If the knowledge of technical and professional labour is diffused to a much wider group of organisational members, their working practices are also vulnerable to managerial control.

Randle's (1995) study of technical workers in the pharmaceutical industry highlights the tightening of management control through performance related pay and promotion systems in which 'targets' attained determine salary levels and career trajectories. Discretionary activity, such as the 'ten per cent time' or one half day per week to provide 'a greater degree of creative and independent thinking', frequently became subsumed into ordinary working time on 'goals emphasised by line managers'. [. . .] These constraints create tensions between management on the one hand, and technical and professional labour on the other. In the Pirelli case discussed earlier the senior accountants, citing commercial priority, effectively arrested the technical innovations being made to the labour process by systems engineers. With the retreat from the intended factory of the future, a number of these engineers were aggrieved enough to resign their posts (Clark, 1995).

Furthermore, they may be the casualties of organisational restructuring. For example, there is some indication of less rather than more occupational mobility within external and internal labour markets. Instead of technical labour being more footloose as it comes to assert its organisational value, labour turnover in the R&D sections of the pharmaceutical industry is low as recruitment is curtailed by management in order to control labour costs, the result of which is diminished promotion prospects and frustrated workers. The outcome is a 'capping' on the number of current entrants into this occupational category which is surprising given that laboratory technicians are one of the occupations forwarded as indicative of knowledge workers. As competition for promotion intensifies, these workers, it has been noted by Perin (1991:259), then become reluctant to adopt more flexible temporal and spatial patterns of work, believing that presence brings visibility and influence so 'that being absent would be disadvantageous to their careers'.

As we have noted earlier, a key theme of the literature is the extension of collegiality. There is no doubt that technical and professional labour does require some features of this ethos and practice. But it is rather foolish to start calling commercial work environments 'campuses' when universities themselves are becoming far less collegial! Under the impact of the quasi-marketisation of higher education and increased bureaucratic regulation through a variety of 'quality' audit procedures, university academics are subject to tighter work specification, intensification of labour and vertical 'line management' complementing if not replacing horizontal co-ordination. As Wilson (1991:254) explains; 'most higher education systems [within the industrialised countries] are experiencing similar trends towards management assertiveness, far greater use of casualised labour . . . devolution of budgetary responsibility . . . within tight institutional guidelines and greater sensitivity to market forces'. As a result, there are deteriorating terms and conditions of employment, a weakening of the academic ethos, and low-trust relations emerging between university management and academics.

There have also been demands for medical doctors to shift their loyalties away from their profession to the employing organisation (Brindle, 1994). [. . .] In 1996, the British Association of Medical Managers recommended a contractual obligation on all doctors to inform on poorly performing colleagues. The 'shopa-doc' proposal caused anger amongst members of the British Medical Association with its council chair claiming that the initiative was 'totally contrary . . . to the concept of the profession . . . and utterly unacceptable' (Turner, 1997:11). Nevertheless, in this regard, a number of professors and heads of departments in higher education are now indeed required to take on budgetary responsibility and the performance evaluation of colleagues, and may even be incorporated into management strategies.

Taking these factors into account, the traditional tension between bureaucracy and professionalism has been recast rather than eliminated. Senior management still requires the capacity for creativity and intuitive exploration, but there is greater pressure in both public and private sectors for marketable outcomes and competitive working practices.

[. . .] Going further, there can also be tighter bureaucratic controls on software developers, downsizing resulting in work intensification as fewer workers do more work and some software companies routinise work with the use of 'standardised adaptations of generic systems for clients'.

Nevertheless, it would be wrong to assume that the impact of the changes has been evenly experienced by technical and professional labour. There are divisions and hierarchies within this, as any other set of occupational categories. Such labour can be divided with, for example, the use of different employment contracts [. . .] or through the technical and/or a gendered division of labour. [. . .] Similarly we need to grasp the dynamics of change over time as the labour process is constantly redivided and reassembled [. . .] but which still reflect a managerial desire for control. Greenbaum also suggests that moves towards the new workplace have resulted in little more than work intensification for some professionals, such as computer systems analysts. Other technical workers, however, can informally reskill themselves [. . .] through trial and error, these workers correct and improve flawed software systems – indicating that managerial control is neither absolute nor, in some situations, efficacious. All these processes can have contradictory aspects. For example there has been increasing formal opportunity for upskilling in previous 'teaching only' universities in the UK as staff are encouraged to develop research profiles. But given the squeeze on existing resources and the expansion of student numbers, such opportunities are either impossible to operationalise or lead only to even greater workloads and burned-out staff.

In conclusion therefore, it is more accurate to say that some of the benchmarks set for routine workers are more likely to be applied to technical and professional labour. Certainly they do not offer a cohesive and coherent occupational group which is in a position to assume organisational and economic dominance. Commentators need to be more cautious in their mapping of these varied groups into an assumed model of their labour within the contemporary workplace.

MANAGEMENT AND THE MIDDLE LAYERS

If there are substantial constraints on employees further down the organisational hierarchy, what about those in the middle? It has been suggested that it is possible and desirable to delayer management levels within organisations because there are alternative means of co-ordination. Middle management are often described as a prime obstacle to change. In fact in recent years, as Scarbrough and Burrell observe, they have been redefined *as* the problem:

> They are costly, resistant to change, a block to communication both upwards and downwards. They consistently underperform; they spend their time openly politicking rather than in constructive problem-solving. They are reactionary, undertrained and regularly fail to act as entrepreneurs.
>
> (1996:178)

However, we should be extremely cautious concerning tales of the death of the middle manager. The early 1990s' recession hit not only manufacturing employees, as in the early 1980s' recession, but also this time service sector employees. It is true that recession and restructuring have hit those industries within the service sector that offered a 'job for life' with good remuneration and promotion prospects, such as the civil service and the media. But only 14 per cent of managers, professionals and white-collar employees generally had experienced unemployment in the five years to 1995. The figure for unskilled manual workers was more than double at 29 per cent (Smith, 1997). More typically, the proportion of managers within the British employment structure has increased in both the public and private sectors throughout the post-war period and shows no sign of slowing down. By the early 1990s, there were 2.75 million managers in the UK with a further 90 000 new managers swelling that number every year (Thomas, 1993). While some layers have been taken out, others have been added, particularly to collect and process information connected to the already discussed growth in monitoring performance, quality and outputs. The burgeoning bureaucracy in the British National Health Service is a case in point. Between 1989 and 1994 the NHS lost 50 000 nurses and midwives but gained over 18 000 managers, an increase of 400 per cent (Milhill, 1996). Management, business and related courses now have the largest student enrolments in British higher education (*Department for Education and Employment, 1996*). As any survey of occupational earning demonstrates, the pay of managers is still relatively high compared to other groups of employees (see, for example again *Labour Market Trends*, 1996).

Nevertheless, evidence does indicate some important changes with regard to managers and management. A managerial version of the search for greater innovation and cost-effectiveness among routine workers is compelling organisations to attack some of the traditional forms of functional responsibilities, 'organisational chimneys' and hierarchical decision making: 'The traditional . . . approach was to manage through levels and tasks, now the intention is to manage across levels and projects' (Starkey and McKinlay, 1994:986) 'Delayering' is a reality in many companies. Nationally British Telecom have reduced their management layers from twelve to six, at branch level WH Smith from four to two, GM (Saturn plant) from six to four and Pirelli (Aberdare plant) have collapsed eight levels into three. This frequently involves new titles and responsibilities. As a result of reorganisation at the British retail group WH Smith, branch managers are 'team leaders' and 'coaches' (*IRS Employment Trends, 1995*). Co-ordinators and conduits of information between production and senior managers may be rendered superfluous by greater organisational transparency via information technology or delegated decision making. Retail sales data that can be collected through EPOS systems means that senior managers can have real time information about the performance of stores and make rapid responses. As a result decisions previously taken by store managers – pricing, space allocation and promotion for example – are displaced to head office (ibid.).

However, we would argue that current perspectives misunderstand both the nature and the number of managerial jobs involved. The prime mistake of those promoting the post-bureaucratic organisation is to believe that new horizontal forms of co-ordination have replaced rather than complemented more traditional vertical divisions of labour and command structures. Many, although not all, of the tasks and functions of middle managers have remained, and organisations are still reliant upon their experience and understanding. Managers continue to exist even if their job titles are changed as supervisors become team-leaders, functional managers become project managers and branch managers become customer care champions. Such developments, are, however, more than plays on words. What is happening in many workplaces is the emergence of a dual structure which combines the search for innovation with enhanced financial and operational accountability. Methods of co-ordination and accountability therefore become more complex, but vertical structures remain the backbone of organisations. Given that the horizontal forms are largely project-based and temporary in nature, we prefer to refer to them as a *shadow division of labour*, that cuts across and supplements vertical structures and hierarchies. Managerial and professional labour that communicates and co-ordinates across functions is therefore *at the same time* subject to increased monitoring of performance, financial targets and penalties (Edwards *et al.*, 1996).

It is also difficult to be as unambiguously enthusiastic as business commentators about such developments. Though, as we have indicated, 'delayering' and 'downsizing' are primarily aimed at routine workers, shifts in the nature of managerial hierarchies have made the working lives of many professionals and managers more stressful. An *Observer*

Business/Gallup survey in 1994 demonstrated that 70 per cent of public and private sector managers reported that their organisations had recently restructured with staff cutbacks and cost reduction initiatives, resulting in greater workloads, increased and often unpaid responsibilities, longer hours and less job security. The practice of 'presenteeism', that is working extra long hours to demonstrate commitment and indispensability, is now common amongst middle managers. Twenty per cent of managers were working more than fifty hours a week in 1995, that figure rising to thirty per cent the following year. With no extra reward for middle managers, job satisfaction is dwindling in restructured companies. Worldwide, 85 per cent of managers are now more concerned about the need to lead a balanced life than at the start of the decade, according to Herriot and Pemberton (1995). Attempts to motivate disaffected managers with performance-related pay has also often backfired due to its lack of objectivity and under-funded schemes that circumscribe the levels of pay settlements. The lack of promotion opportunities in flatter organisations further lowers moral amongst managers previously expectant of upward career trajectories.

As a consequence of such developments Herriot and Pemberton go on to argue that if, in the past, managers had an employment *relationship* based upon mutual trust and commitment rather than *contract* with their companies, this relationship is now being replaced by a *transaction* based on mutual instrumentality involving a simple effort–reward bargain. The relative fragility of the new employment relationship is indicated by the frequency with which even senior managers have to reapply for their own jobs or be evaluated through assessment centres – as managers in a variety of manufacturing and service companies such as LucasVarity, British Gas and House of Fraser can testify.

However, [. . .] managers are not a homogeneous group – even middle managers – and the experiences of these different managers within the restructuring of organisations also varies. There are, of course, both various vertical levels and horizontal occupational group-ings of managers, each with differing functions and organising logics. Organisational change may be driven by any of these levels or groups of managers, though not without the form and logic informing that restructuring being contested amongst those levels and groupings. Similarly, different levels or groups of managers can both benefit from and become victims of that organisational restructuring.

Finally, it is worth noting an increasing recognition in business and the business press that we may have reached the limits of managerial delayering and downsizing. In the US, companies are realising that experience and organisational memory is being lost in an exercise that has done little to really improve productivity.

[. . .]

CONCLUSION

When I was growing up, we used to read that by the year 2000 everyone would have to work only 30 hours a week and that the rest would be leisure time. But as we approach the year 2000, it seems likely that half of us will work 60 hours a week and the rest of us will be unemployed.

(Bridges, 1995b:20).

Little is heard about work in contemporary policy debates. The days when leisure opportunities and job enrichment were the stuff of official government and business reports are mostly long gone. Getting a job is, understandably, a priority and the 1990s' reports are much more likely to be on labour market flexibility or insecurity.

Nevertheless, the experience of work and workplace remains a central one in most people's lives. We have tried to capture the complexity of current trends. Powerful forces *have* been reshaping the world of work; notably intensified competition within a more global political economy, expanded technological and information resources, new managerial ideologies and practices, and the spread of market relations within the state sector and large private firms. Interacting with the limits to old Taylorist and Fordist forms, an imperative to organisational innovation has been created which is the prime source of initiatives to change the nature of labour utilisation and work co-ordination. In order to retain some vertical structure of command and accountability, managers have sought to develop a variety of organisational coping mechanisms in the form of crossfunctional and on-line teams, thus creating a shadow division of labour.

References to the 'new workplace', then, are not out of place, if kept firmly *in* place. For this is not the 'paradigm shift' beloved of academics and commentators looking for a conceptual peg to launch their latest publication. Continuity is as pervasive as change, if for no other reason than because new ideas and practices are by definition built on the legacy of the old. Despite the bewildering number of change programmes and grand new titles for people and practices, the 'new workplace' is still easily recognisable for the vast majority who too often remain poorly motivated, overworked and undervalued. There is, however, no single or simple future work/place. Variation by firm, sector or country co-exists with the powerful structural tendencies to standardise through business-defined 'best practice', as workplace actors struggle to adapt to the constraints and opportunities of their own environments.

In developing the arguments in this chapter, we are aware that they are somewhat 'against the grain'. The world of work has always been something that can be portrayed in terms of high drama. For every popular commentator such as Drucker or Handy that talks soothingly about a future where work for the majority will be more autonomous, creative and professionalised, there is a doom merchant proclaiming that work, at least as we know it, is dead and buried. So Rifkin in *The End of Work* (1995) is the latest to predict the wipe-out of employment by the march of technology; while Bridges in *Jobshift* (1995a) focuses more realistically on the threat to the traditional employment package we call a 'job'.

Jobshift touches on important themes – job insecurity, the blurred edges between employment and self-employment as a 'contract culture' develops and the stunted career paths available in large organisations. Certainly, redundancy is a standard feature of 'employment' for an increasing number of workers; manual, non-manual, professional and managerial. Over five million people have been made redundant in Britain since 1990. In financial services, for example, there have been massive job losses, over 80,000 in banking alone between 1990 and 1994 (Sinden, 1996). Many banks no longer pretend that they offer a career structure, let alone a 'job for life'. But Bridges spoils a good argument in search of *the* future trend, asserting that 'everyone' is now a contingent worker and that all employees must act like people in business for themselves, maintaining self-development career plans. We are back on the territory of Handy's portfolio people.

Our territory in this book is the labour process rather than the labour market, so we have not had the space to consider in detail the extent and character shifts in employment. But from looking inside the workplace such claims do not mirror the experience of most of the workforce. In truth most workers are struggling to survive in and make sense of routine jobs and there are few employees communicating from electronic cottages or happily hawking their portfolios around companies. Full-time work still dominates employment, accounting for 76 per cent of all jobs and declining only 2.2 per cent over the ten years to 1993 (Ash and Rainnie, 1995).

If anyone has become a portfolio person it is more likely that he or she is a conscript of organisational restructuring than a new breed of entrepreneurs. Becoming the victims of downsizing, subcontracting, out-sourcing, contingent contracts and other forms of organisational restructuring is not a situation favoured by most, and given the opportunity such workers – manual, non-manual and managerial – would happily return to the ranks of full-time permanent employment in the big battalions.

This chapter has only been able to touch on some of these issues through the interfaces between the labour process and the employment relationship, but we recognise that people's experience of work develops from what they bring to it in orientations from the wider social structure and what they take out of it in terms of rewards and an employment package. Nevertheless, practices in the labour process shape that wider picture. [. . .] [A] new politics of production can develop as issues of health and safety and work organisation are foregrounded as capital and labour attempt to reconfigure industrial relations in the image of the 'new workplace'.

It is important to get the trends right, because accurate, realistic knowledge can inform policy choices. Politicians too often take their agendas from 'policy entrepeneurs', management gurus and think-tankers who have a vested interest in the sweeping statement, popular slogan and digestible knowledge-gobbitt, regardless of how inconsistent with or embedded in existing bodies of knowledge [they are] (Thompson and du Gay, 1997). But that is hardly surprising when academics, particularly in Britain, absent themselves from the policy arena in search of texts to deconstruct, or to keep their world-weary cynicism about politics and the public realm intact.

Choices are there whether academics keep their heads in the theoretical sand or not. For all the hassles and hardships at work, employees at all levels, when and where encouraged to participate and innovate in a climate of trust and reasonable security, welcome real change – a point made evident in the surveys conducted by Clark (1995). [. . .] And there is ample evidence that management failure to implement their own rhetoric of better human resource policy, training or service quality is often used by staff as part of their armoury of tactics to improve workplace life. A new politics and policy agenda cannot, however, be confined to the workplace. It requires a supportive institutional environment. Reforming governments need to find ways of rewarding innovation and partnership in the workplace. Models are available from the way in which the Swedish Work Environment Fund or the Australian Productivity Commission have encouraged collaboration on workplace innovation between employers, unions and researchers (Mathews, 1994). Nor is this purely theoretical. Evidence from the US (Bluestone and Bluestone, 1992; Levine, 1995) demonstrates that it is stakeholding firms with strong unions and a 'mutual gains' agenda that are at the cutting edge of change, with a vested interest in ensuring competitiveness through investment in skills and equipment.

The existence of policy discussion implies that the future is not set or determined by impersonal forces whether technology or markets, or by overarching theoretical models. As we approach the end of the century it is time to take stock of the nature and future of work, and what options that creates for different kinds of workplace transformation. For those willing to take that opportunity, there are plenty of choices and places between utopia and dystopia.

NOTE

* This chapter has been adapted from, Thompson, P. and Warhurst, C. (1998) *Workplaces of the Future*, Basingstoke: Macmillan.

REFERENCES

Ackroyd, S. and Proctor, S.J. (1996) 'Identifying the New Flexible Firm: Technology, Labour and Organisation in Contemporary British Manufacturing', unpublished paper.

Adler, P.S. (1993) 'Time-and-Motion Regained', *Harvard Business Review*, January–February, 97–107.

Adler, P. and Cole, R. (1995) 'Designed for Learning: A Tale of Two Auto Plants' in Sandberg, A. (ed.) *Enriching Production*, Aldershot: Avebury.

Ash, S. and Rainnie, A. (1995) 'Stress Management and the End of the Full Time Job', paper to the

Restructuring of the Local Economy of Lancashire Conference, University of Central Lancashire with Lancashire County Council.

Barley, S. (1996) *The New World of Work*, Pamphlet, British–North American Committee, London.

Bluestone, B. and Bluestone, I. (1992) *Negotiating the Future: A Labor Perspective on American Business*, New York: Basic Books.

Bridges, W. (1995a) *Jobshift: How to Prosper in a Workplace without Jobs*, London: Nicholas Brealey.

Bridges, W. (1995b) 'The Death of the Job', *Independent on Sunday*, 5 February, 19.

Clark, J. (1995) *Managing Innovation and Change*, London: Sage.

Coopey, J. (1995) 'Managerial Culture and the Stillbirth of Organisational Commitment', *Human Resource Management Journal*, 5:3, 56–76.

Despres, C. and Hiltrop, J-M. (1995) 'Human resource management in the knowledge age: current practice and perspectives on the future', *Employee Relations*, 17:1, 9–23.

Drucker, P. (1986) 'The Changed World Economy', *Foreign Affairs*, 64:4, 768–91.

du Gay, P. (1996) *Consumption and Identity at Work*, London: Sage.

Edwards, P., Armstrong, P., Marginson, P. and Purcell, J. (1996) 'Towards the Transnational Company?' in Crompton, R., Gallie, D. and Purcell, K. (eds) *Corporate Restructuring and Labour Markets*, London: Routledge.

Elger, T. (1991) 'Task Flexibility and the Intensification of Labour in UK Manufacturing in the 1980s' in Pollert, A. (ed.) *Farewell to Flexibility*, Oxford: Blackwell.

Frenkel, S., Korczynski, M., Donohue, L. and Shire, K. (1995) 'Re-constituting Work', *Work, Employment and Society*, 9:4, 773–96.

Gallie, D. (1991) 'Patterns of Skill Change: Upskilling, Deskilling or the Polarisation of Skills?' *Work, Employment and Society*, 5:3, 319–51.

Hamel, G. and Prahalad, C.K. (1996) 'Competing in the New Economy: Managing Out of Bounds', *Strategic Management Journal*, 17, 237–42.

Handy, C. (1995) *The Future of Work*, WH Smith Contemporary Papers 8.

Harrison, B. (1994) *Lean and Mean: The Changing Landscape of Corporate Power in the Age of Flexibility*. New York: Basic Books.

Henwood, D. (1996) 'Work and its future', *Left Business Observer*, 72, Internet edition.

Herriot, P. and Pemberton, C. (1995) *New Deals*, Chichester: John Wiley & Sons.

Hochschild, A.R. (1983) *The Managed Heart*, Berkeley: University of California Press.

Ingersoll Engineers (1996) *The Way We Work*, London.

IRS Employment Trends (1995) 'Putting the customer first: organisational change at WH Smith', 596, 5–9.

Jacques, R. (1996) *Manufacturing the Employee*, London: Sage.

Jain, R.K. and Triandis, H.C. (1990) *Management of Research and Development Organisations*, Chichester: John Wiley & Sons.

Jones, O. (1997) 'Changing the Balance? Taylorism, TQM and Work Organisation', *New Technology, Work and Employment*, 12:1, 13–24.

Kanter, R.M. (1983) *The Change Masters*, New York: Simon & Schuster.

Kumar, K. (1996) *From Post-Industrial to Post-Modern Society*, Oxford: Blackwell.

Kyotani, E. (1996) 'The Bright and Dark Sides of the Japanese Labour Process', unpublished paper.

Labour Market Trends (1996) May, London: Great Britain Office for National Statistics.

Leidner, R. (1993) *Fast Food, Fast Talk: Service Work and the Routinisation of Everyday Life*, Berkeley, CA: University of California Press.

Levine, D. (1995) *Reinventing the Workplace*, The Brookings Institute, Washington DC.

Lyon, D. (1994) *The Electronic Eye*, Oxford: Polity Press.

Marks, A., Findlay, P., Hine, J., McKinlay, A. and Thompson, P. (1997) 'Whisky Galore: Teamworking and Workplace Transformation in the Scottish Spirits Industry', paper to the *15th International Labour Process Conference*, University of Edinburgh.

Mathews, J. (1994) *Catching the Wave: Workplace Reform in Australia*, New York: ILR Press.

McKinlay, A. and Taylor, P. (1997) 'Foucault and the Politics of Production' in McKinlay, A. and Starkey, K. (eds) *Foucault, Management and Organisation*, London: Sage.

McRae, H. (1996) 'You can't treat a skill-force like a workforce', *Independent on Sunday*, Business Section, 3 March, 4.

Milhill, C. (1996) 'NHS managers up 400pc on 1989', *Guardian*, 18 January, 6.

Nichols, T. (1991) 'Labour Intensification, Work Injuries and the Measurement of the Percentage Utilisation of Labour (PUL)', *British Journal of Industrial Relations*, 29:3, 569–92.

OECD (1994) *Jobs Study: Evidence and Explanations* Pts 1 & 2, Paris: OECD.

Osterman, P. (1991) 'Impact of IT on Jobs and Skills' in Morton, M.S.S. (ed.) *The Corporation of the 1990s*, Oxford: Oxford University Press.

Quah, D. T. (1997) 'Weightless economy packs a heavy punch', *Independent on Sunday*, 18 May, 4.

Perin, C. (1991) 'The Moral Fabric of the Office: Panoptican Discourse and Schedule Flexibilities', *Research in the Sociology of Organisations*, 8, London: JAI Press.

Randle, K. (1995) 'The Whitecoated Worker: Professional Autonomy in a Period of Change', paper to the *13th Annual International Labour Process Conference*, University of Central Lancashire, Preston.

Reich, R. (1993) *The Work of Nations*, London: Simon & Schuster.

Rifkin, J. (1995) *The End of Work: the Decline of the Global Labour Force and the Dawn of the Post-Market Era*, New York: G.P. Putnam's Sons.

Ritzer, G. (1997) 'McJobs: McDonaldization and Its Relationship to the Labour Process' in Ritzer, G. (ed.) *The McDonaldisation Thesis*, London: Sage.

Rosenthal, P., Hill, S. and Peccei, R. (1997) 'Checking Out Service: Evaluating Excellence, HRM and TQM in Retailing', *Work, Employment and Society*, forthcoming.

Routh, G. (1987) *Occupations of the People of Great Britain 1801–1981*, Basingstoke: Macmillan.

Scarbrough, H. and Burrell, G. (1996) 'The Axeman Cometh: the Changing Roles and Knowledges of Middle Managers' in Clegg, S.R. and Palmer, G. (eds) *The Politics of Management Knowledge*, London: Sage.

Segal-Horn, S. (1993) 'The Internationalisation of Service Firms', *Advances in Strategic Management*, 9, 31–55.

Sinden, A. (1996) 'The Decline, Flexibility and Geographical Restructuring of Employment in British Retail Banks', *The Geographical Journal*, 162:1, 25–40.

Smith, D. (1997) 'Job insecurity and other myths', *Management Today*, May, 38–41.

Starkey, K. and McKinlay, A. (1994) 'Managing for Ford', *Sociology*, 28:4, 975–90.

Summers, D. (1993) 'Management – the Right Attitude – Staff Surveys Are Popular, But Can Be Fraught With Pitfalls', *Financial Times*, 14 June, 8.

Thomas, A.B. (1993) *Controversies in Management*, London: Routledge.

Thompson, P. and Ackroyd, S. (1995) 'All Quiet on the Workplace Front? A Critique of Recent Trends in British Industrial Sociology', *Sociology*, 29:4, 1–19.

Thompson, P. and du Gay, P. (1997) 'Future Imperfect', *Renewal*, 5:1, 3–8.

Thompson, P. and Findlay, P. (1996) 'The Mystery of the Missing Subject', paper to the *14th International Labour Process Conference*, University of Aston, Birmingham.

Thompson, P., Wallace, T., Flecker, J. and Ahlstrand, R. (1995) 'It Ain't What You Do, It's the Way that You Do it: Production Organisation and Skill Utilisation in Commercial Vehicles', *Work, Employment and Society*, 9:4, 719–42.

Thompson, P., Jones, C., Nickson, D. and Wallace, T. (1996) 'Internationalisation and Integration: A Comparison of Manufacturing and Service Firms', paper to *The Globalisation of Production and Regulation of Labour Conference*, University of Warwick.

Turner, S. (1997) 'Senior doctors slam medical managers' contractual "shop-a-doc" proposals', *BMA New Review*, August, 11.

Wilson, T. (1991) 'The proletarianisation of academic labour', *Industrial Relations Journal*, 22:4, 250–62.

Wright, C. and Lund, J. (1996) 'Best-Practice Taylorism: "Yankee Speed-Up" in Australian Grocery Distribution', *Journal of Industrial Relations*, 38:2, 196–212.

14

FAILURE*

Richard Sennett

Failure is the great modern taboo. Popular literature is full of recipes for how to succeed but largely silent about how to cope with failure. Coming to terms with failure, giving it a shape and a place in one's life history, may haunt us internally but seldom is discussed with others. Instead we reach for the safety of clichés; champions of the poor do so when they seek to deflect the lament "I have failed" by the supposedly healing reply "No you haven't; you are a victim." As with anything we are afraid to speak about forthrightly, both internal obsession and shame only thereby become greater. Left untreated is the raw inner sentence "I am not good enough."

Failure is no longer the normal prospect facing only the very poor or disadvantaged; it has become more familiar as a regular event in the lives of the middle classes. The shrinking size of the elite makes achievement more elusive. The winner-take-all market is a competitive structure which disposes large numbers of educated people to fail. Downsizings and reengineerings impose on middle-class people sudden disasters which were in an earlier capitalism much more confined to the working classes. The sense of failing one's family by behaving flexibly and adaptively at work [. . .] is more subtle but equally powerful.

The very opposition of success and failure is one way of avoiding coming to terms with failure itself. This simple division suggests that if we have enough evidence of material achievement we won't be haunted by feelings of insufficiency or inadequacy – which wasn't the case for Weber's driven man, who felt that whatever is, is not enough. One of the reasons it is hard to assuage feelings of failure with dollars is that failure can be of a deeper kind – failure to make one's life cohere, failure to realize something precious in oneself, failure to live rather than merely exist. [. . .]

On the eve of the First World War, the commentator Walter Lippmann, unhappy with the reckoning of success in dollars which preoccupied his contemporaries, pondered their unsettled lives in a vigorous book he called *Drift and Mastery*. He sought to transmute the material reckoning of failure and success into more personal experiences of time, opposing drifting, erratic experience to mastery of events.

Lippmann lived in the era when the giant industrial firms of America and Europe consolidated. Everyone knows the evils of this capitalism, Lippmann said: the death of small firms, the collapse of government conducted in the name of the public good, the masses fed into the capitalist maw. The problem with his fellow reformers, Lippmann observed, is that they "knew what they were against but not what they were for" (Lippmann, 1914, p. xvi). People suffered, they complained, but neither the nascent Marxist program nor renewed individual enterprise offered a promising remedy. The Marxists proposed a massive social explosion, the individual entrepreneurs greater freedom to compete; neither was a recipe for an alternative *order*. Lippmann, however, was in no doubt over what to do.

Surveying the resolute, hardworking determination of the immigrants then swelling America, he proclaimed in a memorable phrase, "All of us are immigrants spiritually" (ibid., p. 211). The personal qualities of resolve invoked by Hesiod and Virgil, Lippmann saw embodied again in the relentless hard work of immigrants on New York's Lower East Side. What Lippmann hated was the sensitive aesthete's distaste for capitalism, personified, he thought, in Henry James, who looked at the New York immigrants as an alien if energetic race, disheveled and anarchic in their struggles (James, 1968).

What should guide people, cut loose from home, now trying to create a new life narrative? For Lippmann, it was the conduct of a career. Not to make a career out of one's work, however modest its content or its pay, was to leave oneself prey to the sense of aimlessness which constitutes the deepest experience of inadequacy – one must, in modern slang, "get a life." Thus he recovered the oldest meaning of career, which I cited at the opening of this essay, career as a well-made road. Cutting that road was the antidote to personal failure.

Can we practice this remedy for failure in flexible capitalism? Though we may think today of a career as syonymous with the professions, one of its elements – the possession of skill – has not been limited to the professional or even bourgeois realm. The historian Edward Thompson points out that in the nineteenth century even the least favored workers, whether poorly employed, unemployed, or simply foraging from job to job, tried to define themselves as weavers, metalworkers, or farmers (Thompson, 1978). Status in work comes from being more than just "a pair of hands"; manual laborers as well as upper servants in Victorian households sought it in using the words "career," "profession," and "craft" more discriminately than we might think admissible. The desire for such status was equally potent among middle-class employees of the new corporations; as the historian Olivier Zunz has shown, people in the business world first sought in Lippmann's era to elevate their work by treating accounting, salesmanship, or managing as akin to the doctor's or engineer's professional activities (Zunz, 1990).

The desire for the status of a career is thus nothing new. Nor is the sense that careers, rather than jobs, develop our characters. But Lippmann raised the stakes of "getting a life." In Lippmann's view, the life narrative of a career is a story of inner development, unfolding through both skill and struggle. "We have to deal with [life] deliberately, devise its social organization, alter its tools, formulate its method . . ." (ibid, p. 267). The person pursuing a career defines long-term purposes, standards of professional or unprofessional behavior, and a sense of responsibility for his or her conduct. I doubt Lippmann had read Max Weber when he wrote *Drift and Mastery*; the two writers, though, shared a similar concept of career. In Weber's usage, *Beruf*, which is the German equivalent for "career," also stresses the importance of work as a narrative and the development of character possible only by long-term, organized effort. "Mastery means," Lippmann declares, "the substitution of conscious intention for unconscious striving" (ibid., p. 267).

Lippmann's generation believed that they stood at the beginning of a new age of science as well as of capitalism. They were convinced that the proper use of science, technical skills, and, more generally, professional knowledge could help men and women to form stronger career histories, and thus to take firmer control of their own lives. In this reliance on science for personal mastery Lippmann resembled other progressive contemporaries in America, and Fabian socialists like Sidney and Beatrice Webb in Britain, or the young Leon Blum in France, as well as Max Weber.

Lippmann's recipe for mastery also had a specific political aim. He observed the New York immigrants struggling to learn English and to educate themselves in order to begin their careers, but shut out of the institutions of higher learning in the city, which at the time were closed to Jews and blacks and hostile to Greeks, Italians, and the Irish. In calling for a more career-oriented society, he was demanding that these institutions open their doors, an American version of the French motto "careers open to talent."

Lippmann's writing constitutes a massive act of faith in the individual, in making something of *oneself* [. . .] In his writings Lippmann thus tended to pit the Goliath of corporate capitalism against the David of personal will and talent.

The pleasures of reading Lippmann are their own justification; his voice is that of an upright, clean-living Edwardian schoolteacher who has seemingly also spent many hours on picket lines or in the company of men whose words he can barely understand. Still, is his belief in career a viable prescription for us, nearly a century later? In particular, is it a remedy for failure – failure of the sort which consists of aimlessness, of not getting one's life together?

We know different forms of bureaucracy from those Lippmann and Weber knew; capitalism now acts on different productive principles. The short-term, flexible time of the new capitalism seems to preclude making a sustained narrative out of one's labors, and so a career. Yet to fail to wrest some sense of continuity and purpose out of these conditions would be literally to fail ourselves.

Lippmann has often been on my mind in attending to a group of middle-aged programmers I've come to know, men who recently were downsized at an American IBM office. Before they lost their jobs, they – rather complacently – subscribed to belief in the long-term unfolding of their professional careers. As high-tech programmers, they were meant to be the masters of the new science. After they were let go, they had to try out different interpretations of the events which wrecked their lives; they could summon no self-evident, instant narrative which would make sense of their failure. And yet, by means Lippmann perhaps did not foresee, they've rescued themselves from the sense of aimless drift, and indeed found in their very failure a certain revelation of their life career.

Let me first set their company context, since it is distinctive. Up to the mid-1980s, IBM practiced paternal capitalism with a vengeance. The man responsible for IBM's growth, Thomas Watson, Sr., ran the company like a personal fief and spoke of himself as the "moral father" of the firm. The old company song went, "With Mr. Watson leading, To greater heights we'll rise, And keep our IBM, Respected in all eyes" (DeLamarter, 1986, p. 3). The company was run like an army, and Watson's personal decisions about all aspects of the corporation became instant company law. "Loyalty," he said, "saves the wear and tear of making daily decisions as to what is best to do" (Rodgers, 1969, p. 100). Institutionally, IBM resembled a state-run company in France or Italy, with lifetime employment for most employees and a kind of social contract between management and labor.

In 1956, Thomas Watson, Jr., took over from his father. He delegated more and listened better, but the social contract remained in force. IBM gave its workers excellent health insurance, education and pension benefits; it supported workers' social lives with company golf courses, child care, and mortgages; above all, it provided a lifetime ladder of employment, all the stages of a career laid out for people who were expected to stay and to climb. IBM could do so because it exercised a near monopoly in its markets.

Due to grave miscalculations about the growth of the computer industry in the 1980s – IBM virtually threw away its control of the personal computer – by the early 1990s the company was in the throes of upheaval. Watson Jr. had retired; new chairmen foundered. In 1992 the firm suffered a massive loss ($6.6 billion), whereas eight years before it had racked up the largest American corporate profit on record. An elaborate internal bureaucracy had proved immobilizing as the company was outmaneuvered by Bill Gates's Microsoft. IBM also faced stiff competition from Japanese and American upstarts. In 1993, it began, with yet another new chairman, Louis Gerstner, to fashion itself into a competitive corporate machine, and made an equally dramatic turnaround. It sought to replace the rigid hier-archical structure of work with more flexible forms of organization, and with flexible production oriented to getting more products more quickly to market.

The tenure of its 400,000 workers was a prime target in this campaign. At first some were enticed, then many more were forced to go. In the first six months of 1993, a third of the employees in the three IBM plants located in the Hudson Valley in New York were laid off, and the company downsized other operations wherever possible. The new management closed the golf courses and clubs and withdrew from supporting the communities in which IBM operated.

I wanted to know more about what this great turn toward a leaner, more flexible IBM was like, in part because many of the managers and middle-aged engineers caught in the change are my neighbors in upstate New York. Made redundant at a too early age, they have carved out employment as "consultants," which means working their address books in the often vain hope that contacts outside the corporation still remember they exist. Some have gone back to work for the corporation, but as short-term workers on contracts, lacking company benefits and standing in the institution. However they've managed to survive the last four years, they can't live without attending to the brute facts of corporate change and its effects on their own lives.

The River Winds Café, not far from my neighbors' old offices, is a cheery hamburger joint, formerly tenanted during daylight hours only by women out shopping or sullen adolescents wasting time after school. It is here that I've heard these white-shirted, dark-tied men, who nurse cups of coffee while sitting attentively as if at a business meeting, sort out their histories. One knot of five to seven men sticks together; they were mainframe programmers and systems analysts in the old IBM. The most talkative among them were Jason, a systems analyst who had been with the company nearly twenty years, and Paul, a younger programmer whom Jason had fired in the first downsizing wave.

I began spending occasional late afternoons with them in 1994, a year after all but Jason had been let go. [. . .] At the River Winds Café, the engineers' attempt to make sense of what had happened fell roughly into three stages. When I entered the discussions, the men felt themselves passive victims of the corporation. But by the time the discussions came to a conclusion, the dismissed employees had switched focus to their own behavior.

When the pain of dismissal was still raw, discussion revolved around IBM's "betrayals," as if the company had tricked them. The programmers dredged up corporate events or behavior in the past that seemed to portend the changes which subsequently came to pass. These acts of recall included such bits of evidence as a particular engineer's being denied use of the golf-course for a full eighteen rounds, or unexplained trips by a head programmer to unnamed destinations. At this stage the men wanted evidence of premeditation on the part of their superiors, evidence which would then justify their own sense of outrage. Being tricked or betrayed means a disaster is hardly one's own fault.

Indeed, the sense of corporate betrayal struck most outside observers who came to the company at the time. It was a dramatic story: highly skilled professionals in a paternalistic company now treated with no more regard than lowly clerks or janitors. The company seemed to have wrecked itself in the process. The English journalist Anthony Sampson, who visited the company's home offices in the mid-1990s, found social disorganization rife within the company, rather than a reinvigorated workforce. One official admitted, "There's much more stress, domestic violence and need for mental services – directly linked to the layoffs. Even inside IBM the environment has changed radically: they have great unease, without their security" (Sampson, 1995, p. 224). People who had survived behaved as though they lived on borrowed time, feeling they had survived for no good reason. As for the dismissed, a local pastor and former IBM worker commented to Sampson, "They feel bitter and betrayed. . . . were made to feel as if we were the cause of their failure, while the big guys were making millions."

Paul Carroll, another student of this debacle, reports that on an anonymous employee morale survey, one person responded to the company's new insistence on its respect for individual effort rather than corporate loyalty, "What respect? . . . IBM is a very inconsistent company, making grand public statements on respect, sincerity, and sensitivity while practicing oppressive, discriminatory administration at a lower level." "Corporate loyalty is dead," a management consultant flatly declared (ibid., p. 256). And at ATT, a sister corporate monster which went through the same process, there was, in the words of one executive, "a climate of fear. There was fear in the old days too, but when they cut 40,000 jobs who is going to criticize a supervisor?"

But in the River Winds Café these first reactions didn't hold. The programmers found that as an explanation, *premeditated* betrayal wouldn't wash logically. For one thing, many of the superiors who fired them in the early phases of corporate restructuring were themselves fired in later phases; like Jason, they could also now be found at the River Winds. Again, since the company was in fact doing badly through much of the 1980s and early 1990s, the unpalatable facts were all too amply recorded in its annual balance sheet; the dysfunctions of the old corporate culture were plainly on display, rather than hidden.

Most of all, as reasonable adults the programmers came to understand that the theory of betrayal, planned or unplanned, converted the bosses into stick figures of evil. When Paul cited for the fourth or fifth time the mysterious trips of the head programmer, the other people at the table finally jumped on him. "Come on," Jason said, "you know he was a decent guy. He was probably visiting his girlfriend. No one knew what was coming." To this proposition, others had come to agree. And the effect of this consensus was to make the ills of the corporate albatross more real in fact than in fantasy.

So in a second stage of interpretation they focused on finding external forces to blame. At the River Winds Café, the "global economy" now appeared the source of their misfortunes, particularly in its use of foreign workers. IBM had begun "outsourcing" some of its programming work, paying people in India a fraction of the wages paid to the Americans. The cheap wages paid to these foreign professionals were cited as a reason the company had made the Americans redundant. More surprisingly, the company's communications network served as something like the Indians' Ellis Island, their port of immigration, since code written in Amenadabab arrived on a supervisor's desk as rapidly as code written inhouse. (In this regard, Jason told me a rather paradoxical fact he had learned from survivors of his own wave of down-sizing: people in this high-tech company rarely put on-line their judgments or criticisms; they wanted to leave no traces for which they could be held accountable.)

The fear that foreigners undermine the efforts of hardworking native Americans is a deeply rooted one. In the nineteenth century, it was very poor, unskilled immigrant workers who seemed to take away jobs, by their willingness to work for less. Today, the global economy serves the function of arousing this ancient fear, but those threatened at home seem not just the unskilled, but also the middle classes and professionals caught up in the flux of the global labor market. Many American physicians have cited, for example, the flood of "cheap doctors" from Third World countries as one of the reasons their own security can be menaced by insurers and health-maintenance companies. Economists like Lester Thurow have sought to generalize this threat, in arguing that the shift of work to low-wage sites around the world drags down wages in advanced economies like the United States. Rationally, this fear of the global labor market can be debated; Paul Krugman points out, for instance, that only 2 percent of the national income in America comes from imports from low-wage economies elsewhere in the world. But the belief in personal jeopardy caused by external threat is deep-seated and discounts fact.

For instance, in this "protectionist" phase of the discussion, which lasted for several months, the men at the café sought to explain their own troubles by equating foreign influence and American "outsiders" taking over the corporation: they noted repeatedly the fact that the new president of IBM, Louis Gerstner, was Jewish. Unfortunately this phase occurred during the elections of 1994: several of the men voted for extreme right-wing candidates whom they would have found absurd in more secure times.

Yet again, though, this shared interpretation would not hold. The turning point in rejecting the perfidy of outsiders came when the employees first began to discuss their own careers, particularly their professional values. As scientist-engineers, the programmers believed in the virtues of technological developments like digital global communications. They also acknowledged the quality of the work coming out of India.

These acknowledgments meant more than paying abstract obeisance to professional standards. The fact that the men were talking together mattered. During the stage in which the programmers constructed the perfidy of the Indian wagebusters and the machinations of IBM's Jewish president, the men had little to share with one another about the content of their work. Silences frequently fell over the table; betrayal within the company and external victimization both kept talk within the confines of complaining. Focusing on external enemies indeed gave the programmers no professional standing at all. The story referred only to the actions of others, unknown and unseen elsewhere; the engineers became passive agents of global forces.

Jim, the oldest of the IBM employees, and therefore the one who has had the most trouble reestablishing himself, remarked to me, "You know, during the Korean War, I thought, 'I'm just a pawn, no one, in this mud.' But I became more of a pawn at IBM." As the third stage of interpretation began, Paul, who had once suspected the perfidy of a voyaging superior, rounded on Jim, whom he greatly admired. He reminded Jim that they hadn't just been putting in their hours at IBM. Sure, once they had believed in the company, but even more to the point, Paul said, "we love our work." To which Jim replied. "That's quite true. I still love doing it – when I can." And so gradually the men began to speak in a different way.

This third stage of explanation restored some of their sense of integrity as programmers, but at a high cost. Now the focus was more on the history of high-tech work, on its immense recent growth, on the skills needed to deal with industrial and scientific challenges. Something happened to the voices of the men speaking at the café as they abandoned their obsession with how they had been hurt by others. As they focused on the profession, the programmers began to speak about what they personally could and should have done earlier in their own careers in order to prevent their present plight. In this third stage, the discourse of career had finally appeared, career as Walter Lippmann might have imagined it. Matters of personal will and choice, professional standards, narratives of work, all emerged – save that the theme of this career discourse was failure rather than mastery.

These discussions were indeed premised on the fact that IBM had stayed committed to mainframe computers at a time when growth in the industry occurred in the personal-computer sector; most of the programmers were mainframe men. The IBM men began to blame themselves for having been too company-dependent, for having believed in the promises of corporate culture, for having played out a career scenario not of their own creation. "Blame" may suggest guilt. I didn't hear that in the men's voices, at least not guilt of the florid, selfpitying sort. The talk was of mainframes, workstations, the possibilities of Java, the problems of bandwidth – and self. In this third stage, the unemployed recited the successes of people who ten or twelve years ago went into the personal-computer sector via risky small businesses, or who foresaw the possibilities of the Internet. This is what the programmers at the River Winds Café think they should have done. They should have become entrepreneurs like kids in Silicon Valley, the home of small technology start-ups.

[. . .]

For the last year, the story of what happened to IBM and to them has rested here. And this last interpretation, I've noticed, has coincided with a change in my neighbors' behavior in the community. Formerly town aldermen and school board members, they have now dropped out from pursuing these offices. They aren't afraid of holding up their heads in the community, since so many people in our town have been dismissed by IBM or suffered financially as shop owners and tradesmen from the shake-up. They've just lost interest in civic affairs.

The one community engagement the men do keep up, indeed pursue with ever greater vigor, is membership in and stewardship of their local churches. This is important to them because of the personal contact they have with other church members. In this part of the countryside as elsewhere, fundamentalist and evangelical forms of Christianity have been sharply on the rise. The youngest, Paul, told me, "When I was born again in Christ, I became more accepting, less striving." If my neighbors have taken responsibility for their life histories, that ethical act has taken their conduct in a particular direction; they have turned inward.

A successful entrepreneur from Silicon Valley reading this account might well comment. "This shows indeed that they should have taken more risks. Once these men understood the nature of a modern career, they were right to hold themselves accountable. They failed to act." Of course, that harsh judgment assumes the programmers were endowed with foresight. Even so, the discussions at the River Winds Café could thus be taken simply as a cautionary tale about the aggravated vulnerability built into careers today.

But to leave the matter here would exclude the real work these men were engaged in: facing up to their failure, making sense of it in terms of their own characters. In an interview Michel Foucault gave shortly before he died, the philosopher asked his interviewer a question: how does one "govern oneself"?

> How does one "govern oneself" by performing actions in which one is oneself the object of those actions, the domains in which they are applied, the instruments to which they have recourse and the subject which acts?
>
> (Foucault, 1989, p. 123)

The programmers needed to answer that question by finding ways to confront the reality of failure and self-limits. That effort of interpretation is also in Lippmann's spirit of "master," of ceasing to suffer change passively and blindly. To be sure, the action they take is talking to each other. But it's real action none the less. They are breaking the taboo on failure, bringing it out into the open. For this reason, the way they talk is important to understand.

The men try out three stories. All three versions revolve around a crucial turning point; in the first the turning point occurs when existing management begins to betray the professionals, in the second when intruders arrive on the scene, in the third at the moment when the programmers fail to get out. None takes the form of a story in which personal disaster is long and slow in the making, from the time of Thomas Watson, Sr., onward.

[. . .]

[T]he convention of the defining, clarifying moment helps the programmers make sense of the shape of their careers. Their discussions were, of course, not three neat, well-made chapters; relaxed chat inevitably wanders and weaves. But in the first two versions, nagging truths get in the way of the defining events. The first version is deflated by the men's factual knowledge of IBM's condition, the second by the men's belief in technological progress and their sense of professional quality. The third version, however, frees the people talking to take control of the narrative. Now the story can flow: it has a solid center, "me," and a well-made plot, "What I should have done was take my life into my own hands." The defining moment occurs when the programmers switch from passive victimhood to a more active condition. Now their own actions matter to the story. Being fired is no longer the defining event of the third version; the crucial action is the action they should have taken in 1954 or 1985. That defining moment becomes their own responsibility. It is only by making this shift that they can begin to face the fact they failed in their careers.

The taboos surrounding failure mean that it is often a deeply confusing, ill-defined experience. A single, sharp blow of rejection won't contain failure. In a superb study of the downwardly mobile middle-class, the anthropologist Katherine Newman observes that "despite its various outcomes, managerial downward mobility generates a floating, ambiguous, liminal condition." To be a downwardly mobile executive, she says, "is first to discover that you are not as good a person as you thought you were and then to end up not sure who or what you are (Newman 1988, p. 93–94). The men at the River Winds Café eventually rescued themselves from that subjective ambiguity.

It might appear that this narrative working out of failure is arbitrary. Nietzsche says in *Thus Spake Zarathustra* that the ordinary man is an angry spectator of the past, and lacks the power to "will backwards" (Nietzsche, 1969, p. 163). The programmers could not live as angry spectators of their past, however, and so they indeed bent their wills backward in time. And in the evolution of the narrative the men at the River Winds Café eventually ceased to speak as the children of a paternalistic company: they let go of the view that the powerful are scheming demons, their Bombay replacements illegitimate intruders. Their interpretation became in these ways more realistic.

How does this narrative *form* break the sense of aimless inner drift which Lippmann thought so corrosive? Consider another kind of narrative which might be better attuned to contemporary circumstances. The novelist Salman Rushdie asserts that the modern self is "a shaky edifice we build out of scraps, dogmas, childhood injuries, newspaper articles, chance remarks, old films, small victories, people hated, people loved" (Rushdie 1991, p. 21). To him, a life narrative appears as a collage, an assemblage of the accidental, the found, and the improvised. The same emphasis on discontinuity appears in the writings of the philosopher Zygmunt Bauman and the theologian Mark Taylor; they celebrate the efforts of novelists like Joyce or Calvino to subvert well-made plots as a way to render the flow of ordinary experience (Bauman, 1993; Taylor, 1993). The psyche dwells in a state of endless becoming – a selfhood which is never finished. There can be under these conditions no coherent life narrative, no clarifying moment of change illuminating the whole.

Such views of narrative, sometimes labeled "postmodern," indeed mirror the experience of time in the modern political economy. A pliant self, a collage of fragments unceasing in its becoming, ever open to new experience – these are just the psychological conditions suited to short-term work experience, flexible institutions, and constant risk-taking. But there is little room for understanding the breakdown of a career, if you believe that all life history is just an assemblage of fragments. Nor is there any room for assaying the gravity and pain of failure, if failure is just another incident.

The fragmentation of narrative time is particularly marked in the programmers' professional milieu. In *City of Bits*, the architect William Mitchell describes cyberspace as like "a city unrooted to any definite spot on the surface of the earth . . . and inhabited by disembodied and fragmented subjects who exist as collections of aliases and agents" (Mitchell, 1995). The technology analyst [. . .]

The programmers have recovered in talk the connectedness absent onscreen. Their narrative appears indeed pre-postmodern in its striving for coherence and a solid authorial "I." [. . .]

The programmers spoke in the end with an air more of resigned finality than of anger about being "past it," about having blown their chances, even though they are in their physical prime. In this third version, the men felt relieved of struggling anymore – felt a deep-seated fatigue with life which overcomes many middle-aged people. Anyone who has deeply tasted failure will recognize the impulse: given the destruction of hope and desire, the preservation of one's own active voice is the only way to make failure bearable. Simply declaring one's will to endure will not suffice. [. . .] The advice the engineers give to themselves consists of such locutions as "I should have known . . ." and "if only . . .". In this diction, relief is no stranger to resignation. And resignation is an acknowledgment of the weight of objective reality.

Their narrative thus attempted a kind of self-healing. Narrative in general does the work of healing through its structure, however, not through offering advice. Even great allegories, even those so unashamed in moralizing as Bunyan's *Pilgrim's Progress*, transcend the intent to show a reader how to act. Bunyan, for example, makes the temptations of evil so complicated that the reader dwells on Christian's difficulties rather than seeks to imitate his solutions. The healing of narrative comes from precisely that engagement with difficulty. The healing work of making a narrative does not limit its interest to events coming out the "right" way. Instead a good narrative acknowledges and probes the reality of all the wrong ways life can and does turn out. The reader of a novel, the spectator at a play, experiences the particular comfort of seeing people and events fit into a pattern of time; the "moral" of narrative lies in the form, not in advice.

It could be said, finally, that these men have confronted failure in the past, elucidated the values of their careers, but found no way to go forward. In the flexible, fragmented present it may seem possible only to create coherent narratives about what has been, and no longer possible to create predictive narratives about what will be. The fact that the men at the River Winds Café have withdrawn now from active engagement in the local community may seem only to confirm this past-tense condition. The flexible regime may seem to beget a character structure constantly "in recovery."

Ironically, these are the Davids confronting a Goliath of the flexible regime. It is as individuals of the sort Walter Lippmann admired that programmers found a way to discuss failure with each other, and thereby find a more coherent sense of self and time. While we should admire that individual strength, their turn inward and to intimate relations shows the limits of the coherence they achieved. A larger sense of community, and a fuller sense of character, is required by the increasing number of people who, in modern capitalism, are doomed to fail.

NOTE

* This chapter has been adapted from, Sennett, R. (1998), *The Corrosion of Character*, Norton, New York.

REFERENCES

Bauman, Z. Cf., (1993), *Postmodern Ethics*, Blackwell, Oxford.

DeLamarter, R. T. (1986), *Big Blue: IBM's Use and Abuse of Power*, Dodd, Mead, New York.

Foucault, M. (1989), *Résumé des cours, 1970–1982*, p. 123, my translation, Julliard, Paris.

James, H. (1968), *The American Scene*, Indiana University Press, Bloomington, Indiana.

Lippmann, W. (1914), *Drift and Mastery*, Mitchell Kennerly, New York.

Mitchell, W. (1995), *City of Bits*, p. 28, MIT Press, Cambridge, Mass.

Newman, K. (1988), *Falling from Grace: The Experience of Downward Mobility in the American Middle Class*, pp. 93–4, Free Press, New York.

Nietzsche, F. (1969), *Thus Spoke Zarathustra*, p. 163, translated by R. J. Hollingdale, Penguin, London.

Rodgers, W. (1969), *Think: A Biography of the Watsons and IBM*, p. 100, Stein and Day, New York.

Rushdie, S. (1991), *Imaginary Homelands*, p. 12, Granta Books, London.

Sampson, W. (1995), *Company Man*, Random House, New York.

Taylor, M. (1993), *Disfiguring*, University of Chicago, Chicago.

Thompson, E. (1978), *The Making of the English Working Class*, Vintage, New York.

Zunz, O. (1990), *Making America Corporate*, Oxford University Press, New York.

INDEX

Printed in the United States
by Baker & Taylor Publisher Services